Cambridge Lower Secondary
Science

TEACHER'S RESOURCE 8

Mary Jones, Diane Fellowes-Freeman & Michael Smyth

CAMBRIDGE
UNIVERSITY PRESS & ASSESSMENT

Shaftesbury Road, Cambridge CB2 8EA, United Kingdom

One Liberty Plaza, 20th Floor, New York, NY 10006, USA

477 Williamstown Road, Port Melbourne, VIC 3207, Australia

314–321, 3rd Floor, Plot 3, Splendor Forum, Jasola District Centre, New Delhi – 110025, India

103 Penang Road, #05–06/07, Visioncrest Commercial, Singapore 238467

Cambridge University Press & Assessment is a department of the University of Cambridge.

We share the University's mission to contribute to society through the pursuit of
education, learning and research at the highest international levels of excellence.

www.cambridge.org
Information on this title: www.cambridge.org/9781108785181

© Cambridge University Press & Assessment 2021

First published 2014
Second edition 2021

20 19 18 17 16 15 14 13 12 11 10 9 8 7 6

Printed in Great Britain by Ashford Colour Press Ltd.

A catalogue record for this publication is available from the British Library

ISBN 978-1-108-78518-1 Paperback with Digital Access

Additional resources for this publication at www.cambridge.org/go

〉 Contents

Introduction   v

About the authors   vi

How to use this series   viii

How to use this Teacher's Resource   x

About the curriculum framework   xv

About the assessment   xvi

Approaches to learning and teaching   xvi

Setting up for success   xix

Teaching notes

1   Respiration   2

2   Properties of materials   21

3   Forces and energy   37

4   Ecosystems   63

5   Materials and cycles on Earth   78

6   Light   100

7   Diet and growth   123

8   Chemical reactions   139

9   Magnetism   161

Glossary   177

Acknowledgements   183

Digital resources

The following items are available on Cambridge GO. For more information on how to access and use your digital resource, please see inside front cover.

Active learning

Assessment for Learning

Developing learner language skills

Differentiation

Improving learning through questioning

Language awareness

Metacognition

Skills for Life

Letter for parents – Introducing the Cambridge Primary and
                        Lower Secondary resources

Lesson plan template and examples of completed lesson plans

Curriculum framework correlation

Scheme of work

Mid-point test and answers

End-of-year test and answers

Answers to Learner's Book questions

Answers to Workbook questions

Answers to English Language Workbook questions

Glossary

You can download the following resources for each unit:

Differentiated worksheets and answers

Language worksheets and answers

Resource sheets

End-of-unit tests and answers

> Introduction

Welcome to the new edition of our Cambridge Lower Secondary Science series.

Since being launched, Cambridge Lower Secondary Science has been used by teachers and children in over 100 countries around the world for teaching the Cambridge International Lower Secondary Science Curriculum Framework.

This exciting new edition has been conceived and designed by speaking to Lower Secondary Science teachers all over the world, looking to understand their needs and difficulties, and then carefully designing and testing the best ways of meeting these needs. As a result of this research, we've made some important changes to the series. This Teacher's Resource has been carefully redesigned to enhance its usability and accessibility to teachers, with careful focus on navigation and the incorporation of pages from the Learner's Book. This Teacher's Resource is also available digitally through our Cambridge GO platform, along with extra support and more teaching resources.

The series is built around well-known teaching pedagogies, and we provide full guidance within this Teacher's Resource for using child-centred teaching approaches which develop active learning and metacognition, and which are brought to life in the classroom through illustration and questioning.

Get to know your learners better with frequent and effective formative assessment opportunities and guidance, starting with clear learning objectives and success criteria as well as an array of assessment actions, including advice on self- and peer assessment.

Ensure that all learners are able to progress in the course with clear, consistent differentiation in the form of tiered activities, differentiated worksheets and advice about supporting learners' different needs.

All our resources are written for teachers and learners who use English as a second or additional language. This has meant the careful avoidance of unnecessarily complex vocabulary and expression, while the series provides a major focus on building up functional and subject vocabulary.

We hope you enjoy using this course and that it is beneficial in advancing the learning of your students. Please get in touch if you have any questions for us, as your views are essential for us to ensure our schemes meet your needs as a teacher.

Eddie Rippeth

Head of Primary and Lower Secondary Publishing, Cambridge University Press

› About the authors

Mary Jones

Mary obtained an MSc in Zoology from the University of Oxford. She has worked as a teacher and a lecturer in different types of educational institution, teaching students of all ages.

Mary's greatest interest is in sharing her love of science with young learners. She has written many textbooks, in which she aims to encourage learners to 'think like a scientist'. Her long involvement in examining and in international training has given her insight into the difficulties that learners all over the world have in understanding some topics in science, and this has informed her writing approach. She is passionate about the need to develop skills rather than just accumulating knowledge – skills that are vital for students to be successful as they move into higher education or the world of work.

Diane Fellowes-Freeman

Diane was a teacher for almost 40 years, mostly as Head of the Science Department at several large state schools in the south of England. She has taught all three sciences to students of all abilities up to GCSE and biology and chemistry to A Level. With so many changes in science courses over this time she has developed many new resources to meet the new specifications and to help her students. When her own children were young she spent some time teaching (mainly science) at their primary school, which was a new, fascinating and enjoyable experience.

She is passionate about engaging students in science so that they are able to understand and appreciate more about the world around them. It is important they see the relevance of science to their future.

Throughout her career she loved learning from other teachers and trying new techniques. One of the most enjoyable and rewarding parts of her job was mentoring many teacher training students and teachers who were newly qualified.

Whilst still teaching full time she did some work for Cambridge University Press but the first big project was for the previous Cambridge Checkpoint Science edition. She has been fortunate to be invited to speak at a number of Cambridge overseas training events in Dubai, Malaysia, Indonesia and Vietnam. It is always a delight to meet so many teachers and share ideas and skills.

Her hope is that teachers will find this new edition gives them more help to develop their skills and provide an excellent foundation in science for all their learners.

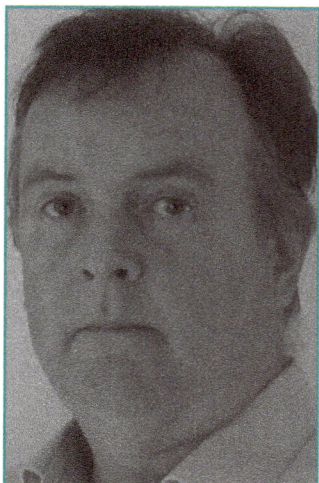

Michael Smyth

Michael graduated with a PhD in Biophysics and began his career in research at the University of Oxford. His enthusiasm for both science and education then led him into full-time teaching. Michael spent most of his teaching career as a Head of Science in a leading UK private school, which taught across the age ranges from kindergarten to A Level. He significantly raised attainment in the sciences at this school.

With publications spanning four decades, Michael's work includes articles in high-impact journals and secondary science learning aids for the 11–19 age groups. His work has been featured in major newspapers and he has won international awards for his work in science education. A senior examiner for over 20 years, Michael currently writes and marks exam papers, trains teachers and examiners and writes books and articles on science.

Michael remains passionate about the sciences and science education, realising that teachers of today are preparing the scientists of tomorrow. He feels this series will greatly benefit teachers and learners alike. The Learner's Books give clear explanations with accompanying pictures and diagrams. The Workbooks give learners practice at answering test-style questions, and these questions are fully differentiated. Taken together, Michael believes these components conspire to be the most powerful learning tool available for the 11–14 age group.

> How to use this series

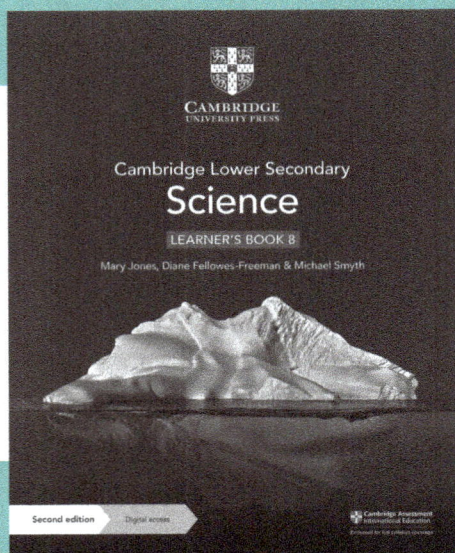

The Learner's Book is designed for students to use in class with guidance from the teacher. It contains nine units which offer complete coverage of the curriculum framework. A variety of investigations, activities, questions and images motivate students and help them to develop the necessary scientific skills. Each unit contains opportunities for formative assessment, differentiation and reflection so you can support your learners' needs and help them progress.

The Teacher's Resource is the foundation of this series and you'll find everything you need to deliver the course in here, including suggestions for differentiation, formative assessment and language support, teaching ideas, answers, unit and progress tests and extra worksheets. Each Teacher's Resource includes:

- a print book with detailed teaching notes for each topic
- an Elevate edition with all the material from the book in digital form, plus editable planning documents, extra guidance, downloadable worksheets and more.

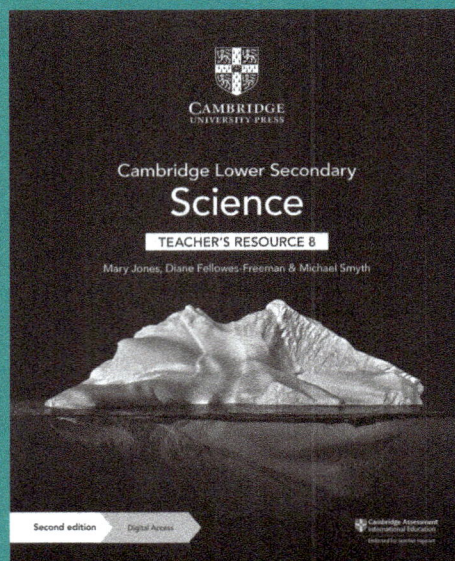

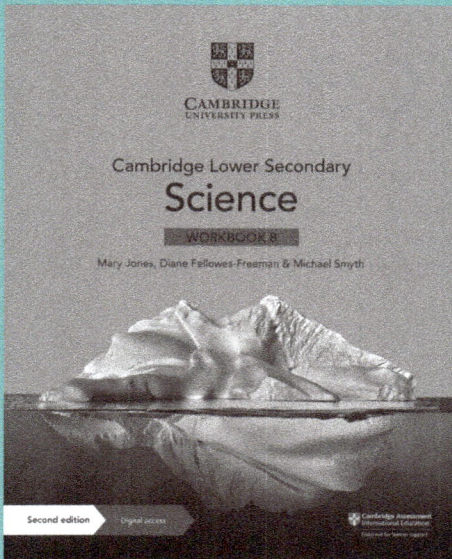

The skills-focused write-in Workbook provides further practice of all the topics in the Learner's Book and is ideal for use in class or as homework. A three-tier, scaffolded approach to skills development promotes visible progress and enables independent learning, ensuring that every learner is supported.

English language skills are the single biggest barrier to students accessing international science. The English Language Skills Workbook helps learners understand scientific terms and express themselves effectively in English. Activities range from choosing the right word in a list of possible answers to writing longer responses.

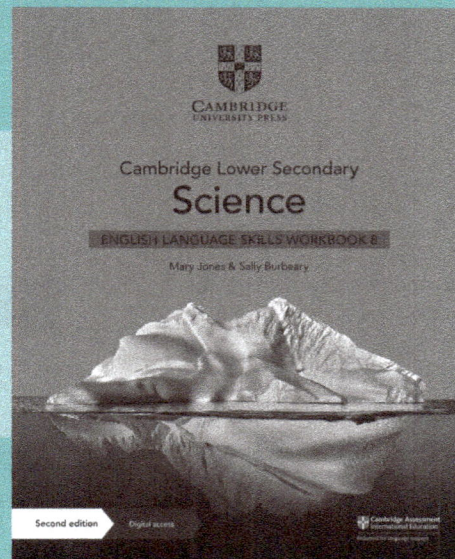

A letter to parents, explaining the course, is available to download from Cambridge GO (as part of this Teacher's Resource).

> How to use this Teacher's Resource

This Teacher's Resource contains both general guidance and teaching notes that help you deliver the content in our Cambridge Primary Science resources. Some of the material is provided as downloadable files, available on **Cambridge GO**. (For more information about how to access and use your digital resource, please see inside front cover.) See the Contents page for details of all the material available to you, both in this book and through Cambridge GO.

Teaching notes

This book provides **teaching notes** for each unit of the Learner's Book and Workbook. Each set of teaching notes contains the following features to help you deliver the unit.

The **Unit plan** summarises the topics covered in the unit, including the number of learning hours recommended for the topic, an outline of the learning content and the Cambridge resources that can be used to deliver the topic.

Topic	Learning hours	Learning content	Resources
1.1 The human respiratory system	2-3	Structure of the respiratory system	**Learner's Book:** Questions 1–2 Think like a scientist: Looking at lungs Activity: What does the larynx do?

The **Background knowledge** feature explains prior knowledge required to access the unit and gives suggestions for addressing any gaps in your learners' prior knowledge.

Learners' prior knowledge can be informally assessed through the **Getting started** feature in the Learner's Book.

The **Teaching skills focus** feature covers a teaching skill and suggests how to implement it in the unit.

Reflecting the Learner's Book, each unit consists of multiple sections. A section covers a learning topic.

BACKGROUND KNOWLEDGE

Learners should be familiar with many of the ideas in this unit and are going to need their knowledge of particle theory to help them understand the ideas behind solutions and solubility

TEACHING SKILLS FOCUS

Lesson starters 3

An effective lesson starter sets the mood for the lesson and, as well as influencing learning can also influence behaviour and therefore be a powerful tool for classroom management.

At the start of each section, the **Learning plan** table includes the learning objectives, learning intentions and success criteria that are covered in the section.

It can be helpful to share learning intentions and success criteria with your learners at the start of a lesson so that they can begin to take responsibility for their own learning

LEARNING PLAN

Learning objective	Learning intentions	Success criteria
8Cc.05 Describe how the solubility of different salts varies with temperature.	• Plan an investigation.	• Identify different types of variable.

There are often **common misconceptions** associated with particular learning topics. These are identified in a table, along with suggestions for identifying evidence of these misconceptions in your class and suggestions for how to overcome them.

Misconception	How to identify	How to overcome
Many learners think weather and climate are the same thing.	Ask learners: *What is the difference between weather and climate?*	Explain the difference carefully and reinforce the difference by the correct use of the terms.

For each topic, there is a selection of **Starter ideas**, **Main teaching ideas** and **Plenary ideas**. You can pick out individual ideas and mix and match them depending on the needs of your class. The activities include suggestions for how they can be differentiated or used for assessment. **Homework ideas** are also provided.

Starter ideas

1 Getting started (10 minutes)

Description: Ask learners, in pairs, to suggest as many words as they can that are concerned with weather. Take feedback from the class. You could compile a list, as this will be useful for various tasks in the Learner's Book. It would be a good opportunity to discuss the meanings and spelling of these terms.

Main teaching ideas

1 Recording the weather (40 minutes, plus time to take readings every day for a week; this could be done at break or before or after school)

Learning intention: To give learners practical experience of recording weather information and basic understanding of the importance of standardisation when comparing data.

Thinking and Working Scientifically skills are woven throughout the Learner's Book. In the teaching notes, the ***Thinking and Working Scientifically* guidance** identifies these sections from the Learner's Book and provides more detail about the skills that it supports.

Science in Context skills are addressed in the Projects at the end of each unit in the Learner's Book, where learners can use what they have learned in the context of the wider world, and these Projects are supported by the *Project Guidance* sections in the Teaching Notes.

The **Language support** feature contains suggestions for how to support learners with English as an additional language. The vocabulary terms and definitions from the Learner's Book are also collected here. Note that the definitions provided in the Teacher Resource may be a little more detailed than in the Learner's Book.

LANGUAGE SUPPORT

Learners will use the following words:

primary colours: the name given to red, green and blue light as they cannot be made from the addition of any other colours of light

Digital resources to download

This Teacher's Resource includes a range of digital materials that you can download from Cambridge GO. (For more information about how to access and use your digital resource, please see inside front cover.) This icon ⬇ indicates material that is available from Cambridge GO.

Helpful documents for planning include:

- **Letter for parents – Introducing the Cambridge Primary and Lower Secondary resources:** a template letter for parents, introducing the Cambridge Lower Secondary Science resources.
- **Lesson plan template:** a Word document that you can use for planning your lessons. Examples of completed lesson plans are also provided.
- **Curriculum framework correlation:** a table showing how the Cambridge Lower Secondary Science resources map to the Cambridge Lower Secondary Science curriculum framework.
- **Scheme of work:** a suggested scheme of work that you can use to plan teaching throughout the year.

Each unit includes:

- **Differentiated worksheets:** these worksheets are provided in variations that cater for different abilities. There are 3 levels of Worksheet: A, B and C. 'A' support the less confident, and 'C' are designed to challenge the more confident. Answer sheets are provided.
- **Language worksheets:** these worksheets provide language support and can be particularly helpful for learners with English as an additional language. Answer sheets are provided.
- **Resource sheets:** these include templates and any other materials that support activities described in the teaching notes.
- **End-of-unit tests:** these provide quick checks of the learner's understanding of the concepts covered in the unit. Answers are provided. Advice on using these tests formatively is given in the Assessment for Learning section of this Teacher's Resource.

Additionally, the Teacher's Resource includes:

- **Mid-point test and answers:** a test to use after learners have studied half the units in the Learner's Book. You can use this test to check whether there are areas that you need to go over again.
- **End-of-year test and answers:** a test to use after learners have studied all units in the Learner's Book. You can use this test to check whether there are areas that you need to go over again, and to help inform your planning for the next year.
- **Answers to Learner's Book questions**
- **Answers to Workbook questions**
- **Answers to English Language Skills Workbook**
- **Glossary**

> CAMBRIDGE LOWER SECONDARY SCIENCE 8 UNIT 4: ECOSYSTEMS

Name _____   Date _____

Worksheet 4.4

...y in an Arctic food web

...a food web in the Arctic Ocean.

polar bear

seal

> CAMBRIDGE LOWER SECONDARY SCIENCE 8 UNIT 2: PROPERTIES OF MATERIALS

Name _____   Date _____

Worksheet 2.3(ii)

The results of an investigation

Marcus and Sofia have collected data from an...
They measured how much lead nitrate would...
Here are their results.

Temperature	lead ...
20	52
40	72
50	30
60	
70	100

1 Display these results neatly and cor...

2 What pattern is there in these re...

3 What would you advise Sophi...

Cambridge Lower Secondary Science 8 – Mary J...

> CAMBRIDGE LOWER SECONDARY SCIENCE 8 UNIT 5: LANGUAGE DEVELOPMENT

Name _____   Date _____

...heet 5.1

...meanings

...ge that apply to the atomic structure, the weather or climate change.

proton

tropical   **polar**

nucleus

wind

Weather	Climate change

...tomorrow.

> CAMBRIDGE LOWER SECONDARY SCIENCE 8: END-OF-UNIT TEST

Name _____   Date _____

Disclaimer: This test and mark scheme have been written by the authors.

End-of-unit test

Unit 7

1 a   A balanced diet should include the correct amount of energy each day.

     What else should be included in a balanced diet?   [1]

_____

_____

Marcus wanted to know if cashew nuts contain...

- He measured 20 cm³ of water into a test tube...
- He measured the temperature of the water.
- He held a cashew nut in a flame until it star...
- He held the burning nut under the test tube...
- When the nut finished burning, he measure...

Cambridge Lower Secondary Science 8 – Mary Jones, Diane...

> CAMBRIDGE LOWER SECONDARY SCIENCE 8: END-OF-YEAR TEST

Name _____   Date _____

Disclaimer: This test and mark scheme have been written by the authors.

End-of-year test

Questions

Biology

1   The diagram shows a side view of the human skeleton

   a   On the diagram, use a label line and the letter **H** to identify a hinge joint.
   b   On the diagram, use a label line and the letter **B** to identify a ball-and-socket joint.   [1]
   c   Two muscles work together to move the bones at a hinge joint.   [1]
       What is the term used to describe these two muscles?

                                                                                                               [1]

_____

Cambridge Lower Secondary Science 8 – Mary Jones, Diane Fellowes Freeman and Michael Smyth © Cambridge University Press 2021   1 >

> About the curriculum framework

Cambridge International have developed their Cambridge Lower Secondary Science curriculum framework to support learners in developing their understanding about the natural world, particularly how to explain and investigate phenomena.

The curriculum framework incorporates three components:

- four content strands (Biology, Chemistry, Physics, and Earth and Space)
- a skills strand called Thinking and Working Scientifically
- a context strand called Science in Context.

Biology, Chemistry, Physics and Earth and Space provide the scientific knowledge content, which gradually develops from stage 7 to stage 9 and provides a smooth progression towards Cambridge IGCSE™ study.

The Thinking and Working Scientifically learning objectives focus on the key scientific skills that are developed throughout the course. This strand is split into three types of scientific enquiry:

- Models and representation
- Scientific enquiry
- Practical work.

Science in Context allows for personal, local and global contexts to be incorporated into scientific study, making science relevant to the contexts that learners are familiar with. This element of the curriculum offers great flexibility to teachers and learners around the world, exploring development of scientific knowledge over time; the evaluation of issues; ideas of peer review and the ideas surrounding specific environmental impacts from the uses of science..

The Cambridge Lower Secondary Science curriculum framework promotes a learner-led, enquiry-based approach. Practical work is a valuable part of science learning and develops learners' investigation skills such as observation, measurement and equipment handling.

> About the assessment

Information about the assessment of the Cambridge International Lower Secondary Science curriculum framework is available on the Cambridge Assessment International Education website: https://www.cambridgeinternational.org/lowersecondary

> Approaches to learning and teaching

The following are the key pedagogies underpinning our course content and how we understand and define them.

Active learning

Active learning is a pedagogical practice that places the learner at its centre. It focuses on how learners learn, not just on what they learn. We, as teachers, need to encourage learners to 'think hard', rather than passively receive information. Active learning encourages learners to take responsibility for their learning and supports them in becoming independent and confident learners in school and beyond.

Assessment for Learning

Assessment for Learning (AfL) is a teaching approach that generates feedback which can be used to improve learners' performance. Learners become more involved in the learning process and, from this, gain confidence in what they are expected to learn and to what standard. We, as teachers, gain insights into a learner's level of understanding of a particular concept or topic, which helps to inform how we support their progression.

Differentiation

Differentiation is usually presented as a teaching practice where teachers think of learners as individuals and learning as a personalised process. Whilst precise definitions can vary, typically the core aim of differentiation is viewed as ensuring that all learners, no matter their ability, interest or context, make progress towards their learning outcomes.

It is about using different approaches and appreciating the differences in learners to help them make progress. Teachers, therefore, need to be responsive, willing and able to adapt their teaching to meet the needs of their learners.

Language awareness

For many learners, English is an additional language. It might be their second or perhaps their third language. Depending on the school context, students might be learning all or just some of their subjects through English.

For all learners, regardless of whether they are learning through their first language or an additional language, language is a vehicle for learning. It is through language that students access the learning intentions of the lesson and communicate their ideas. It is our responsibility, as teachers, to ensure that language does not present a barrier to learning.

Metacognition

Metacognition describes the processes involved when learners plan, monitor, evaluate and make changes to their own learning behaviours. These processes help learners to think about their own learning more explicitly and ensure that they are able to meet a learning goal that they have identified themselves or that we, as teachers, have set.

Skills for Life

How do we prepare learners to succeed in a fast-changing world? To collaborate with people from around the globe? To create innovation as technology increasingly takes over routine work?

To use advanced thinking skills in the face of more complex challenges? To show resilience in the face of constant change? At Cambridge, we are responding to educators who have asked for a way to understand how all these different approaches to life skills and competencies relate to their teaching.

We have grouped these skills into six main Areas of Competency that can be incorporated into teaching, and have examined the different stages of the learning journey and how these competencies vary across each stage.

These six key areas are:

- Creativity – finding new ways of doing things, and solutions to problems
- Collaboration – the ability to work well with others
- Communication – speaking and presenting confidently and participating effectively in meetings
- Critical thinking – evaluating what is heard or read, and linking ideas constructively
- Learning to learn – developing the skills to learn more effectively
- Social responsibilities – contributing to social groups, and being able to talk to and work with people from other cultures.

Cambridge learner and teacher attributes

This course helps develop the following Cambridge learner and teacher attributes.

Cambridge learners	Cambridge teachers
Confident in working with information and ideas – their own and those of others.	**Confident** in teaching their subject and engaging each student in learning.
Responsible for themselves, responsive to and respectful of others.	**Responsible** for themselves, responsive to and respectful of others.
Reflective as learners, developing their ability to learn.	**Reflective** as learners themselves, developing their practice.
Innovative and equipped for new and future challenges.	**Innovative** and equipped for new and future challenges.
Engaged intellectually and socially, ready to make a difference.	**Engaged** intellectually, professionally and socially, ready to make a difference.

Adapted from Approaches to learning and teaching series, courtesy of Cambridge University Press and Cambridge Assessment International Education: cambridge.org/approachestolearning.

More information about these approaches to learning and teaching is available to download from Cambridge GO

Series-specific approaches

Cambridge Lower Secondary Science has been developed with scientific investigation at its heart, to support learners to understand and explain the world around them. *Think like a scientist* features offer engaging opportunities for learners to predict, observe and identify the patterns in what they see. Encouraging learners to see and investigate for themselves promotes active learning and deep understanding.

Opportunities for active learning are included throughout the series, in Activities and Questions at every point. Learners are also encouraged to self-assess and reflect on their learning, to develop their metacognitive skills and their awareness of their own progress.

Projects provide valuable opportunities to delve deeper into learners' own personal and local contexts, as well as global contexts as they progress through the course. This ensures that scientific learning is relevant for every learner.

〉 Setting up for success

Our aim is to support better learning in the classroom with resources that allow for increased learner autonomy while supporting teachers to facilitate student learning.

Through an active learning approach of enquiry-led tasks, open-ended questions and opportunities to externalise thinking in a variety of ways, learners will develop analysis, evaluation and problem-solving skills.

Some ideas to consider to encourage an active learning environment are as follows:

- Set up seating to make group work easy.

- Create classroom routines to help learners to transition between different types of activity efficiently, e.g. move from pair work to listening to the teacher to independent work.

- Source mini-whiteboards, which allow you to get feedback from all learners rapidly.

- Start a portfolio for each learner, keeping key pieces of work to show progress at parent–teacher days.

- Have a display area with learner work and vocab flashcards.

Planning for active learning

We recommend the following approach to planning.

1   Plan learning intentions and success criteria: these are the most important feature of the lesson. Teachers and learners need to know where they are going in order to plan a route to get there.

2   Plan language support: think about strategies to help learners overcome the language demands of the lesson so that language doesn't present a barrier to learning.

3   Plan starter activities: include a 'hook' or starter to engage learners using imaginative strategies. This should be an activity where all learners are active from the start of the lesson.

4   Plan main activities: during the lesson, try to: give clear instructions, with modelling and written support; coordinate logical and orderly transitions between activities; make sure that learning is active and all learners are engaged; create opportunities for discussion around key concepts.

5   Plan assessment for learning and differentiation: use a wide range of Assessment for Learning techniques and adapt activities to a wide range of abilities. Address misconceptions at appropriate points and give meaningful oral and written feedback which learners can act on.

6   Plan reflection and plenary: at the end of each activity and at the end of each lesson, try to: ask learners to reflect on what they have learnt compared to the beginning of the lesson; build on and extend this learning.

7   Plan homework: if setting homework, it can be used to consolidate learning from the previous lesson or to prepare for the next lesson

To help planning using this approach, a blank Lesson plan template is available to download from Cambridge GO (as part of this Teacher's Resource). There are also examples of completed lesson plans.

For more guidance on setting up for success and planning, please explore the Professional Development pages of our website www.cambridge.org/education/PD

❯ 1 Respiration

Unit plan

Topic	Learning hours	Learning content	Resources
1.1 The human respiratory system	2-3	Structure of the respiratory system	**Learner's Book:** Questions 1–2 Think like a scientist: Looking at lungs Activity: What does the larynx do? **Workbook:** Exercise 1.1, Structure and function in the respiratory system **Teacher's Resource:** Worksheet 1.1, Journey into the lungs
1.2 Gas exchange	2-4	Structure of air sacs; movement of oxygen and carbon dioxide between air sacs and blood; comparing the composition of inspired and expired air	**Learner's Book:** Activity: Gases in and out Think like a scientist: Why are air sacs so small? Think like a scientist: Comparing the carbon dioxide content of inspired air and expired air **Workbook:** Exercise 1.2, Lung surface area and body mass
1.3 Breathing	2-2.5	How air is moved into and out of the lungs	**Learner's Book:** Questions 1–2 Think like a scientist: Measuring the volume of air you can push out of your lungs Think like a scientist: Using a model to represent breathing movements **Workbook:** Exercise 1.3A, Measuring lung volumes Exercise 1.3B, Looking at data on lung volumes Exercise 1.3C, Lung volume at different ages **Teacher's Resource:** Worksheet 1.3, Respiratory system leaflet

Topic	Learning hours	Learning content	Resources
1.4 Respiration	2-4	How useful energy is released from glucose inside mitochondria	**Learner's Book:** Questions 1–3 Think like a scientist: Investigating respiration in peas, including questions 1–6 Activity: Thinking about a thermogram Activity: Explaining the difference between breathing and respiration **Workbook:** Exercise 1.4, Respiration by yeast **Teacher's Resource:** Worksheets 1.4A–C An investigation using hydrogencarbonate indicator Template 1.4: Graph axes for *Think like a scientist: Investigating respiration in peas*
1.5 Blood	2-2.5	Structure of blood and functions of its components; how blood transports oxygen and glucose for respiration	**Learner's Book:** Questions 1–5 Activity: Making a picture of blood **Workbook:** Exercise 1.5A, The components of blood Exercise 1.5B, Functions of blood components Exercise 1.5C, Rats at altitude **Teacher's Resource:** Worksheets 1.5A–C Adapting to high altitude
Cross-unit resources			**Learner's Book:** Check your Progress **Project:** Helping white blood cells to protect us from pathogens **Teacher's Resource:** Language development worksheets 1.1 Completing sentences about respiration 1.2 Explaining the meanings of words

BACKGROUND KNOWLEDGE

Learners will know that respiration is one of the characteristics of living organisms. Some may also know that it involves the release of energy from glucose. They learnt about the structure of cells in Stage 7, and so should be aware of mitochondria.

Learners who followed the Cambridge programme at Stage 6 learnt the basic structure of the human respiratory system, and they should know that oxygen moves from air into the blood in the lungs. They are unlikely to know about air sacs, or the movement of carbon dioxide from the blood to the air inside the lungs.

At Stage 5, they will have used the particle model to describe solids, liquids and gases, which will help them to understand how particles of oxygen and carbon dioxide can move between air sacs and the blood. They are unlikely to know about diffusion, which is covered later in this book in Topic 3.7, Particles on the move.

The movement of air into and out of the lungs by breathing movements is a difficult topic at this level, and should be approached with care, giving learners time to absorb the concepts involved. The relationship between pressure and volume will be covered in more detail in Topic 3.6, Pressure in liquids and gases.

At Stage 6, learners will have learnt about the human circulatory system, including its function in transporting oxygen. This topic covers only the structure and functions of blood; there is no need to consider the heart or blood vessels in any detail. Learners will have learnt about the structure and function of red blood cells at Stage 7, Topic 1.3.

TEACHING SKILLS FOCUS

Organising practical work 1

Hands-on practical activities are an extremely important component of any modern science course. Learners experience for themselves how a variety of scientific apparatus and procedures are used. For many learners, doing an experiment themselves makes it much easier for them to understand the topic they are studying.

Thinking carefully about how you organise practical work with your class can make the experience for both you and your class much more enjoyable and successful. Here are some ideas you might like to consider.

- Before attempting to do any practical work, it is essential that learners understand the rules for behaviour in a laboratory. Schools should have their own set of rules, which are the same in every laboratory, and display them prominently on the wall. They must be fully enforced by every science teacher.

- You may like to have a supply of safety glasses and laboratory coats for learners to use when they are doing practical work. Putting on a laboratory coat can help them to feel responsible as they work.

- It is very unlikely that you will have an emergency, but you should have in place a procedure with which you and the learners are familiar. You should be able to tell learners to stop what they are doing immediately, and know that they will respond appropriately. This may require practice. It is important, however, not to scare learners and make them nervous of doing practical work. Laboratories can often be among the safest places in the school, because learners know how to behave sensibly there.

- Some basic apparatus (such as test tubes, retort stands) can be stored so that learners can find and collect it for themselves when asked to do so. Label each cupboard with the name of the apparatus that is kept inside; you can include a drawing or photograph of the apparatus on the cupboard door as well, to help learners who are not sure of the names.

- It is a good idea to keep the apparatus on trays inside the cupboards. You can then take a tray of, for example, small beakers out of the cupboard when needed and place it on the bench, to make it easier for learners to collect one. Make sure that you place the trays at different places around the room, to avoid learners all standing in the same place as they collect their apparatus.

- When working in groups, one person can take responsibility for collecting the apparatus, to avoid everyone crowding around at the same time. If there is a lot to collect, then arrange for one person from each group to collect some of it, and another to collect the rest. You can also ask one group at a time to collect their apparatus, rather than everyone at once. Make sure that different groups do this in different sequences each time.

- If you have a large class, or a class where learners are not used to being able to move around in the room, or are unfamiliar with laboratory rules, problems may arise if they are asked to collect their own materials. Instead, you can take a tray of the required apparatus to each group or each bench. Later, as learners get more used to working in a laboratory, you can move towards expecting them to collect their own apparatus.

As a challenge, in this unit you could try the *Think like a Scientist* tasks in Topic 1.2, *Think like a scientist: Why are air sacs so small?* and *Think like a scientist: Comparing the carbon dioxide content of inspired air and expired air*. Settle the groups at their places, then take the prepared apparatus in trays to each group. Then, in Topic 1.4, *Think like a scientist: Investigating respiration in peas*, set out the apparatus at the front of the laboratory, and ask one person from each group to come and collect it.

Plan how you will clear up when the practical session is over. Will learners do their own washing up, or will you or a laboratory technician do this? Where will learners place dirty or washed apparatus? Have a method in place to trap any solids that might be thrown away, to stop them going down the sink – you can tie a sieve (the type that you use in a kitchen) to each tap, for convenience.

Topic 1.1: The human respiratory system

LEARNING PLAN

Learning objectives	Learning intentions	Success criteria
8Bs.03 Describe how the structure of the human respiratory system is related to its function (in terms of lung structure and the action of the diaphragm and intercostal muscles) and understand the difference between breathing and respiration.	• Learn about the structure of the human respiratory system.	• Name the parts of the respiratory system on a diagram.
8TWSc.07 Collect and record sufficient observations and/or measurements in an appropriate form.	• Use a range of senses to observe the structure of lungs.	• List, in order, the parts of the respiratory system that air passes through.

LANGUAGE SUPPORT

Learners will use the following words:

respiration: a series of chemical reactions that take place in all living cells, in which energy is released from glucose

respiratory system: the system involved with providing oxygen to the blood and removing carbon dioxide, so that respiration can take place in cells

trachea: a tube leading from the back of the throat, through which air travels into the lungs; it has C-shaped rings of cartilage in it to support it

windpipe: another name for the trachea

cartilage: a tough but bendy material that provides support to the trachea

bronchus: one of two tubes that convey air from the trachea into the lungs

bronchiole: one of many small tubes that carry air through the lungs, from the bronchi

air sac: a tiny blind-ending sac in the lungs, in which gas exchange takes place between the air and the blood; also known as an alveolus

larynx: the organ at the top of the trachea that contains the vocal cords

voicebox: another name for the larynx

vocal cords: bands of muscle that stretch across inside the larynx, which we vibrate to make sounds

Common misconceptions

Misconception	How to identify	How to overcome
Learners may think that the lungs are where respiration takes place; it is very common for there to be confusion between gas exchange and respiration.	Ask learners to do the *Getting started* activity. You can ask questions as you demonstrate the structure of sheep or goat lungs.	Constant reinforcement is likely to be required, to emphasise the difference between gas exchange and respiration and also (later) breathing.

Starter ideas

1 Getting started (10 minutes, including sharing ideas)

Description: Ask learners to work with a partner to decide which statements are correct. There is no need to write down answers. Then ask some of the pairs to give their suggested answers, orally. Use their ideas to discover any wrong preconceptions about respiration, which you can address later in the lesson. Any wrong decisions, or slight uncertainty about this, will reveal misconceptions.

2 Lungs (5–10 minutes)

Resources: Lungs from a sheep or a goat, to be used later in the demonstration, *Think like a scientist: Looking at lungs*.

Description: Before learners enter the room, place the lungs on a dissecting board or in a large container, and cover them.

Invite learners to the front of the class. Ask them to guess what is under the cover. They can ask questions, but you can only answer 'yes' or 'no'. You can give clues if they do not get close.

Uncover the lungs. Ask learners what they think they are, and what they do. There may be incorrect ideas about respiration happening only in the lungs.

You could now go straight into the *Think like a scientist* demonstration, or put the lungs on one side and start the main lesson using the diagram of the respiratory system in the Learner's Book.

Main teaching ideas

1 The parts of the human respiratory system (20–25 minutes)

Learning intention: To be able to identify and name the different parts of the human respiratory system, and to outline their functions.

Resources: Learner's Book Topic 1.1, diagrams of positions of lungs in the body and of the human respiratory system.

If possible, show a large copy of the second diagram on the board or screen.

If available, a model of the human body with removable organs would be useful.

Description: Use the diagrams and modules to talk about the structure of the respiratory system. Say the names of each part carefully, repeating them often. Use questioning to involve learners, and encourage them to say the names of the parts.

You could provide learners with an unlabelled version of the diagram, for them to stick into their notebooks and label.

Ask learners to answer questions 1 and 2, either orally or by writing the answers in their notebooks.

> **Differentiation ideas:** Some learners may need help to label the diagram, and to answer the questions. Learners who need a challenge could draw the diagram in their notebook, rather than being provided with an unlabelled version to stick in.

> **Assessment ideas:** Check that learners are confident in pronouncing the names of the parts of the respiratory system. Check answers to Questions 1 and 2.

2 Think like a scientist: Looking at lungs (15–20 minutes)

Learning intention: To consolidate understanding of the structure of the respiratory system.

Resources: A fresh set of lungs obtained from a butcher – sheep or goat lungs are ideal (if you have to obtain these the day before the lesson, make sure that they are kept in a fridge so that learners are not put off by strong smells); a dissecting board or large bowl in which to place the lungs; access to warm water, soap and towels, for washing hands; clipboards for learners to make notes or drawings, if appropriate.

Description: Bring learners to the front. If any learners say that they do not want to watch, do not attempt to persuade them, but simply allow them to sit quietly at the back of the class, where they cannot see the lungs. These learners may decide to watch the demonstration once it has begun.

Demonstrate the structure of the lungs and the tubes leading into them. Allow learners to touch the lungs while wearing gloves and safety glasses – they should feel how soft and spongy they are. They can also feel the cartilage rings in the trachea.

Talk through the questions and encourage learners to suggest their answers.

When the demonstration has finished, make sure that everyone washes their hands thoroughly.

Learners can then return to their places and write the answers to the questions.

If no set of lungs is available, a series of images showing the different parts of the lung, or a video clip showing the different structures of the lung, or a video clip of a lung dissection, can be used.

> **Differentiation ideas:** This task works well with learners of all abilities. Differentiation is by outcome, where there will be a range of answers to the questions.

> **Assessment ideas:** Listen to any questions as you demonstrate the structure of the lungs. Listen to answers from learners, and mark their written answers to the questions.

3 What does the larynx do? (5–10 minutes)

Learning intention: To practise observing carefully through touch and hearing

Description: Ask each learner to follow the instructions in the Learner's Book for this activity.

They can do this individually, at their desks.

This idea is good for helping learners to appreciate that observations can be made with all of our

senses, not just sight. It is also helpful for linking what learners have learnt about the respiratory system to their own body. If learners cannot locate their larynx, then the vibration from it can be felt at the front of the neck while speaking.

> **Differentiation ideas:** Some learners may need help finding their larynx and feeling differences in its position when they make different sounds. Some learners may be able to relate the higher frequency of vibration to the higher pitch of a sound.

Plenary ideas

1 Naming the parts of the respiratory system (5 minutes)

Description: Draw or project an unlabelled image of the respiratory system on the board. Ask a learner to name a part of the system. Ask another learner to come and label this part on the board. Repeat with each part.

> **Assessment ideas:** Use answers to check learners' ability to recognise and name the parts of the respiratory system.

Check that learners can pronounce and spell the names correctly.

2 Mastermind (5 minutes)

Resources: A card for each learner, with a tick (✓) on one side and a cross (✗) on the other side

Description: Choose a learner (or ask for a volunteer) to be 'Mastermind'.

Ask this learner a question about the respiratory system, based on the work done in this lesson.

The Mastermind gives an answer – they can choose to give a wrong answer if they wish to.

The other members of the class hold up their cards, with the tick or cross showing, to show whether they think the answer is correct or incorrect.

You can then interrogate the rest of the class to find the correct answer if necessary, or to find out why a learner has identified a correct answer as a wrong one.

Repeat with more questions to the same Mastermind.

> **Assessment ideas:** Use responses of the class to identify any misunderstandings.

Homework ideas

1 Workbook exercise 1.1
2 Worksheet 1.1

Topic worksheets

Worksheet 1.1 A, journey into the lungs

Topic 1.2: Gas exchange

LEARNING PLAN

Learning objectives	Learning intentions	Success criteria
8Bs.03 Describe how the structure of the human respiratory system is related to its function (in terms of lung structure and the action of the diaphragm and intercostal muscles) and understand the difference between breathing and respiration. 8Bs.04 Describe the diffusion of oxygen and carbon dioxide between blood and the air in the lungs. 8TWSm.01 Describe what an analogy is and how it can be used as a model. 8TWSp.05 Make risk assessments for practical work to identify and control risks. 8TWSm.02 Use an existing analogy for a purpose. 8TWSc.05 Carry out practical work safely, supported by risk assessments where appropriate. 8TWSc.07 Collect and record sufficient observations and/or measurements in an appropriate form. 8TWSa.02 Describe trends and patterns in results, including identifying any anomalous results.	• Learn how gas exchange takes place. • Use a model and analogies to explore why alveoli are very small. • Do an experiment to compare the carbon dioxide content of inspired and expired air. • Analyse data on lung surface area and suggest explanations for relationships.	• Describe how gas exchange takes place in the alveoli. • Relate the results of an experiment using agar jelly and dye to gas exchange in the lungs. • Interpret results of an experiment to compare the proportion of carbon dioxide in expired air with inspired air.

CONTINUED

Learning objectives	Learning intentions	Success criteria
8TWSa.03 Make conclusions by interpreting results and explain the limitations of the conclusions. 8TWSa.05 Present and interpret observations and measurements appropriately.		

LANGUAGE SUPPORT

Learners will use the following words:

alveoli: air sacs in the lungs, where gas exchange takes place with the blood

capillaries: the smallest type of blood vessel

gas exchange: the movement (by diffusion) of gases into and out of organisms; in the lungs, oxygen diffuses into the blood and carbon dioxide diffuses out

diffusion: the net movement of a substance from a place of higher concentration to a place of lower concentration, as a result of the random movement of particles

haemoglobin: a red pigment in red blood cells that combines reversibly with oxygen and transports oxygen from the lungs to all respiring cells

analogy: the use of one structure, idea or process to explain another

limewater: a dilute solution of calcium hydroxide; it goes cloudy when mixed with carbon dioxide

expired air: air that is breathed out

inspired air: air that is breathed in

Common misconceptions

Misconception	How to identify	How to overcome
Learners can become confused between gas exchange, respiration and breathing.	When learners are asked to describe these processes and where they take place.	Constant reinforcement to emphasise the difference between gas exchange and respiration and also (later) breathing.
Learners may think that diffusion involves substances purposely moving from one place to another.	When answering questions throughout this topic.	Remind learners what they know about particles, and that particles move randomly; they cannot 'think' or 'know' where they are going
Learners may think that expired air 'is' carbon dioxide, and does not contain any oxygen.	During discussion; when answering questions at the end of *Think like a scientist: Comparing the carbon dioxide content of inspired and expired air* and working through the self-assessment.	See the following notes about this experiment.

Starter ideas

1 Getting started (10 minutes, including sharing ideas)

Learning intention: To find out what learners already know about the behaviour of particles in a gas.

Description: Ask learners to work with a partner to identify the diagrams, and to complete the sentences.

2 Alveoli (5–10 minutes)

Resources: Search the internet for video clips or images of alveoli.

Description: Show learners the video clip(s) and/or images. Ask: *What do you think this is? How does this relate to what you saw when we looked at lungs in the previous lesson? Why are some of the capillaries shown red, and others blue?* Answers could reveal misunderstandings about respiration and gas exchange.

Main teaching ideas

1 Activity: Gases in and out (15 minutes)

Learning intention: understand how oxygen and carbon dioxide move between the alveoli and the blood.

Resources: Learner's Book, diagram of air sacs in the lungs.

Description: This activity encourages learners to focus on the detailed structure of the barrier between the air in the alveoli and the blood in a capillary; it reinforces understanding of how and where gas exchange takes place.

Talk to learners about how gas exchange takes place, using the text and diagram in the Learner's Book. Use questioning to involve them in the discussion, and to check that they remember about haemoglobin (which was mentioned at Stage 7 when they learned about red blood cells). Emphasise the link between the structure and the function of the air sacs, such as having thin walls to allow rapid diffusion of gases.

Then ask learners to do *Activity: Gases in and out.*

> **Differentiation ideas:** You could provide a diagram for some learners who need support, ready for them to complete. Those who are able to complete the task easily and quickly could add annotations to their diagram, with more detail about how the process takes place.

> **Assessment ideas:** Mark the diagrams to determine how well learners understand the process of gas exchange.

2 Think like a scientist: Why are air sacs so small? (up to 30 minutes)

Learning intention: To understand why there are many very small alveoli in the lungs, rather than a few large ones.

Resources: Per group: two Petri dishes each filled with agar jelly; some coloured dye, e.g. methylene blue, ink; a dropper pipette; paper towel.

Per class: at least two cork-borers, one with a diameter of 10 mm and one with a diameter of 5 mm.

If you do not have cork-borers to cut large and small holes in the agar, you can improvise, for example, using drinking straws and an apple corer. However, note that making 10 mm and 5 mm holes ensures that approximately equal volumes of dye will be added to each dish.

Description: Ask each group to follow the instructions in the Learner's Book. After they have set up the experiment, they can predict what they think will happen.

Learners should find that the jelly absorbs the dye faster in the dish with many small holes than in the dish with fewer, larger holes. This is because the dye contacts a larger surface area around the sides of the smaller holes.

> **Practical guidance:** The dishes of agar jelly can be made up in advance. Keep them in the fridge, covered, so that bacteria do not grow on them.

Results can normally be seen within 10 minutes, but this depends on various factors such as the room temperature and the dye used.

> **Differentiation ideas:** Some learners will need help making the holes in the jelly. A small twisting movement can help to remove the jelly from the hole without damaging the rest.

Learners who need a challenge could be asked to calculate the total surface area and volume of the holes in each dish.

3 Think like a scientist: Comparing the carbon dioxide content of inspired and expired air (15 minutes)

Learning intention: To understand that there is more carbon dioxide in expired air than in inspired air.

Resources: Apparatus as shown in the diagram in the Learner's Book.

Conical flasks can be used instead of test tubes.

You will need several pieces of clean rubber tubing, as each learner should use a new piece.

Note: it is very important that the lengths of the glass tubing are as shown in the diagram. The central tube, which leads into both tubes, has one long piece of tubing that dips down into the limewater in one tube, and a short piece that finishes in the air space above the limewater in the other. The other glass tubes in each test tube make contact with the air or liquid respectively.

Description: Ask learners to follow the instructions in the Learner's Book. Warn them how to avoid sucking in limewater. Limewater is a mild irritant, so the volume of the liquid should be as small as possible to avoid the risk of sucking it in.

> **Differentiation ideas:** Some learners will need a lot of help to understand why the air they breathe out goes into one tube, and the air they breathe in goes into the other.

Learners who need a challenge can continue breathing in and out to see if the limewater in the other tube eventually goes cloudy. It should, which shows that there is some carbon dioxide even in inspired air.

Plenary ideas

1 Key words (5 minutes)

Description: Give learners 3 minutes to write down as many key words as they can think of from this lesson.

Then ask a learner to read out their first key word, and ask the class if they can explain its meaning.

Repeat until all key words have been covered.

> **Assessment ideas:** Use answers to check that learners understand all of the new words used in the lesson.

2 Voiceover (5 minutes)

Resources: Search the internet for an animation or video clip of alveoli.

Description: Show the animation or video clip of alveoli. Ask learners to write a voiceover for the clip.

> **Assessment ideas:** Use the voiceovers to check understanding.

Homework ideas

1 Workbook exercise 1.2
2 Self-assessment for the limewater experiment.

Topic 1.3: Breathing

LEARNING PLAN

Learning objectives	Learning intentions	Success criteria
8Bs.03 Describe how the structure of the human respiratory system is related to its function (in terms of lung structure and the action of the diaphragm and intercostal muscles) and understand the difference between breathing and respiration.	• Learn how the intercostal muscles and diaphragm muscles change the volume of the chest cavity, moving air into and out of the lungs. • Measure how much air can be pushed out of the lungs in one breath, and look for patterns in results, and plan a further experiment based on this technique.	• Correctly answer questions about the actions of intercostal muscles and diaphragm muscles. • Plan a suitable experiment to test the hypothesis in *Think like a scientist*, question 2.

CONTINUED

Learning objectives	Learning intentions	Success criteria
8TWSp.04 Plan a range of investigations of different types, while considering variables appropriately, and recognise that not all investigations can be fair tests.	• Use a model to show how breathing movements take place. • Display data from secondary sources (as results charts and graphs), and analyse it to draw conclusions.	• Provide suitable explanations for what happens when using the balloon in a syringe model. • Answer questions in Workbook exercise 1.3 successfully.

LANGUAGE SUPPORT

Learners will use the following words:

breathing: movements caused by muscles, which cause air to move into and out of the lungs

contract: of muscles: get shorter

relax: (of a muscle) stop contracting

Common misconceptions

Misconception	How to identify	How to overcome
Learners may think that the lungs themselves can move, rather than muscles causing the movements involved in breathing.	During discussion of breathing movements; when answering the questions in *Think like a scientist: Using a model to represent breathing movements.*	The use of a syringe and balloon as a model to illustrate breathing movements may help. Learners could also be shown the balloon in a bell jar model.
Learners may think that it is the movement of air into the lungs that makes the chest cavity expand, rather than the cause and effect being the other way round.		

Starter ideas

1 Getting started (10 minutes, including sharing ideas)

Description: Ask learners to write answers to the five questions. Allow no more than five minutes, then ask learners to give you their answers. Use answers to identify any missing knowledge, or lack of understanding.

2 Balloons in a bell jar (5 to 10 minutes)

Learning intention: To begin to think about how breathing happens, by looking at a model.

Resources: Search the internet for a video clip of balloons in a bell jar being used to represent lungs (or you could make a model yourself).

Description: Show learners the video clip, or demonstrate the model yourself. Ask if anyone can explain why the balloons inflate when the rubber is pulled downwards. This will help learners to begin to appreciate that the lungs inflate because of something happening to them, rather than by making it happen themselves.

Main teaching ideas

1 Activity: What happens when you breathe in? (10 minutes)

Learning intention: To appreciate that the chest cavity moves up and out as you breathe in.

Description: Ask learners to sit quietly and relax. Then ask each of them to place one hand on their rib cage (practise this yourself first, so that you can show them the best place to put their hands). Ask them to think about what happens as they breathe slowly in, and then out again.

> **Differentiation ideas:** All learners can do this activity. Differentiation is by outcome; some learners will have difficulty observing what happens when they breathe in and out, while others will identify both that the rib cage moves up and that the diaphragm moves down as they breathe in. Some learners may also be able to recognise that breathing in requires effort, whereas breathing out does not.

2 Think like a scientist: Measuring how much air you can push out of your lungs (20–30 minutes)

Learning intention: To make a volume scale on a bottle; to measure and record volumes of air breathed out; to plan an experiment to test a hypothesis.

Resources: Per group (or per class if done as a whole-class activity): a large plastic bottle that can hold $3\,dm^3$ of liquid, with a lid; a big bowl that can hold water; a piece of sterilised bendy tubing; a $100\,cm^3$ measuring cylinder; a waterproof pen that can write on the plastic bottle.

See also the diagrams in the Learner's Book.

Description: See the instructions in the Learner's Book.

> **Practical guidance:** This experiment can cause a lot of excitement and result in water on the floor, so you may prefer to do this as a class activity. Beware

of very small learners who play wind instruments, who may have a surprisingly large lung capacity.

Do not ask any learners to do this experiment if they do not want to, or if there is a health reason why they should not.

The planning exercise in question 2 of *Think like a scientist: Measuring how much air you can push out of your lungs* could be done as a class discussion, in groups, or as an individual homework task.

> **Differentiation ideas:** All learners should be able to do the experiment successfully. You could have an outline results chart available to give to anyone who has difficulty constructing their own. You could also provide a planning help sheet if needed – see Template 1.3.

> **Assessment ideas:** Use the results charts to assess ability to organise and display results. Use the planning task to assess understanding of experimental design, including the control of variables.

3 Think like a scientist: Using a model to represent breathing movements (10–15 minutes)

Learning intention: To use a model to explain how movement of the diaphragm causes air to move into the lungs.

Resources: See the diagram in the Learner's Book. This apparatus can be made up in advance. The size of the syringe does not matter. It is very important that the balloon fits tightly over the rubber bung, and that the plunger makes an airtight seal with the syringe barrel.

Description: Learners can follow the instructions in the Learner's Book. They need to move the plunger steadily and firmly, and watch carefully to see what happens. When the diaphragm (plunger) moves downwards, air moves into the lungs (balloons). This can help learners to understand breathing movements.

> **Differentiation ideas:** All learners should be able to do the experiment and observe the balloons inflating and deflating as they pull and push the plunger.

Most learners will be able to answer question 3 in *Think like a scientist*. Question 4 is more demanding, and it is likely that only some learners will be able to explain what is happening in terms of pressure and volume changes in the syringe barrel. Most will need a lot of support to help them to understand this concept.

> **Assessment ideas:** Use answers to questions 3, 4 and 5 in *Think like a scientist* to determine how well learners understand how breathing movements move air into and out of the lungs.

Plenary ideas

1 Summarising breathing (5 minutes)

Resources: Learner's Book.

Description: Ask all learners to write down answers to questions 1 and 2, allowing enough time for most to finish. Then ask some individuals to tell the class their answers.

> **Assessment ideas:** Use the answers to the questions to determine how well learners understand how breathing movements move air into and out of the lungs.

2 Pelmanism (10 minutes)

Resources: Set of cards with the names of each structure shown in the diagram of the respiratory system in Topic 1.1, and another set with a unique function for each of these structures.

Description: Learners work in groups to try to collect pairs of cards that match structure and function.

Ask learners to reflect on what they found difficult in this lesson.

It is not easy to link the idea of muscles contracting with an increase in volume, and then link the increase in volume with a decrease in pressure, which results in air moving into the lungs. Ask learners: *How well do you feel you understand this? Did using the model help? What do you feel you could do now, to help you to understand it better?*

Homework ideas

1 Workbook exercises 1.3A–C
2 Worksheet 1.3

Topic worksheets

Worksheet 1.3, Respiratory system leaflet

Topic 1.4: Respiration

LEARNING PLAN		
Learning objectives	**Learning intentions**	**Success criteria**
8Bp.04 Know that aerobic respiration occurs in the mitochondria of plant and animal cells and gives a controlled release of energy. **8Bp.05** Know the summary word equation for aerobic respiration (glucose + oxygen → carbon dioxide + water). **8Bs.03** (part) Understand the difference between breathing and respiration. **8TWSp.03** Make predictions of likely outcomes for a scientific enquiry based on scientific knowledge and understanding.	• Find out how every living cell gets the energy it needs to stay alive. • Do an experiment to investigate how, in respiration, some energy is released as heat. • Think about the difference between breathing and respiration.	• Correctly answer questions 1–4 about the respiration equation. • Obtain and display results clearly from *Think like a scientist: Investigating respiration in peas*, and use these results to draw an appropriate conclusion. • Make good suggestions, with reasons, about how to improve this experiment.

CONTINUED

Learning objectives	Learning intentions	Success criteria
8TWSc.05 Carry out practical work safely, supported by risk assessments where appropriate. **8TWSc.07** Collect and record sufficient observations and/or measurements in an appropriate form. **8TWSa.02** Describe trends and patterns in results, including identifying any anomalous results. **8TWSa.03** Make conclusions by interpreting results and explain the limitations of the conclusions. **8TWSa.04** Evaluate experiments and investigations and suggest improvements, explaining any proposed changes. **8TWSa.05** Present and interpret observations and measurements appropriately.	• Use secondary sources to consider results from an experiment using hydrogencarbonate indicator to determine carbon dioxide concentration.	• Contribute to an explanation of the difference between breathing and respiration. • Complete Workbook exercise 1.4, giving mostly correct answers. • Complete Worksheet 1.4, giving mostly correct answers.

LANGUAGE SUPPORT

Learners will use the following words:

glucose: a sugar that is used in respiration

mitochondria: small structures (organelles) found in the cells of animals, plants and fungi, in which aerobic respiration takes place

aerobic respiration: the controlled release of energy from glucose (and other nutrient molecules) through a series of reactions using oxygen, inside mitochondria

Common misconceptions

Misconception	How to identify	How to overcome
Learners may confuse breathing and respiration.	When working on *Activity: Explaining the difference between breathing and respiration.*	Talk to learners as they work on this activity. Ask questions about what they are doing and how they are intending to explain the difference between these two processes.

Misconception	How to identify	How to overcome
Learners may say that respiration 'produces' energy.	As learners talk about respiration, as they answer questions (written or oral) and as they work on *Activity: Explaining the difference between breathing and respiration*.	Learners have learnt about energy in physics, and should be aware that it is not created or destroyed. Remind them of this, and reinforce by using the term 'release energy', and correcting any learner who uses the incorrect term.

Starter ideas

1 Getting started (10 minutes, including sharing ideas)

Description: Ask learners to work in pairs to discuss the question in *Getting started*. Then ask one or more pairs to share their ideas with the rest of the class. This helps learners to remember what they have learnt about energy in physics lessons, so that they are ready to use these concepts in this new situation.

2 Thermogram (5 minutes)

Resources: Learner's Book thermogram image.

Description: Ask learners to look at the thermogram, and to follow the instructions in the book. Can they answer question 1? Can anyone suggest an answer to question 3? It is fine if answers are wrong at this stage – they will find out the correct answers as the lesson continues.

Note: Alternatively, this activity can be done *after* learners have found out about respiration and what it is, later in the lesson.

Main teaching ideas

1 Why do we need energy? Where does it come from? (10–15 minutes)

Learning intention: To understand what aerobic respiration is, where it happens and why it happens.

Resources: Learner's Book.

Description: Use the text, photographs and diagrams in the Learner's Book to help learners to understand that aerobic respiration is a chemical reaction, that it uses oxygen and that it releases energy from glucose. Use questioning to draw out ideas from learners, for example, about energy

changes (as covered in Stage 7), about mitochondria (also dealt with briefly in Stage 7) and about the various reasons why organisms need energy. You could end by asking all learners to answer questions 1, 2 and 3.

> **Differentiation ideas:** Some learners will need help to answer these questions, especially question 3 which requires an explanation.

Learners who need a challenge could be asked to relate what they have just learnt about respiration to work they have done in Stage 7 on chemical reactions, and how we can tell that a reaction has taken place. What observations would show them that the chemical reactions of respiration have taken place?

2 Think like a scientist: Investigating respiration in peas (10 minutes to set up the experiment; a few minutes each day over the next four or five days, to read temperatures)

Learning intention: to collect, display and interpret results of an experiment about respiration; to evaluate the experiment and suggest improvements.

Resources: See the diagram in the Learner's Book. As an alternative to conical flasks with insulation, you could use a vacuum flask (the type used to keep a drink warm or cold).

Description: If you are doing this as a group experiment, ask groups to follow the instructions in the Learner's Book. If done as a class experiment, show the apparatus to everyone, and put it together so that they can see this being done.

Learners can construct their results chart at this point, ready to fill it in.

Try to collect at least five, and preferably more, temperature readings from each flask over the next few days.

Provide learners with 2 mm graph paper, or a copy of *Template 1.4 Graph axes for Think like a scientist: Investigating respiration in peas*, to construct their graphs.

> **Practical guidance:** The 'dead peas' can be dried peas or beans. The germinating peas (or beans) should be soaked in water for a few hours, and then left in a warm place to germinate. This can be done one or two days before the experiment is to be carried out. You need enough to fill one third to one half of a conical flask or other container.

> **Differentiation ideas:** Some learners will need help to construct their results chart and to draw the graph. Template 1.4 contains an outline grid for these results, with the axes labelled (but no scales). Learners who need a challenge could calculate the mean temperature change per day for each flask.

> **Assessment ideas:** You can use learners' work to assess graph drawing skills.

3 Activity: Explaining the difference between breathing and respiration (30 minutes or more; learners could begin the task in class and perhaps spend some homework time on it)

Learning intention: To consolidate understanding of the difference between breathing and respiration.

Resources: Different groups are likely to require different resources. They may want: large sheets of coloured paper; marker pens in different colours; paper, glue, stapler, paper clips, scissors, and so on; access to the internet; access to a printer; access to a projector.

Description: Ask learners to follow the instructions in the Learner's Book. Give them a short period of time to think about what they will do – no more than 5 minutes. Then ask them to collect what they think they will need (it is fine if they change their minds later) and make a start.

Move between groups and ask questions about what they are doing; ensure that all members of each group are contributing.

> **Differentiation ideas:** Differentiation will be by outcome. Some learners will produce a basic display or poster, while others will be more imaginative and be able to find novel and engaging ways of explaining these two terms.

Plenary ideas

1 Remembering the equation for aerobic respiration (5 minutes)

Description: Write the word equation for aerobic respiration on the board (or ask a learner to do this). Ask: *What can you do to help you remember this equation?*

Make a list of ideas that learners put forward, then ask everyone to decide which ones they will use when they try to learn and remember the equation.

2 Breathing and respiration (5 minutes)

Description: Learners should sit in groups (group size is not important).

Ask the first group to say a sentence about breathing. Does the rest of the class think the sentence is correct? If not, what needs to be changed?

Now go to the next group and ask them to say a sentence about respiration. Does the rest of the class think the sentence is correct? If not, what needs to be changed?

Now go to the next group, who have to say a *different* sentence about breathing. And so on, until each group has suggested a sentence.

> **Assessment ideas:** This is a good way of discovering any confusion between respiration and breathing.

Homework ideas

1 Workbook exercise 1.4
2 Worksheets 1.4A–C

Topic worksheets

Worksheet 1.4A–B, An investigation using hydrogencarbonate indicator

Topic 1.5: Blood

LEARNING PLAN

Learning objectives	Learning intentions	Success criteria
8Bs.02 Describe the components of blood and their functions (limited to red blood cells transporting oxygen, white blood cells protecting against pathogens and plasma transporting blood cells, nutrients and carbon dioxide).	• Learn about the structure of blood. • Find out about the functions of red blood cells, white blood cells and blood plasma. • Interpret data from a secondary source and apply knowledge about red blood cells in a new situation.	• Contribute to making a picture to show the components of blood. • Complete a table to summarise the components of blood and their functions.

LANGUAGE SUPPORT

Learners will use the following words:

blood plasma: the liquid part of blood

red blood cells: the most common type of cell in blood; they have no nucleus; they transport oxygen

white blood cells: blood cells with a nucleus; they help to protect against pathogens

oxyhaemoglobin: the compound formed when oxygen combines with haemoglobin

pathogens: organisms that cause disease, e.g. bacteria, viruses

phagocytosis: the actions of phagocytes, certain white blood cells, when they take in and destroy pathogens (the terms phagocyte and phagocytosis are not required in the specification)

antibodies: chemicals produced by white blood cells, that bind with pathogens and help to destroy them

Common misconceptions

Misconception	How to identify	How to overcome
Learners may think that antibodies are alive, or that they are cells.	When discussing the ways in which white blood cells protect from pathogens.	Refer to antibodies as chemicals, and encourage learners to do the same.

Starter ideas

1 Getting started (10 minutes, including sharing ideas)

Description: Ask learners to discuss the three questions with a partner. Allow four or five minutes, then ask for answers. You could ask a learner to draw a red blood cell on the board, and then add annotations to it according to suggestions from other learners.

2 Red blood cells animation (10 minutes)

Learning intention: To help learners recall what they have previously learnt about red blood cells.

Resources: Search the internet for an animation or video clip showing red blood cells.

Description: Show learners the animation or video clip and ask them: *What are these cells? What do they do? What special features do they have that help them to perform this function?*

Main teaching ideas

1 Components of blood and their functions (20–30 minutes)

Learning intention: To be able to describe the different components of blood and their functions.

Resources: Learner's Book text, illustrations and questions; search the internet for an animation or a video clip of blood flowing through a vessel.

Description: Show learners the animation. Use questioning to help them to identify red blood cells. Concentrate on identifying the white blood cells, and the wall of the blood vessel. (If the animation also shows platelets you could mention them and say that they help blood to clot, but learners do not need to know about that at this stage.)

Next, or alternatively, show the video clip of blood flowing through vessels. Point out the red blood cells, and the cells in the tissues around them. You could liken the blood flowing through the vessel to a fleet of delivery trucks moving along a road.

Now use the text and diagrams in the Learner's Book to discuss the components of blood and their functions. Use questioning to involve learners. Learners can also answer questions 1, 2 and 3.

> **Differentiation ideas:** Some learners will need help to answer the questions successfully, particularly question 3. You could use questions to build scaffolding for them, such as: *Do you remember what mitochondria are? Do you remember what mitochondria do?* (aerobic respiration). *What do they use to do this?* (oxygen). *So, what would happen to the oxygen in a red blood cell, if it had mitochondria?*

> **Assessment ideas:** Use answers to oral and written questions to assess understanding of the components of blood and their functions.

2 Activity: Producing a voiceover for phagocytosis video (20 minutes)

Learning intention: To understand phagocytosis. Note, however, that knowledge of this term is not required in the specification at this stage.

Resources: Search the internet for a video clip of a human white blood cell engulfing a foreign object (phagocytosis).

Description: Show learners the video clip. Talk about what is happening. Now ask learners, in small groups, to write a voiceover for the video clip.

When everyone has finished, ask each group to speak their voiceover as the clip plays. This idea is good for arousing interest in phagocytosis; and for developing a good understanding of the process.

> **Differentiation ideas:** Organise groups so that learners who need more support are in a group with others who are able to provide it. Move around the groups and use questioning to encourage all learners to contribute to writing the voiceover, and to challenge confident learners to think more deeply about what is happening in the video.

> **Assessment ideas:** The voiceovers will give a good idea of how well learners understand the process of phagocytosis.

3 Activity: Making a picture of blood (20–30 minutes)

Learning intention: To reinforce understanding of the structure of blood.

What idea is good for: A hands-on activity that helps learners to understand the different components of blood, and their appearance, fully.

Resources per group: Whatever materials you have available for making a picture of blood, for example: a sheet of plain paper; some red card; some white card; scissors; glue.

Description: This is a hands-on activity that helps learners to understand the different components of blood, and their appearance, fully. Learners should follow the instructions in the Learner's Book.

> **Differentiation ideas:** Some learners may need help deciding how to make their picture; for example, making more red cells than white cells, or the relative sizes of red and white cells.

Learners who need a further challenge could think about how they would make a model to show how red blood cells transport oxygen from the lungs to body cells; if time allows, they could make this model.

Plenary ideas

1 Mind map (20–30 minutes)

Resources: Large sheets of paper.

Description: Ask learners to make a mind map of everything they have learnt in this unit. They could do this individually, or work in pairs.

When each learner or pair has finished, display the mind maps on the wall. Learners can move along the wall and look at other people's mind maps. Ask: *Which one do you think is best? Why?*

> **Assessment ideas:** The mind maps can be used to indicate any misconceptions or misunderstandings in this unit.

2 Summarising the lesson (5 minutes)

Description: Give learners 1 minute to think of a sentence summarising one thing that they have learned in this lesson.

Then ask some of them to share their sentence with you and the rest of the class.

> **Assessment ideas:** Use learners' statements to determine recall and understanding of the components of blood and their functions.

Homework ideas

1 Worksheets 1.5A–C
2 Workbook exercises 1.5A–C

Topic worksheets

Worksheets 1.5A–C, Adapting to high altitude

PROJECT GUIDANCE

Helping white blood cells to protect us from pathogens

This project addresses the following learning objectives:

8SIC.01 Discuss how scientific knowledge is developed through collective understanding and scrutiny over time.

8SIC.02 Describe how science is applied across societies and industries, and in research.

8SIC.03 Evaluate issues which involve and/or require scientific understanding.

This project focuses on one transmissible disease with global importance – rabies – and provides learners with an opportunity to research various aspects of it. This relates to the way in which white blood cells help to protect us from pathogens.

Learners will work in groups on one particular aspect of the discovery and application of the causes and treatments for rabies.

Each group will then make a presentation (as a poster or illustrated talk) of their chosen or allocated topic(s).

Decide whether you will ask each group to work on a particular topic and to present their findings in a particular way, or if you will allow them to choose.

Decide how to divide the class into groups. You may also like to allocate roles to each member within the group.

Find and select suitable references for groups to use. These could include library books and relevant web pages.

Explain to the whole class what the project is about, and how the groups will contribute to the final set of presentations.

Tell the groups what they need to include in their poster or presentation.

Ask each group to present their work. It is probably best to do this in the sequence of the topics in the Learner's Book, as the sequence in the Learner's Book already follows what happened in the correct order in terms of time.

> 2 Properties of materials

Unit plan

Topic	Learning hours	Learning content	Resources
2.1 Dissolving	2.5-3.5	Solutions: use of vocabulary and properties of solutions	**Learner's Book:** Questions 1–5 Think like a scientist: Dissolving and mass **Workbook:** Exercise 2.1A, Using the correct scientific term Exercise 2.1B, What is the difference between these terms? Exercise 2.1C, Explaining observations **Teacher's Resource:** Worksheet 2.1, Extracting salt Template 2.1: Peer assessment for *Activity: Explaining dissolving and forming a solution*
2.2 Solutions and solubility	2.5-3.5	Understanding differences in concentration; using particle theory; investigating solubility	**Learner's Book:** Questions 1–11 Think like a scientist: Making different concentrations of solutions Think like a scientist: Solubility in water **Workbook:** Exercise 2.2A, Using the correct scientific term Exercise 2.2B, Looking at the solubility of three solutes Exercise 2.2C, Making up a solution
2.3 Planning a solubility experiment	2.5-3.5	Planning an investigation; carrying out an investigation	**Learner's Book:** Questions 1–6 Think like a scientist: Planning an investigation Think like a scientist: Carrying out your plan **Workbook:** Exercise 2.3A, Dissolving salt Exercise 2.3B–C Comparing the solubility of two salts **Teacher's Resource:** Worksheets 2.3 (i) A–C, Solubility

Topic	Learning hours	Learning content	Resources
			Worksheet 2.3 (ii), The results of an investigation Template 2.3A: Planning an investigation Template 2.3B: Using the results of an investigation
2.4 Paper chromatography	2.5-3.5	Use of chromatography to separate dissolved substances; interpretation of chromatograms	**Learner's Book:** Questions 1–7 Think like a scientist: Separating the colours in ink Think like a scientist: Is the green colour in plant leaves pure? Activity: Using the correct words **Workbook:** Exercise 2.4A, Wordsearch Exercise 2.4B, Paper chromatography Exercise 2.4C, Paper chromatography with plant material **Teacher's Resource:** Worksheets 2.4A–C, Vocabulary Template 2.4A: Peer assessment for chromatology Template 2.4B: Terms and definitions
Cross-unit resources			**Learner's Book:** Check your Progress **Project:** The secret formula **Teacher's Resource:** Language development worksheets 2.1 Elements, mixtures and compounds 2.2 Names, units and measurements

BACKGROUND KNOWLEDGE

Learners should be familiar with many of the ideas in this unit and are going to need their knowledge of particle theory to help them understand the ideas behind solutions and solubility.

The learners will also have opportunities to build on their practical skills, such as selecting suitable equipment and making risk assessments in the various practical opportunities in the unit. There is opportunity to improve their investigation skills in topics such as the investigation of solubility and work on chromatography. To help learners with the investigation skills, two support templates are provided. These templates have outlines and guidance about both planning an investigation and dealing with the results.

Learners are unlikely to have met chromatography in any detail, but study of solubility in topics 2.3 and 2.4 will provide enough background for learners to understand the different solubilities.

Plenaries 1

Plenaries are a tool that can be used to ensure you have an overview of learners' progress and understanding during the lesson and can be used to inform you what your next teaching steps should be.

Science teachers can lack the time to use plenaries effectively in lessons. This is because the lessons are usually so full, especially in practical sessions. When the lesson is busy, with learners trying to complete practical work and especially towards the end when learners are clearing up, a plenary session often gets squeezed out. At best you may have time to say: *What did we learn today?* or merely to state what the lesson has been about. As science teachers, we need to acknowledge this. If your timetabled sessions are not very long, it becomes more important to complete the practical work or to clear up. In these circumstances you would need to start your next session with some reflection by the learners on what they learned or understood from the practical session and do a revision/recap idea at the start of the next lesson.

It may be more useful in some sessions to have mini-plenaries as you progress through the lesson. For example, at the start of a practical, asking learners what measures they are taking to be safe or accurate, or checking they have the names of equipment correct. This will enable you to be clear about learners' knowledge as they work.

It may be that, during a unit with lots of practical work, you plan a meaningful plenary after a couple of sessions.

The main points for a good plenary are:

- it has to be planned
- you have to have enough time
- the learners have to do the work.

A range of plenaries is suggested throughout all units.

A very useful quick plenary is 'the emoji exit card'. This can be set up fairly quickly and, if it is used regularly, the learners get used to doing it. The learners always get asked the same three questions.

- How well did you understand today's material?
- What did you learn in today's class?
- Please answer the teacher's question.

The first point can be quickly answered by drawing a suitable emoji or just a smiling, sad or neutral face. The final point is a good assessment opportunity for you, with perhaps three tiered questions written on the board, or printed on paper, with only one question differentiated, for your main groups of learners.

Aim to use the emoji exit card and at least two different plenaries from those suggested in this unit.

- Did the use of the emoji exit cards help you to understand better what the learners got from the lesson?
- How could you frame a good question for the emoji card?
- How will the information from the emoji card help you to plan your next lessons?

Use one of the vocabulary plenaries.

1 *Focus on key words*, as in Topic 2.3 Planning a solubility investigation.

   Ask learners to write down as many key words to do with investigations as they can. Give them a time limit, perhaps 1 or 2 minutes. Then ask learners to read out three words and then move on, asking for three more – but they must be different. You need to ensure that those less confident in using English can contribute, perhaps by asking them early in the process or asking them to repeat the words they just heard.

2 *Using the correct words* as in Topic 2.4 Chromatography.

   This activity is about a matching words with meanings.

Did the use of these word-based plenaries help to improve the learners' scientific vocabulary? Can you think of any other ways to improve the use of scientific language?

Topic 2.1: Dissolving

LEARNING PLAN

Learning objectives	Learning intentions	Success criteria
8TWSc.04 Take appropriately accurate and precise measurements, explaining why accuracy and precision are important. **8TWSc.05** Carry out practical work safely, supported by risk assessments where appropriate. **8TWSc.07** Collect and record sufficient observations and/or measurements in an appropriate form. **8TSWa.05** Present and interpret observations and measurements appropriately.	• Use scientific terms associated with solutions. • Investigate the properties of solutions. • Practise measuring mass and volume.	• Use the terms 'solvent', 'solute' and 'solution' appropriately. • Use particle theory to explain some of the properties of solutions. • Measure mass and volume of liquids accurately.

LANGUAGE SUPPORT

Learners will use the following words:

dissolving/dissolve: the complete mixing of a solid with a liquid

solution: a mixture in which particles of a substance (solute) are mixed with particles of a liquid so that the substance can no longer be seen

solute: a substance that is dissolved

solvent: a liquid in which other substances will dissolve

transparent: a material through which light can pass in a way that produces clear images

opaque: a material through which light cannot pass

conserved: no change happens; used in this unit with regard to mass and volume

Common misconceptions

Misconception	How to identify	How to overcome
Often learners do not fully understand the idea that the solute is still present in the solution; they think it has disappeared. This is especially true of colourless solutions.	Ask learners directly: *What has happened? Where has the solute gone?*	You could demonstrate conservation of mass. Find the mass of a solute (such as sodium chloride). Place the beaker of solvent (water) on a top pan balance, and record its mass. Add the solute. Note that the new mass is the mass of solute plus mass of solvent.

Misconception	How to identify	How to overcome
Learners sometimes confuse melting and dissolving.	Ask learners to compare the difference between melting and dissolving.	You may need to go over this several times and on different occasions. You could ask learners to explain this as a starter or plenary activity.

Starter ideas

1 Getting started (10 minutes)

Description: Ask learners to explain the differences to a partner and, between them, reach an answer, which they can share with the class. Ask each pair to draw a diagram to show the arrangement of particles in a liquid. Ask them to hold them up for peer assessment between groups. Look for confusion over compounds and mixtures, especially the idea of mixtures of compounds. Also ensure that the diagrams of particles in a liquid are correct. The Workbook Exercise 2.1A also addresses this subject, and would be a suitable introduction to the topic.

2 Find words starting with… (10 minutes)

Resources: Learner's Book.

Description: Write the word 'solution' vertically on the board and challenge learners to find scientific terms starting with each of the letters in the word. You could allow the learners to use the glossary in the Learner's Book or not, or you could differentiate the task for those who find language difficult. Take feedback from the class. You could award a point for each correct answer and two points if no one else has that answer.

Main teaching ideas

1 Dissolving (10–15 minutes, depending on what learners understand)

Learning intention: To understand what a solution is and some of its basic properties.

Resources: Beakers of water; solute that is colourless in solution (such as salt or sugar); solute that forms a coloured solution (such as copper sulfate); milk (keep hidden).

Description: Dissolve the sugar or salt in a beaker of water, using the correct vocabulary to explain what you are doing. Ask learners what they think is happening. Use the particle model to explain what happens. Do the same with copper sulfate and

again ask: *Is this a solution? Has the copper sulfate dissolved?* Bring out the milk and ask: *Is this a solution?* You could ask the learners to answer this in pairs and share answers. A class discussion about what a solution is would be useful.

> **Differentiation ideas:** All learners need to understand this idea so it may be necessary to go over it more than once for learners who need support. Ask learners directly: *Where has all the solid gone? Why can't you see it any more?* You could ask learners to explain what happens when a solid dissolves in water, in pairs or to the whole class. You could ask them to draw diagrams to help explain and to demonstrate which learners may need extra support. This is important for the less confident learners. When asking questions to the whole class, ensure that the more confident learners do not dominate, and those who are shy have their opportunity to answer.

You could stretch learners by asking them why, when you add copper sulfate crystals to water and they dissolve, there is evidence that they have not disappeared.

> **Assessment ideas:** Ask for a simple 'one piece of paper' explanation of what a solution is and what happens when something dissolves. You could use these for peer assessment; you could use Template 2.1 Peer assessment for *Activity: Explaining dissolving and forming a solution*.

2 Explaining dissolving and forming a solution (20 minutes)

Learning intention: To explain how a solution is formed.

Resources: Template 2.1 Peer assessment for *Activity: Explaining dissolving and forming a solution*

Description: Ask learners to use particle theory to explain how a solution is formed. This could be done without reference to the Learner's Book. It could be done as a poster, computer slide show or on paper.

> **Practical guidance:** This could be done after carrying out the practical session or as homework. The peer assessment could then be done as a separate task.

> **Differentiation ideas:** If necessary, less confident learners could be given a few minutes with the Learner's Book, just to check particle theory. This should not be necessary for the more confident learners.

> **Assessment ideas:** The peer assessment on the template can be used to point out where improvement is needed.

3 Think like a scientist: Dissolving and mass (20–30 minutes)

Learning intention: To understand that the solute does not disappear – it just can't be seen in a solution.

Resources: Learner's Book; filter paper (or watch glass); top pan balance; salt; beaker of water; stirring rod.

Description: Follow the instructions in the Learner's Book and lead learners through the task. You may want to get the class to do each step at the same time, depending on how skilled they are.

> **Practical guidance:** It may be easier to have samples of salt or sugar already on filter paper for the class, to save them all trying to pour a suitable quantity themselves. If you have watch glasses available, learners may find it easier to use them to handle the small quantity of solute and successfully transfer more of it safely to the beaker. Discourage too much vigorous stirring and spilling liquid. It is important that you stress the careful use of the top pan balance.

> **Differentiation ideas:** It would be helpful to prepare the equipment in advance for learners who need more support, so that they do not need to move around the classroom too much.

As learners do the practical, circulate and ask them about what they are doing and why. Ask questions such as: *How accurately have you measured the water? How sure are you that you have added all the solute?* This will help them stay focused and remember that the measurements need to be accurate as they need to account for all the solvent and solute. Try to match the level of complexity of the questions with the confidence of the learners.

> **Assessment ideas:** Use questions 1–4 in *Think like a scientist: Dissolving and mass* to assess the understanding of the ideas.

Plenary ideas

1 Dissolving and melting (10 minutes)

Description: Ask learners to produce a quick guide to explaining the difference between melting and dissolving. They could do this in pairs or individually. Collect learners' guides as they leave and place them on the wall. Identify any learners who need more input on this idea. Look for inconsistencies, poor use of scientific language and poor explanations.

2 Lucky dip words (10 minutes)

Resources: Pieces of card or paper with key words from the topic.

Description: Learners work in pairs. One learner takes a card and describes the word or term to the other learner. Then they swap roles.

Homework ideas

1 Workbook exercises 2.1A–C

N.B. the Workbook exercises for this topic all help reinforce prior knowledge, so that the whole class can study the topic with good understanding of the content.

Topic worksheets

Worksheet 2.1, Extracting salt

Topic 2.2: Solutions and solubility

LEARNING PLAN

Learning objectives	Learning intentions	Success criteria
8Cp.01 Understand that the concentration of a solution relates to how many particles of the solute are present in a volume of the solvent. **8Cc.05** Describe how the solubility of different salts varies with temperature. **8TWSc.04** Take appropriately accurate and precise measurements, explaining why accuracy and precision are important. **8TWSc.05** Carry out practical work safely, supported by risk assessments where appropriate.	• Use particle theory to describe the difference between dilute and concentrated solutions. • Make solutions of different concentrations. • Compare solubility of various solutes. Describe the solubility of a solute at different temperatures.	• Describe how to make solutions of different concentrations. • Compare the number of solute particles in solutions of different concentrations. • Compare the solubility of different solutes. • Carry out an investigation safely. Explain that a change in temperature changes the solubility of a solute.

LANGUAGE SUPPORT

Learners will use the following words:

concentrated (solution): a solution in which a large mass of solute is dissolved

dilute (solution): a solution in which a small mass of solute is dissolved in a large volume

soluble: a substance that will dissolve in a given solvent

insoluble: a substance that will not dissolve in a given solvent

saturated solution: a solution in which no more of the solute will dissolve; note, this term is extension material

solubility: a measure of how soluble a solute is in the particular solvent

Common misconceptions

Misconception	How to identify	How to overcome
Some learners struggle with the use of all the similar sounding terms (such as solvent, solute, solubility).	Continually ask learners to explain the terms.	Use repetition and various activities suggested in the Learner's Book and the Teacher's Resource to ensure familiarity with the terms.

Starter ideas

1 Getting started (10 minutes)

Description: Give learners 1 minute to think about the meanings of the words 'solvent', 'solute' and 'solution'. Do not allow any talking, writing or looking up during this time. Now give them one minute to discuss the meanings with a partner. Then ask learners to write the meanings on different pieces of paper. If you place a group of definitions for the same word together, the class can compare them.

2 What do you mean by 'it's stronger'? (10 minutes)

Resources: A range of concentrations of liquids such as fruit squash, tea (without milk) that are very obviously at different concentrations

Description: This task teaches learners to use the terms 'more concentrated' or 'less concentrated' (more dilute) rather than 'it's stronger' and to understand the idea of concentration. Show learners the range of liquids and ask them which is the most concentrated or to place them in order of concentration. This will depend on how many liquids you have available. Ask them to think about what they mean by 'more concentrated'. You could ask them, in pairs, to discuss this in terms of particles and share ideas with the class.

Main teaching ideas

1 Think like a scientist: Making different concentrations of a solution (30 minutes)

Learning intention: To practise accurate measurements, show the need for accurate measurements and to reinforce the idea of different concentrations.

Resources: Test tubes; test tube rack; two measuring cylinders; suitable for measuring 10 cm³; pipette; concentrated solution of a food dye (the colour is unimportant, but make it fairly dark so that there is an obvious change in colour when the dilutions are made up); beaker of water.

Description: Go through the method for the task with the class and demonstrate the correct use of a measuring cylinder. Emphasise the accuracy needed and discuss the table to show them the volumes required. Make it clear how to use the pipette to get the meniscus exactly right by adding or removing the last few drops of solution or water as appropriate.

> **Differentiation ideas:** All learners should be able to do this activity, but some will need more help than others. You could work directly with these learners and demonstrate the technique for using a measuring cylinder. Learners who need a challenge could produce a solution that is half the concentration of the last solution they made.

> **Assessment ideas:** Use questions 1–6 from *Think like a scientist: Making different concentrations of a solution* to assess understanding.

2 Think like a scientist: Solubility in water (30 minutes)

Learning intention: To investigate the solubility of various solutes.

Resources: Test tubes; test tube rack; measuring cylinder; spatula; a range of solutes such as sodium chloride, potassium sulfate and sugar.

Description: Demonstrate the activity, emphasising the need to control the variables as much as possible. Useful hints could be the volume of the water used and the reliability of using spatulas as a measure. It would be useful to ask how learners can ensure the shaking or stirring of the test tube can be kept the same.

> **Differentiation ideas:** All learners should be able to do this activity, but some will need more help, particularly with the organisational skills. As you circulate, observe what they are doing and/or ask them to explain what learners are doing. Think about how you will group learners (mixed levels so that there is support for those with lower organisational skills, or a smaller range of levels so they can become self-reliant). Some learners may need reminding about the loading of the spatula and not to mix solutes. You could use a few more 'less soluble' solutes, or even an insoluble substance, to stretch those who need a challenge.

> **Assessment ideas:** Use questions 7–9 from *Think like a scientist: Solubility in water* and the results table.

3 Illustrating different concentrations (20–30 minutes)

Learning intention: To reinforce the ideas of particle theory and concentration.

Resources: Poster materials or felt and sticky materials.

Note: Alternatively, this could be completed as a computer task.

Description: Ask learners to draw or cut out 'particles' of a solute and a solvent and then arrange them to show the relative numbers in different solutions. They should use different coloured paper for the different particles. They could do this as an interactive task, perhaps using felt and fastening material such as Velcro, so that others could make a very concentrated solution, a very weak solution, and so on.

> **Differentiation ideas:** Learners who need a challenge could do this as an interactive task, perhaps on the computer. Other learners may need support to manage the task, as in the illustration in the Learner's Book. Work with learners to help them make several different concentrations and present them as a labelled poster.

Plenary ideas

1 Explain the difference between… (10 minutes)

Description: Ask learners to explain the difference, in particle terms, between a concentrated solution and a less concentrated one. They must use the words: 'solvent', 'solute', 'particle'.

2 How to remove …? (10 minutes)

Description: Ask learners to list solvents, other than water, that are used to remove stains such as ballpoint pen, grass or nail polish from clothing. Ask learners to do this as a discussion with a partner and then to produce a 'top tip' to remove stains. Take feedback from the class. This could be a starting point for a piece of research homework.

Homework ideas

1 Workbook exercise 2.2A–C

2 Research stain removal and solvents

Topic 2.3: Planning a solubility investigation

LEARNING PLAN		
Learning objectives	**Learning intentions**	**Success criteria**
8Cc.05 Describe how the solubility of different salts varies with temperature. 8TWSp.04 Plan a range of investigations of different types, while considering variables appropriately, and recognise that not all investigations can be fair tests. (part) 8TWSc.04 Take appropriately accurate and precise measurements, explaining why accuracy and precision are important. 8TWSc.05 Carry out practical work safely, supported by risk assessments where appropriate. 8TWSc.07 Collect and record sufficient observations and/or measurements in an appropriate form. 8TWSa.02 Describe trends and patterns in results, including identifying any anomalous results.	• Plan an investigation. • Carry out an investigation safely. • Take enough accurate and precise measurements and explain why these are important. • Describe the trends and patterns in the results of an investigation. • Describe how the solubility of salts varies with temperature.	• Identify different types of variable. • Plan an investigation. • Carry out an investigation safely. • Measure accurately and precisely, explaining why this is important. • Describe the trends and patterns in the results. • Describe how the solubility of different salts varies with temperature.

CONTINUED

Learning objectives	Learning intentions	Success criteria
8TWSa.03 Make conclusions by interpreting results and explain the limitations of the conclusions. 8TSWa.05 Present and interpret observations and measurements appropriately.		

LANGUAGE SUPPORT

Learners will use the following words:

variables: factors that can be changed in an investigation

independent variable: the variable that is directly changed by the investigator in an experiment

dependent variable: the variable that changes in an investigation as a result of changing the independent variable; this variable is measured

control variables: factors that are kept the same in an investigation so that the test is fair

range: the difference between the highest and lowest values

interval: the size of the gap between measurements

Common misconceptions

Misconception	How to identify	How to overcome
Some learners confuse the terms dependant variables and independent variables.	Ask frequently about the variables using the correct terms.	Reinforce that the dependent variable **depends** on what the independent variable does.
Some learners find difficulties with using data and interpreting graphs.	Watch carefully when learners are working on exercises involving these areas. Ask: *Why do you think that? What does this mean?*	Provide plenty of practice in these areas so that it becomes familiar.

Starter ideas

1   Getting started (10 minutes)

Description: In this task, learners think about the difference between 'accurate' and 'reliable' results. Ask learners, in pairs, to discuss what these terms mean. Take feedback from the class. The idea that a set of results is reliable is something they should be familiar with. What many do not realise, however, is that they can get similar results for each repetition as a result of not measuring accurately and doing the same inaccurate thing each time. This may be an opportunity to revisit basics such as measuring with a ruler; some learners will measure from the end of the ruler and not the zero. Their results will be reliable but not accurate.

2   Science words starting with … (10 minutes)

Resources: Learner's Book.

Description: Write the chosen word (such as 'variable' or 'independent') vertically on the board and challenge learners to find science words beginning with each letter. Discuss the results in class and award one point for a correct word, or two points if no other learner has the same word. You could let learners use of the glossary, or not. You could choose to restrict words to those linked with investigations.

Main teaching ideas

1 Preparation for the investigation (10–20 minutes)

Learning intention: To prepare learners to think about what they need to include in their investigation plan.

Resources: Learner's Book; water; beakers; test tubes; thermometers; salt; spatulas; stirring rods; measuring cylinders (different sizes); a means of heating water

Description: Talk learners through the first part of the text and the speech bubbles, and the outline of how to do the investigation. Demonstrate the task, but not in too much detail. Avoid measuring accurately. Do not attempt to be consistent, for example, do one test with a beaker and large volume of water, the next using one test tube. You could also be a little careless with the hot water, to further emphasise safety. You could hint at the heat loss from the water while you do the investigation and discuss what could be done.

Then ask learners what they thought about how you carried out the demonstration. Encourage learners to point out what you did wrong and where you were not careful.

> **Differentiation ideas:** All learners need to be able to do the planning task in the next activity. Ensure you include all learners in the discussion of how you carried out the demonstration. Direct questions at the class and only use a learner's name at the end of the question, so they don't know who is expected to answer. As you observe the class, look for those who are unsure. The key questions to see which learners may need support are: *What am I trying to find out? What am I changing? What am I keeping the same?* These should help you identify those learners who are in need of more help. Look for those who are unable to see the significance of the inconsistencies in your practical techniques.

You could challenge those learners who need to be stretched to check their plans with one another.

2 Think like a scientist: Planning an investigation (30–50 minutes, with write up)

Learning intention: To plan the investigation.

Resources: Learner's Book; support sheets; sticky notes.

Description: Group learners in twos or threes and ask them to work through the text and discuss all the listed points before they make their group decision. Then they should write up their plans.

> **Differentiation ideas:** Circulate and listen to the discussions. Prompt where necessary; ask learners why they are doing a particular thing. Ask: *Which is the dependent variable? How exactly will you measure that?*

You may need to provide additional guidance to some learners as they attempt to draw up their results tables. You could refer them to the reference section of the Learner's Book. Learners could use the sticky notes to record the answers to various points in their plan. They can then arrange the notes appropriately, to order their write-up of the plan.

Those who find this task difficult could use the support sheet *Template 2.3 A: Planning an investigation.* You could provide a set of these sheets for each group, for use during discussions. Some of the less confident learners may need to use the planning support sheets to write their plans. Discourage more confident learners from using the planning sheets if they do not need the support.

> **Assessment ideas:** You could use the written plans and/or questions 1–6 from *Think like a scientist: Planning the investigation.*

3 Think like a scientist: Part 2, Carrying out the investigation (40–70 minutes, with graph and discussion of results)

Learning intention: To work on practical skills and analysis skills.

Resources: Read learners' plans before they start this task, to ensure their plans are sensible (logical sequence, all the basics answered, the independent, dependent and control variables identified and considered), with risk assessment and a list of equipment they plan to use. Then you can provide what they have asked for, plus other items so that they can select what they want, particularly if the plan is different from those of other groups.

Include a range of laboratory glassware: measuring cylinders of various sizes; beakers of various sizes; test tubes and test tube racks; means of heating water; thermometers; spatulas; glass rods and/ or paper to dry the spatulas if they are using then to stir the solution. Also include some equipment that is not needed. You could choose to have some insulating materials available.

> **Practical guidance:** Watch out for safety, accuracy and reliability. Allow time for clearing up.

> **Differentiation ideas:** Circulate, watch and question learners while they are carrying out their investigation. Prompt where needed, by asking questions such as: *Why are you doing it that way? What effect will it have if you ...? How are you ensuring this is accurate? How confident are you in your results?*

Work directly with groups that have difficulty carrying out the task. They may need support with accurate measuring. You may need to demonstrate this or ask one of the other groups to do so. Once learners are at the stage of plotting the graph, they could use support sheet *Template 2.3B: Using the results of the investigation*. More confident learners should be able to complete this task with little or no support.

> **Assessment ideas:** Use answers to 1–3 from *Think like a scientist: Carrying out the investigation*.

Plenary ideas

1 What could have been better? (10 minutes)

Description: Ask each group to discuss what could have been better about their investigation. Ask them how they could modify or improve it.

You could do this as an 'exit card' exercise or as feedback to the class. You could use the exit cards as a basis for a starter for the next session.

> **Assessment ideas:** Use the write-ups and the results analysis as an assessment to inform the next piece of practical work.

2 Focus on key words (10 minutes)

Description: Ask learners to write down as many key words about the investigations as they can. Give them a time limit, perhaps 1–2 minutes. Then ask learners to read out three words and then move on, asking for three more, which must be different. You need to ensure that those less confident in using English can contribute, perhaps by asking them early on in the process or asking them to repeat the words they just heard.

Homework ideas

1 Workbook exercise 2.3A

2 Workbook exercise 2.3B–C

3 Complete planning exercise if unfinished in class time

4 Complete results and graph plotting if not completed in class time

Topic worksheets

Worksheets 2.3A–D

Topic 2.4: Paper chromatography

LEARNING PLAN		
Learning objectives	**Learning intentions**	**Success criteria**
8Cp.02 Describe how paper chromatography can be used to separate and identify substances in a sample.	• Separate dissolved substances by using chromatography.	• Describe how to carry out a practical task to separate dissolved substances by using chromatography.

CONTINUED

Learning objectives	Learning intentions	Success criteria
8TWSc.05 Carry out practical work safely, supported by risk assessments where appropriate.	• Interpret chromatograms. • Use the appropriate scientific terms.	• Explain what a chromatogram shows. • Use the appropriate scientific language in the descriptions.

LANGUAGE SUPPORT

Learners will use the following words:

paper chromatography: a method for separating mixtures of dissolved chemicals using special paper

chromatogram: the resulting separation of substances after carrying out chromatography

permanent: fixed; in this case, does not dissolve in water

solvent front: the level the solvent has reached as it travels up the paper, while carrying out chromatography

Common misconceptions

Misconception	How to identify	How to overcome
Some learners may have difficulty with the idea that some inks are not soluble in water.	Some learners may express surprise when it is suggested that other solvents need to be used.	Remind learners about what happens if they get permanent ink on their clothes.

Starter ideas

1 Getting started (10 minutes)

Description: This task reminds learners that paper chromatography is another example of separating mixtures. Ask learners to draw diagrams to show how solutions can be separated. Then they discuss with a partner.

2 Pure or mixture? (10 minutes)

Resources: Cards with various items written on, such as: water from the tap; seawater; sodium; copper chloride; copper sulfate solution.

Note: This could be done as a slide show.

Description: Hold up a card and ask learners to indicate 'mixture' or 'pure'. You could do 'thumbs up' for pure, 'thumbs down' for mixture, or learners could hold up paper or mini whiteboards with P or M on them. After each item, ask: *Why do you think*

that? or *What does the mixture contain?* You will be able to identify learners who find this difficult and remind them about the ideas of pure substances and what a mixture really is.

Main teaching ideas

1 Think like a scientist: Separating the colours in ink (50 minutes)

Learning intention: To explain what chromatography is and how to carry out an investigation into different types of coloured ink.

Resources: Learner's Book; chromatography paper (or filter paper); beaker; water; pencil and ruler; glass rod or wooden spill to hang paper from; coloured ink (pipette needed if it is liquid ink) or a black pen; various other coloured inks and/or food dyes.

Description: Start by explaining that liquids that appear to be one colour may be made up of substances of different colours. Demonstrate how to separate the colours in coloured ink and/or have one that you have prepared earlier, so they can see what happens. You could also try using the colours from various sweets or food dyes.

Learners should follow the instructions from the Learner's Book and/or the demonstration.

> Practical guidance: Make sure you follow the steps in the method described in the Learner's Book. Ask learners to repeat back to you why each step is taken. Be careful to ensure that the ink spot is dry before you add more, so that the spot is not too big. Take time to demonstrate how to hang the strip of chromatography paper, to ensure that the ink spot is above the level of the water or solvent. You could ask different learners to perform each step after you have demonstrated it, to reinforce what they need to do.

Circulate as learners do this task. Watch out for problems with overloading ink, or making the spot too large. Remind learners to allow each application of ink to dry before adding more. Other problems include:

- placing the paper too far into the water so that the ink is below the water line
- not hanging the chromatogram securely
- leaving the chromatogram to run for too long so that the solvent front takes the ink to the far end of the paper.

Ensure the chromatograms are dry before learners attempt to stick them into their notebooks.

> Differentiation ideas: Ask different learners to demonstrate and explain why each step is taken. There should be little difficulty for learners here but be aware of those who are less dextrous and those who have colour perception problems.

Some learners will require more hands-on support with carrying out this task. You can judge this by carefully watching what they are doing and providing advice and support. You could allow those who manage to get this set up correctly and quickly to use other substances and make more than one chromatogram. It is interesting to compare different brands of pen, for example.

> Assessment ideas: Use questions 1–5 from *Think like a scientist: separating the colours in ink.*

2 What is chromatography used for? (20 minutes)

Learning intention: To link chromatography to real-world science.

Resources: Some ready-made chromatograms; a chromatography tank; variety of food dyes; water; pencil and ruler; chromatography paper (or filter paper); large beaker (if a tank is not available); glass rod or wooden spill; pipettes

Description: Set up the tank with a number of different food dyes (or coloured inks: different brands of the same colour inks are interesting), making sure they are labelled in pencil. If possible, allow learners to carry out each stage. As this is likely to take some time, you will need to have one that you made earlier. Discuss why you might need to do this; for example, to compare inks, perhaps in forensics (see the project at the end of the topic) or looking for colourings in food (some colourings are banned in some countries because they are regarded as health risks). Discuss why it is a good idea to place the paper in a tank. (Air movements could result in uneven flow of solvent or the solvent drying out in places.).

Use prepared chromatograms to show what happens and how easy (or not) it is to compare the results.

> Differentiation ideas: It may be necessary to draw around the coloured blobs to make it clearer for less confident learners, or learners with colour perception difficulties. The use of different chromatograms with more or less obvious differences and a bank of questions could be helpful to stretch learners who find these ideas straight-forward.

> Assessment ideas: Use questions 1–4.

3 Think like a scientist: Is the green colour in plant leaves pure? (Paper chromatography with plant materials) (30–40 minutes)

Learning intention: To show chromatography with a solvent other than water.

What idea is good for: Practical skills development and use of an alternative solvent.

Resources: Fresh green plant material such as spinach (leaves should be dark green but without a very thick cuticle); pestle and mortar; ethanol, pipette; chromatography paper (or filter paper); beaker; pencil; glass rod or spill.

Description: Carry out the demonstration, involving learners so they understand clearly what they should do. If necessary, ask learners for the next step and ask others why that step should be taken. Crush the spinach leaves, adding a little ethanol, in the pestle and mortar. Let it stand for about 10 minutes (time for the green pigment to dissolve in the ethanol) – this is important, don't be tempted to rush or there will not be enough pigment for learners to be able to see the separation. Prepare the chromatography paper with a pencil line and a cross, about 1 cm from the end. Use a pipette to load some of the liquid onto the cross. Allow the spot to dry before adding more of the liquid. Place the chromatography paper over a glass rod or pencil and hang it in a beaker containing some ethanol, so that the line is just above the ethanol.

The resulting chromatogram may be very faint and hard to see, so it would be helpful to show learners one you made earlier. The pigment tends to fade in the light so ask learners to stick the paper into their notebooks as soon as it is dry. It can be useful for learners to draw a pencil line around the different areas of the pigments so that, when they do fade, they have a reminder of what happened.

> **Practical guidance:** When using ethanol make sure that the area is well-ventilated and there are no heat sources.

> **Differentiation ideas:** Use questioning as above. Try to include as many learners as possible with the practical tasks and ask questions during the demonstration. While the practical is in progress, circulate and offer advice to those who are having difficulty with the mechanical process. Ask the groups questions such as: *How can you keep the spot as small as possible? Why does that matter?* Answers to this type of question should help to direct your support to where it is most needed.

> **Assessment ideas:** Ask learners to make a step-by-step guide to extracting and separating the pigments, perhaps as a poster, and do a peer review, using *Template 2.4: Peer assessment for chromatography*.

Plenary ideas

1 Using the correct words (10 minutes)

Resources: Cards with terms applying to this topic, as in *Activity: Using the correct words*, from *Template 2.4B: Terms and definitions* could be used.

Timer, or access to a clock with a second hand.

Description: With a partner, learners time how long it takes each person to match the correct terms with the meanings.

2 Mastermind (10 minutes or longer)

Resources: Prepared questions from this unit.

Description: Ask a volunteer to sit in the hot seat as 'Mastermind'. Explain that they can choose to answer correctly or incorrectly and that you do not want them to answer every question correctly. Once the question has been answered, the class members must each hold up a tick (✓) or a cross (✗). You can then ask for further clarification if needed. Ask learners to think how well they did with the questions and where they need to put in some more work to improve. You can get a very quick idea of how the class has understood the material.

Homework ideas

1 Workbook exercises 2.4A–C

Topic worksheets

Worksheets 2.4A–C

PROJECT GUIDANCE

The secret formula

This project addresses the following learning objectives:

8SIC.03 Evaluate issues which involve and/or require scientific understanding.

8SIC.04 Describe how people develop and use scientific understanding as individuals and through collaboration, e.g. through peer review.

The aim of this project is to help learners to see how science is used in investigations of crimes.

You could set up part of the room as a research laboratory environment, with a noticeboard covered with formulae and ideas, a workbench with a range of experimental apparatus and the note. You could use adults to act out this scenario complete with white coats and a disguise.

The point is to interest them and then to discover which pen was used to write the note.

Provide a range of equipment for the groups to carry out the tests.

You need to provide ink 'extracted' from the note and four pens, one of which matches the ink. It might be useful if one pen was a permanent marker pen, in which the ink is insoluble in water.

You could load the inks onto one piece of chromatography paper that can be rolled into a tube, so that it will stand in a large beaker. If you can use this method, the comparison of the inks will be easier – but take care with loading the chromatogram, ensuring the spots are fully dry, and with placing the rolled paper in the beaker to ensure that any part of the paper above the load line does not touch the solvent.

Having discovered who wrote the note, learners move on to the more important part of the project, which is to discuss the evidence. Learners discuss, in groups of three or four: *Does this provide you with evidence that this person has the formula? If not, why not? What other evidence should you look for?* Circulate during group discussion, prompting and keeping the groups focused. After allowing time for group discussion, have a feedback session with the whole class. Take the opportunity to ask the groups to share their results and to be collaborative in their approach. Discuss the role of research scientists and industry as appropriate. Once the groups have some results, ask them to cross question one another along the lines of: *How can you be sure this result is correct? What techniques did you use? Could there have been an error?*

Make a point of 'testing' learners' findings and pointing out the peer review aspect of the learning objective **8SIC.04**.

The main point of this project is to consider: *What evidence do I have? What does it tell me and can I be sure?*

You could extend this investigation to include a shoe or bootprint or fingerprints. It can be exciting for learners to find the laboratory set up with police 'do not cross' tape or evidence that things have been knocked over or broken. Many learners like to engage with solving a puzzle or mystery, so you could add puzzle-solving tasks, such as investigating codes, if you have time or would like to stage an event. Such an event could be organised in a venue outside the classroom, in a hall or public area, where you have more space and you could involve more than one class with the initial crime scene.

You could change the scenario to any type of crime scene, even a murder scene if that is suitable for your situation.

> 3 Forces and energy

Unit plan

Topic	Learning hours	Learning content	Resources
3.1 Forces and motion	2–3	What we mean by balanced and unbalanced forces; the effects of balanced forces on motion; the effects of unbalanced forces on motion	**Learner's Book:** Questions 1–4 Activity: Balanced or unbalanced forces? Think like a scientist: Measuring balanced and unbalanced forces **Workbook:** Exercise 3.1A, Balanced forces Exercise 3.1B, Unbalanced forces Exercise 3.1C, Changing direction **Teacher's Resource:** Worksheet 3.1, Effect of balanced and unbalanced forces Template 3.1: Results table for *Think like a scientist: Measuring balanced and unbalanced forces*
3.2 Speed	2–3	The meaning of the unit of speed and how to work out the unit; know and be able to use the equation for speed	**Learner's Book:** Questions 1–5 Activity: Speed, distance and time Think like a scientist: Calculating speed **Workbook:** Exercise 3.2A, Units of speed Exercise 3.2B, Calculating speed Exercise 3.2C, Calculating distance and time **Teacher's Resource:** Worksheets 3.2A–C, Calculating speed, distance and time Template 3.2: Results table and graph axes for *Think like a scientist: Calculating speed*

Topic	Learning hours	Learning content	Resources
3.3 Describing movement	2-3	How graphs can be used to describe movement; what a distance/time graph shows; how to draw a distance/time graph	**Learner's Book:** Questions 1–3 Activity: My journey Think like a scientist: Walking and running **Workbook:** Exercise 3.3A–C, Distance/time graphs **Teacher's Resource:** Template 3.3: Results tables and graph axes for *Think like a scientist: Walking and running*
3.4 Turning forces	1.5-2	Recognise when a force has a turning effect; know the meaning of and how to use the term moment; be able to calculate moments	**Learner's Book:** Questions 1–5 Activity: Identifying moments Think like a scientist: Calculating moments **Workbook:** Exercise 3.4A, Identifying turning forces Exercise 3.4B, Calculating moments Exercise 3.4C, Moments, force and distance **Teacher's Resource:** Worksheets 3.4A–C, Forces for turning
3.5 Pressure between solids	1.5-2	Recognise that forces can cause pressure on an area; understand what affects this pressure; be able to calculate the pressure caused by a force on an area	**Learner's Book:** Questions 1–5 Think like a scientist: Calculating pressure **Workbook:** Exercise 3.5A, Describing pressure Exercise 3.5B, Calculating pressure Exercise 3.5C, Variables affecting pressure
3.6 Pressure in liquids and gases	1-1.5	Recall how particles move in liquids and gases; understand how particle movement causes pressure in liquids and gases; predict how changes in liquids and gases affects the pressure	**Learner's Book:** Questions 1–5 Think like a scientist: Observing the effects of pressure **Workbook:** Exercise 3.6A, Trends in pressure 1 Exercise 3.6B, Trends in pressure 2 Exercise 3.6C, Trends in pressure 3 **Teacher's Resource:** Worksheets 3.6A–C

Topic	Learning hours	Learning content	Resources
3.7 Particles on the move	1–1.5	Describe how random movement of particles causes diffusion; understand how diffusion happens in liquids and gases	**Learner's Book:** Questions 1–5 Activity: Watching diffusion Think like a scientist: The effect of temperature on the speed of diffusion **Workbook:** Exercise 3.7A, Diffusion in gases and liquids Exercise 3.7B, Diffusion Exercise 3.7C, Variables affecting diffusion
Cross-unit resources			**Learner's Book:** Check your Progress **Project:** Making a balance for weighing **Teacher's Resource:** Language development worksheets 3.1 Forces and energy vocabulary 3.2 Sorting the instructions and the questions

BACKGROUND KNOWLEDGE

Learners will recall some information about forces, including some of the effects of forces. These should include pushing and pulling for Topic 3.1 and turning for Topic 3.4. Learners may also recall the equipment used to measure forces, the unit of force and be able to draw and interpret simple force diagrams. Learners should be familiar with terms such as 'equal', 'opposite', 'balanced' and 'unbalanced'.

For Topics 3.2 and 3.5, learners should recall the meanings of the terms 'distance', 'area' and 'time', together with some of the units of measurement for these quantities. Learners should be able to substitute values into a simple algebraic equation,

and possibly to rearrange this equation or use a formula triangle.

Learners should be able to interpret graphs and understand how graphs are used to show the relationship between two variables for Topic 3.3. While learners may not have met the term 'gradient', they should be able to express this in terms of steepness and whether the line on the graph is sloping up or down, or is horizontal.

For Topics 3.6 and 3.7, learners may find it helpful to recall the arrangement and movement of particles in gases and liquids, and the ways in which the movement of gas particles is affected by changes in temperature.

TEACHING SKILLS FOCUS

Lesson starters 1

An effective lesson starter is the key to a successful lesson. A starter can be a way of engaging learners' interest in the topic and providing the focus for the learning outcomes to be achieved in the main activity that will follow.

Starters should be varied and unpredictable. If learners do not know what to expect at the beginning of your lesson, then that will add interest even before learners arrive. Starters can take place before learners take their seats or as they arrive at their seats. Effective starters can help settle learners and also help to improve behaviour.

Starters should always be linked to the learning objective, or objectives, in the lesson. Starters should not just be a 'fun' activity that is not related to the lesson. If this is the case, learners will be confused as to what they are supposed to be learning.

For example, in a lesson about balanced and unbalanced forces, learners could be instructed to line up across the back wall of the room as they arrive. The width of the classroom will be an agreement line. If learners go to one, specified, side they strongly agree, if they go to the other side then they strongly disagree. In the middle means they do not know. Then make statements, such as: *The unit of force is newtons* and wait for learners to position themselves. Follow simple statements

with more complex ones, such as: *Friction always acts in the same direction as movement* then, when learners have taken their places on the agreement line, ask for justifications of why they took up their chosen position. This activity is fun for learners, it breaks the usual routine of coming in and sitting, yet it allows you to assess prior understanding. By the time learners are seated in their places, learning will have already started and they will be more focussed for the main activity.

As a challenge, if you usually take a very traditional approach to your lesson structure, choose music that is related to the topic and have this playing as learners arrive. Maybe ask them to sing along!

During – or after – the lesson ask yourself questions such as:

- Was this starter activity successful, and if so, why?
- Did the starter activity affect the overall mood of the lesson?
- Did learners engage with the starter activity?
- Did the starter activity help learners engage with the main lesson content?
- What could I change to make this starter even more effective for future lessons?

Don't forget to share good ideas with colleagues and promote the idea of sharing good practice in your department or school.

Topic 3.1: Forces and motion

LEARNING PLAN

Learning objectives	Learning intentions	Success criteria
8Pf.03 Describe the effects of balanced and unbalanced forces on motion. 8TWSm.01 Describe what an analogy is and how it can be used as a model. 8TWSp.04 Plan a range of investigations of different types, while considering variables appropriately, and recognise that not all investigations can be fair tests. 8TWSc.02 Decide what equipment is required to carry out an investigation or experiment and use it appropriately. 8TWSc.04 Take appropriately accurate and precise measurements, explaining why accuracy and precision are important. 8TWSc.07 Collect and record sufficient observations and/or measurements in an appropriate form. 8TWSa.02 Describe trends and patterns in results, including identifying any anomalous results. 8TWSa.03 Make conclusions by interpreting results and explain the limitations of the conclusions.	• Understand how forces act on objects. • Understand that forces have direction. • Understand that forces equal in size and opposite in direction are balanced. • Understand that one or more forces that do not have an equal force acting in an opposite direction are unbalanced. • Recognise that balanced forces will cause no change in motion. • Recognise that unbalanced forces will cause a change in speed or direction of movement. • Understand force diagrams.	• Describe that forces include pushing and pulling objects. • Recognise from force diagrams whether forces are balanced or unbalanced. • Describe what will happen to an object when a balanced or unbalanced force acts. • Draw force diagrams and correctly interpret force diagrams.

LANGUAGE SUPPORT

Learners will use the following words:

force: an action that, if unbalanced, will change the direction of movement of an object or will change the shape of an object

balanced: forces acting on an object are balanced if the sizes of the forces are equal and they are in opposite directions

opposite: the direction of two forces is opposite if the angle between the forces is 180°

direction: the path of movement of an object or the line along which a force acts

unbalanced: forces acting on an object are unbalanced if the effects of the forces do not cancel

slow down: get slower, decelerate or reduce in speed

speed up: get faster, accelerate or increase in speed

change direction: an object moves in a curved path or at an angle to its original movement

Common misconceptions

Misconception	How to identify	How to overcome
If an object is stationary, then there must be no forces acting.	Show an object, such as a book, resting on a desk and ask what forces are acting, or whether there are any forces.	Lift the object and ask what will happen if you let go. Learners will say the object will fall. Ask what causes the object to fall. Learners should say gravity or weight. Set the object on the desk and ask whether gravity has disappeared. Learners should say no. If they say yes, then allow them to lift the object. Can they feel the weight? So does gravity switch on only when they lift something? Then ask why the object does not fall through the desk, so introducing the balanced contact force.
There must be an unbalanced forward force on an object moving at a constant speed.	Ask learners to draw a force diagram for an object moving at a constant speed in a straight line. Prompt for a forward force and friction if necessary.	If the force diagram shows a larger, unbalanced, forward force, then ask for another force diagram for an object getting faster in the forward direction. This should look similar. Ask how you can tell the object is getting faster, then use that idea on the original force diagram.

Starter ideas

1 Getting started (5 minutes)

Description: Learners should recall the unit of force and that forces can be represented by arrows. The last question will identify the misconception that no forces act on a stationary object.

Note: The correct answer to question 3 is true as weight (or the force of gravity) always acts. The contact force from a surface acts when an object is supported by a surface. This idea serves as an introduction to balanced force.

2 Tug of war (5–10 minutes)

Resources: Rope; coloured tape; space where it is safe to do the activity.

Description: Any even number of learners can participate, from two as a demonstration to a whole-class activity. Learners pull on the rope to try to move it in their direction. Ask questions about the forces on the rope. *Are there forces acting even when the rope is not moving?*

Safety: Ensure there is adequate space in case learners fall when pulling.

Some learners may think that there are no forces acting if an object is stationary, so this activity can be used to overcome this misconception.

Main teaching ideas

1 Activity: Balanced or unbalanced forces? (20 minutes, to include reflection and peer assessment)

Learning intention: To understand that objects that are stationary or moving at constant speed have balanced forces acting; objects that are changing speed or direction have unbalanced forces acting.

Resources: The statements could be prepared on cards for the learners, to reduce the writing required.

Description: Learners construct and complete a table, as in the Learner's Book.

> Differentiation ideas: Learners needing more support could be prompted to think whether the speed or direction of the object is changing.

Learners needing more challenge could be asked to think of other examples that show: **a** balanced forces, **b** unbalanced forces that result in a change of speed, **c** unbalanced forces that result in a change of direction.

> Assessment ideas: Learners could swap tables and assess each other's work.

2 Think like a scientist: Measuring balanced and unbalanced forces (20–30 minutes, to include recording results)

Learning intention: To observe the effects of balanced and unbalanced forces and to be able to make measurements.

Resources: See the Learner's Book.

Description: See the Learner's Book.

Learners may find it difficult to make readings from the force meter when the forces are unbalanced, as the readings may fluctuate as the string moves. This can be used to prompt discussion about whether measurements can always be known accurately.

> Practical guidance: Before the experiment, the force meters should be checked to ensure that they are moving freely and are correctly set to

zero. Learners should be encouraged to check this themselves.

The two newton meters/forcemeters do not have to be the same, but this is preferred at the start as one of the questions asks about this.

> Differentiation ideas: Learners needing more support could be asked to attach the forcemeter to either side of a rigid support and to pull them both. Then another learner takes both readings. This will make the meters easier to read as there will be less movement.

Learners needing more challenge could be asked, as an extension to question 6 in *Think like a scientist: Measuring balanced and unbalanced forces*, to give strengths and limitations of this analogy.

> Assessment ideas: Looking at the ways learners approach making measurements (*Are they reading the force meter at eye-level?*) and draw tables (*Are the results and observations recorded neatly and logically?*) can reveal much about their experimental skills.

3 Circus of forces (20+ minutes)

Learning intention: To identify when forces are balanced and when they are unbalanced.

Resources: Sets of objects set up at stations around the class. These can include:

- a forcemeter hanging from a clamp stand and masses to hang
- a toy car to push
- a ball to roll down a ramp
- a ball to be thrown and caught between two learners.

A short set of instructions should be available at each station.

Description: Learners work in approximately equal-sized groups and move around the stations. It is helpful if you sound a signal so all groups move at the same time. At each station, learners observe what happens when the object is used according to the instructions. In each case, learners decide when the forces are balanced and when the forces are unbalanced. Learners should record their observations. Learners should draw force diagrams during the activity.

> **Differentiation ideas:** Learners needing more support could be asked to identify whether speed is changing in each case. The ball being thrown could be omitted, as this example is more complex.

Learners needing more challenge could be asked where the forces are coming from. For example, when they are pushing the toy car the push is obvious, but friction is less obvious. The ball being thrown could be analysed further into the throwing stage, the stage when the ball is in the air and the catching stage, all of which involve unbalanced forces.

Answers: For example, the masses on the forcemeter: when the masses are added the forces are unbalanced as the spring in the meter extends and starts to move down; when the masses stop moving, the forces are balanced; when the masses are removed, the forces are unbalanced as the spring starts to move upward.

> **Assessment ideas:** After the activity, learners can display their results, either on their desks or by the original stations, and a gallery walk can take place with learners giving feedback to each other. A gallery walk is where learners move around the room looking at the work of others.

Plenary ideas

1 Alternative words (3–5 minutes)

Resources: Small pieces of paper, approximately 10 cm by 5 cm. These could have prompts for 'balanced forces' and 'unbalanced forces'.

Description: Ask learners to use as few words as possible to describe what 'balanced forces' and 'unbalanced forces' mean. For example, for balanced forces they could write words such as 'equal' or 'opposite' or 'cancel out'.

> **Assessment ideas:** Reading the words on the cards should make clear how many in the class understand the concepts of balanced and unbalanced forces.

2 What I learned today (1–5 minutes depending on number of statements)

Resources: Paper and pens.

Description: Learners list a minimum of three things they the learned in the lesson.

> **Assessment ideas:** Learners can record this activity in notebooks for assessment at the same time as the next homework or as exit slips.

Homework ideas

1 Learner's Book questions

2 Workbook exercises 3.1A–C

3 Worksheet 3.1

Topic worksheets

Worksheet 3.1, Effect of balanced and unbalanced forces

Topic 3.2: Speed

LEARNING PLAN

Learning objectives	Learning intentions	Success criteria
8Pf.01 Calculate speed $\left(\text{speed} = \dfrac{\text{distance}}{\text{time}}\right)$. 8TWSm.03 Use symbols and formulae to represent scientific ideas. 8TWSp.04 Plan a range of investigations of different types, while considering variables appropriately, and recognise that not all investigations can be fair tests. 8TWSc.03 Evaluate whether measurements and observations have been repeated sufficiently to be reliable. 8TWSc.04 Take appropriately accurate and precise measurements, explaining why accuracy and precision are important. 8TWSc.07 Collect and record sufficient observations and/or measurements in an appropriate form. 8TWSa.02 Describe trends and patterns in results, including identifying any anomalous results. 8TSWa.05 Present and interpret observations and measurements appropriately.	• Understand what we mean by speed. • Learn about the unit of speed. • Be able to calculate speed.	• Describe speed as distance travelled per unit time. • Determine the units of speed, using the units of distance and the units of time. • Recall and use the equation $\text{speed} = \dfrac{\text{distance}}{\text{time}}$ • Rearrange the equation, or use a formula triangle, to calculate distance or time of travel.

LANGUAGE SUPPORT

Learners will use the following words:

unit: part of any physical quantity that defines what is being measured, for example metres, seconds

speed: distance travelled per unit time

metres: the standard scientific unit of length, used to measure distance in this topic

per: in each; the word per can appear between two different units, for example: metres per second

second: the standard scientific unit of time

m/s: metres per second; metres divided by seconds; the standard scientific unit of speed

calculate: use a mathematical process to derive an answer

average speed: calculated by dividing distance travelled by time taken; as actual speed may vary during the journey, the result of the calculation is an average value for the speed

constant: not changing; the word uniform is also used for constant

---

Common misconceptions

Misconception	How to identify	How to overcome
When carrying out division, many learners think that a larger number must always be divided by a smaller number.	Provide some speed calculations where the numerical value of distance is less than that of time.	Remind learners that speed is calculated by dividing distance by time, and not the other way around. Also prompt for the idea that an object could be travelling very slowly and so cover less than 1 m in each second.

Starter ideas

1 Getting started (5 minutes)

Description: Learners can work individually or in pairs to answer the questions. If working individually, they can swap answers for peer discussion and assessment.

Learners may have seen road signs with numbers such as 50 and not consider that these numbers have no meaning without units. In science, units must always be provided with physical quantities.

2 Speed comparison (5–10 minutes)

Resources: Two objects such as tennis balls or toy cars and a flat surface.

Description: Push the two objects at the same time so one goes noticeably faster than the other. Ask: *Which is travelling faster?* Follow this question by asking how learners recognise that it is travelling faster, without using the word 'speed' (the faster one travels a greater distance in the same time interval). This can be made easier by doing this again but in stages. For example, position the two objects close

to you and state this is the start time. Then position the objects at different distances from you and state this is where they are after 1 s. Ask: *Which has gone faster?*

Main teaching ideas

1 Activity: Speed, distance and time (10+ minutes)

Learning intention: To relate the three quantities: speed, distance and time.

Description: See the Learner's Book. Distances could be provided. For example, from home to the shops is 200 m, to another major city is 200 000 m. The speeds range from that of walking to that of an aeroplane to provide a range of answers for their chosen distances.

Answers: Times should be calculated in seconds.

> **Differentiation ideas:** For large time values, learners needing more challenge could convert seconds to minutes or hours. Learners needing more support could be prompted for practicalities, such as why they do not travel from home to school by aeroplane. This can be extended, for those needing more challenge, to comparing actual travel times between cities by train or by aeroplane. The aeroplane may travel faster, but time taken to get to the airport, time waiting at the airport, etc. could make the actual journey time longer. This reinforces the concept of average speed.

> **Assessment ideas:** Learners can check each other's calculations.

2 Think like a scientist: Calculating speed (20–30 minutes, including graph plotting)

Learning intention: To plan an investigation, consider variables, make measurements, record results, make calculations from results, plot a graph and make conclusions.

Description: Learners can work in groups or pairs if required. See the Learner's Book for instructions and questions.

Safety: If this is done on a bench or desk, a barrier should be used to prevent the moving object rolling off the bench onto the floor. The barrier can be a book or pencil case.

> **Differentiation ideas:** Learners needing more support could be asked whether the speed of the object over the distance will be constant. Learners may realise that the object will slow down, due to friction. This can be used to reinforce the concept of average speed.

A challenge could be given by asking whether the results would be improved by using a longer or shorter distance. (Longer distance means longer time, which is easier to measure, but would give a greater speed change and vice versa.)

> **Assessment ideas:** Learners can assess the answers from other pairs or groups.

3 Average speeds (15–20 minutes)

Learning intention: To calculate speed at intervals from measurements of distance and time, then calculate an average.

Resources: Wind-up or remote control cars or other ground-moving objects; metre rule; five stopwatches; adhesive tape; access to a smooth horizontal surface at least 6 m long.

Description: Learners prepare a straight 'race' track by marking 1 m distance intervals from 0 to 5 m. Each vehicle is released individually on the track, starting just before the 0 m mark. As the vehicle travels along the track, one learner measures the time taken for the vehicle to travel along each 1 m interval. The five individual speeds are calculated. The times are then added together and used to calculate the average speed over the total 5 m distance. Ask: *How do the results compare? Did any vehicle noticeably change speed over the 5 m distance?*

> **Differentiation ideas:** Learners needing more support could be asked whether the speed of an object can vary from the average speed that is worked out in this activity.

Learners needing more challenge could be asked whether dividing the track into shorter intervals would make the average more accurate. It would not, because the average speed is the total distance divided by the total time.

> **Assessment ideas:** Ensure that all learners perform at least one speed calculation.

Plenary ideas

1 Give me five (3–5 minutes)

Resources: Small pieces of paper, approximately 10 cm by 5 cm.

Description: Each learner writes their name and five things that they learned in the lesson and hands it in at the end of the lesson.

> **Assessment ideas:** Read the statements to see what has been learned. If anything is missing, recap in the next lesson.

2 Speed questions (5 minutes)

Resources: Small pieces of paper.

Description: Each learner writes a question of their choice about speed on their piece of paper. The questions are swapped and learners write the answers to other learners' questions on the reverse of the paper. The question is returned to the person who wrote it, for the pair to discuss.

> **Assessment ideas:** Ask for volunteers to share their questions (not the answers) for class discussion.

Homework ideas

1 Learner's Book questions

2 Workbook exercises 3.2A–C

3 Worksheets 3.2A–3.2C

4 Give learners information, or ask them to research information, from local or international sporting events, from which they can calculate average speed, distance or time, knowing two of these; for example, they could investigate running, cycling, horseracing or motorsport events

Topic worksheets

Worksheets 3.2A–C

Topic 3.3: Describing movement

LEARNING PLAN

Learning objectives	Learning intentions	Success criteria
8Pf.02 Interpret and draw simple distance/time graphs.	• Learn how to use graphs to describe movement. • Understand what a distance/time graph shows. • Be able to draw a distance/time graph.	• Describe the motion of an object in words using the information from a distance/time graph. • Sketch a distance/time graph, using information in words about the motion of an object. • Draw a distance/time graph using numerical values provided. • Read numerical values from a distance/time graph.

LANGUAGE SUPPORT

Learners will use the following words:

distance/time graph: a type of graph in which the distance moved by an object is displayed on the vertical axis and the time elapsed is on the horizontal axis

stationary: not moving

at rest: not moving

sketch: make a drawing; in the context of a graph, sketch means to show the shape of the graph without plotting values, so there will only be named variables on the axes and not a numbered scale; axes on sketch graphs usually have arrowheads

safety precautions: in an experiment, these are adjustments made to reduce the risk of accident or reduce the risk of injury from an accident; they are specific to the experiment and more than just basic school laboratory rules

Common misconceptions

Misconception	How to identify	How to overcome
Graphs are difficult to interpret.	Many learners lose motivation when graphs are seen or mentioned.	Ask whether learners prefer a non-fiction book with or without pictures. If they prefer pictures, then ask why. Begin to present graphs as pictures that provide a great deal of information at a glance. With some learners, this will not be achieved in one lesson, but must be a continued approach.
An upward/downward sloping line on a distance/time graph means the object is getting faster/slower.	After learning about distance/time graphs, ask learners to describe in words what is happening to an object from a distance/time graph.	Ask learners to suggest a moving object. Ask learners to consider they are watching this object moving at a constant speed away from their position. Ask: *What is happening to the distance? How would this look if you plotted distance against time on a line graph?* The same thing can be done for an object approaching their position. If, and **only if**, learners have covered the gradient of graphs in mathematics, then the concept of the gradient being constant could be mentioned. As the gradient is change in vertical value divided by change in horizontal value, then the gradient is distance divided by time, which is speed.

Starter ideas

1 Getting started (5 minutes)

Resources: Paper, ruler and pencil.

Description: Learners work individually or in pairs. Ask learners needing support to mention a speed in m/s. This need not be a walking speed and could take any value. Then remind them that this speed represents the number of metres that are travelled per second. Any incorrect graph shapes will indicate specific misconceptions.

2 Watch the ball rolling (5–10 minutes, depending on structure of activity)

Resources: Tennis ball; metre rule or tape measure; stopwatches.

Description: Learners put the metre rule or tape measure on a flat surface. They roll the tennis ball slowly, parallel, and close to the distance scale. Learners use stopwatches to time the ball through distance intervals. For example, 10 learners with stopwatches could each time the ball from 0 to 10 cm, 0 to 20 cm, 0 to 30 cm, and so on. Draw axes for distance and time on the board and ask learners to predict what the line would look like. The results could then be used to plot the graph.

Main teaching ideas

1 My journey (10–20 minutes)

Learning intention: To relate learners' own experiences to the construction of a sketch graph.

Resources: Paper, rulers, pencils.

Description: See the Learner's Book for instructions. Encourage learners to share their ideas with you, to ensure that the journeys they choose are suitable and not too complex. If a journey is complex, then possibly one part of it could be used.

Answers: The questions in this activity are self- and peer assessment.

> **Differentiation ideas:** Learners needing more support could be guided as to what some of the parts of their chosen journey may look like on the graph, to start the sketching process. Learners requiring more challenge may be asked to estimate numerical values for distance and time for their journey. This could be done in m and s, or in km and h.

> **Assessment ideas:** The assessment is part of the activity, where learners interpret each other's graphs.

2 Think like a scientist: Walking and running (30 minutes)

Learning intention: To make measurements of distances and times to plot distance/time graphs for slower and faster movements.

Resources: Space to run safely, stopwatches, tape measure, graph paper.

Description: See the Learner's Book for instructions. For the running activity, the runner should start a few metres before the start of the measured distance, to ensure they are travelling at a roughly constant speed over the entire measured distance. Tell learners that the aim is to run at a constant speed and **not** as fast as possible.

> **Differentiation ideas:** Learners needing more support could be asked to predict the difference between the two graphs.

Learners needing more challenge could be asked why the runner starts before the measured distance.

> **Assessment ideas:** Learners' values for the speeds can be self-assessed as being reasonable values. If learners divide distance and time 'the wrong way around' they will get a speed value that is not realistic and this should be pointed out.

3 Rolling marble (15–40 minutes, depending on number of measurements taken)

Learning intention: To make measurements of distances and times and use these to plot distance/time graphs.

Resources: Ramp of adjustable height; smooth horizontal surface; marble or other small ball; adhesive tape or chalk; metre rule; stopwatches; graph paper.

Description: Learners use the ramp to start the marble rolling at various speeds. They use adhesive tape or chalk to mark the start position on the ramp. The marble will continue to roll on the smooth horizontal surface. The measured distance will start at the end of the ramp, or a short distance after the end of the ramp if the marble is likely to bounce. Learners mark distances, with adhesive tape or chalk, at 20 cm, 40 cm, 60 cm, 80 cm and 100 cm. They measure the time taken for the marble to travel the first 20 cm three times and calculate an average. Learners do this again for 40 cm, 60 cm, 80 cm and 100 cm. They can use the average times to plot a distance/time graph. Learners set the ramp to different heights and repeat the experiment.

> **Differentiation ideas:** Learners needing more support can be asked: *What will happen to the speed of the marble on the horizontal surface as the ramp gets steeper?* Learners should say that it would go faster. Then ask learners who need more of a challenge to show you the steepest possible position of the ramp (which is vertical). Ask them to 'roll' the marble down the vertical ramp and explain why the marble does not then continue to roll quickly across the horizontal surface, as they predicted.

> **Assessment ideas:** Ask learners whether they have repeated the measurements a sufficient number of times. Ask: *How do you judge this? Why is the time not just measured at 100 cm but at 20 cm intervals? Why were 5 cm intervals not used instead?*

Plenary ideas

1 Agreement line (2–5 minutes, depending on number of statements)

Description: Learners gather at one side or the back of the room where there is clear space for the length or width of the room. One side represents 'strongly agree' and the other is 'strongly disagree'. Make true/false statements about distance/time graphs and ask the learners to position themselves along the agreement line, according to what each individual thinks. Then ask some individuals why they are at that position. Reflection statements can be used in the activity. For example: 'I feel I really understand distance/time graphs.'

2 Show me the shape (1–2 minutes)

Description: Learners listen to statements about the movement of an object and use one arm to make the shape of the line on a distance/time graph. For example, for 'constant low speed away', learners will make a shallow gradient, with an upward slope, with one arm.

Homework ideas

1 Learner's Book questions

2 Workbook exercises 3.3A–C

Topic 3.4: Turning forces

LEARNING PLAN

Learning objectives	Learning intentions	Success criteria
8Pf.04 Identify and calculate turning forces (moment = force × distance).	• Recognise when a force causes something to turn. • Know how to use the term 'moment'. • Be able to calculate the moment caused by a force.	• Identify when a force will cause something to turn. • Give examples of things that turn when a force is applied. • Calculate moments and determine the unit of moment.

LANGUAGE SUPPORT

Learners will use the following words:

turn: rotate around an axis or change direction

lever: a rigid bar that pivots on a fixed support

pivot: the point about which a lever turns

moment: the turning effect of a force, calculated as the force multiplied by the distance of the force from the pivot

newton metre (N m): the standard unit of moment; other units of moment include N cm and N mm

Common misconceptions

Misconception	How to identify	How to overcome
A force, such as a push, cannot also cause a moment. For example, a push is needed to open a door, so opening a door cannot also involve a moment.	Give learners examples, such as those in Workbook exercise 3.4A and ask which involve moments.	Ask learners to identify when any movement of a rigid object is not in a straight line. Then ask whether there is a fixed point about which the object will turn, such as the hinge on the door. These criteria can be used to identify whether a moment is involved.

Starter ideas

1 Getting started (5 minutes)

Learning intention: To begin to think about the turning effects of forces.

Description: Learners should be able to give examples, such as twisting the top off a bottle. There is the possibility of learners identifying objects that move in circles rather than turn about a pivot.

2 Opening the door (5–10 minutes)

Resources: A swing door that can be pushed.

Description: Ask learners to volunteer to push the door open. They will probably do this by using the handle or pushing in a position far from the hinges. Then either ask them why they push at that position, or ask them to push the door at points closer to the hinges. Some learners may only recognise the push aspect of the force rather than the turning effect.

Main teaching ideas

1 Activity: Identifying moments (20+ minutes)

Learning intention: To identify moments in everyday objects.

Resources: Magazines that can be cut; large sheets of paper; glue; coloured pens.

Description: Learners cut out pictures showing everyday objects that require moments to work. These are to be labelled.

⟩ **Differentiation ideas:** Learners needing more support can be asked to identify the pivot and the point at which the force is applied. The pivot can be recognised as the point about which the object would turn. Learners needing more challenge could be asked to estimate the force and the distance, and therefore the moment for each object. It can be helpful, when estimating forces, to remind learners that the weight of an apple is approximately 1 N. Learners often find estimation of quantities such as this to be challenging.

⟩ **Assessment ideas:** Ask learners to explain where forces are applied to make objects turn, for example, why the hands of a door is far from the hinges.

2 Think like a scientist: Calculating moments (20–30 minutes, depending on structure of activity)

Learning intention: To investigate how the force required to turn an object about a pivot varies with distance from the pivot.

Resources: See the Learner's Book.

Description: See the Learner's Book.

⟩ **Differentiation ideas:** Learners needing support could be given situations and asked to predict the effects; for example, reading a scale from a point above or below eye level. This could be supported by actual scales and objects, or by diagrams.

Learners needing more challenge could be asked to suggest things that make measurements difficult in this investigation; for example, the vertical scale at the end of the metre rule may not be close enough to what is being measured. Also, as the metre rule goes down, the end of the metre rule gets further from this scale.

⟩ **Assessment ideas:** Learners can be observed while doing the investigation and asked additional questions about their method, such as about consistency of results or whether these need to be repeated.

3 Levers for lifting (10–15 minutes)

Learning intention: To demonstrate the effect of changing the distance of the force from the pivot when creating a moment.

Resources: Rigid plank of wood, minimum 1.5 m long and strong enough to support the weight of an adult; 2–3 bricks

Description: Make a lever by placing the plank of wood on the bricks that will form the pivot. Start by having the pivot reasonably central to the plank. Ask one learner to stand on one end of the plank. Ask another learner to attempt to raise the first learner off the ground by using the lever. Repeat this, moving the pivot closer to the first learner and ask how the force needed to raise them off the ground changes. This can be extended by using one learner to raise two – or even three – other learners off the ground, if the plank is long enough or strong enough.

Note: Do **not** ask learners to provide their body weights as this is a qualitative activity only. Discretion should be used, when choosing the volunteers, so as not to cause offence over differing body weights.

Safety: Ensure that learners have something to hold onto when standing on the lever and encourage slow, gradual movements.

⟩ **Differentiation ideas:** Learners needing more support can be asked whether it requires more or less force if the distance from the pivot is increased or decreased. They could be prompted, using phrases such as 'easier' or 'more difficult', before linking this to force, if required.

Learners needing more challenge could be asked to predict what will happen to the required force if the distance from the pivot is doubled or halved. When the pivot is moved, then the distances of both weights on their side change. Ask: *How will this affect the force required?*

⟩ **Assessment ideas:** Ask learners to explain why the force required decreases when the pivot is moved closer to the learner who will be lifted. Learners can also be asked to write up the activity and include drawings, using stick figures to illustrate their work.

Plenary ideas

1 Explain the meanings (3–5 minutes)

Resources: Paper and pen or pencil.

Description: Learners work in pairs. Provide learners with a list of key words or phrases and ask them to take turns explaining the meanings to each other. Include 'moment', 'pivot', 'lever', 'force', 'load', 'distance', 'balanced moments'. Learners can reflect on the relative ease, or difficulty, of explaining each term.

> **Assessment ideas:** Learners who think they have given, or have heard, a particularly good explanation can share these with the class.

2 What did your partner learn? (5 minutes)

Resources: Paper and pen or pencil.

Description: Learners work in pairs. One learner describes three things that they learned in the lesson. Then their partner does the same. Each learner should try to think of something different say, to avoid a 'leader–follower' scenario. Learners can compare what others have learned with what they have learned.

> **Assessment ideas:** Learners can ask each other questions about what the other has learned, or individuals can volunteer to ask the whole class questions about what they have learned.

Homework ideas

1 Learner's Book questions

2 Workbook exercises 3.4A–C

3 Worksheets 3.4A–C

4 Ask learners to make a list of activities at home that use moments

Topic worksheets

Worksheets 3.4A–C, Forces for turning

Topic 3.5: Pressure between solids

LEARNING PLAN		
Learning objectives	**Learning intentions**	**Success criteria**
8Pf.05 Explain that pressure is caused by the action of a force, exerted by a substance, on an area $\left(\text{pressure} = \frac{\text{force}}{\text{area}}\right)$.	• Recognise that forces can cause pressure on an area. • Understand what affects pressure. • Be able to calculate the pressure caused by a force on an area.	• Understand that forces can cause pressure. • Describe how changes in force and area will affect the pressure between solids. • Recall and use the equation $\text{pressure} = \frac{\text{force}}{\text{area}}$

LANGUAGE SUPPORT

Learners will use the following words:

pressure: the result of a force exerted on an area; the pushing effect of a force

sharp: having a pointed end with a small area at the end of the point; having the ability to cut or push into something else

surface area: in the context of pressure between solids, this is the area of contact between the two solids

newtons per metre squared: the international standard unit of pressure; meaning the number of newtons of force on every square metre of area; written as N/m^2

point: in the context of objects, the tip of a sharp object

Common misconceptions

Misconception	How to identify	How to overcome
Increasing the area of contact between two solids must increase the pressure between them.	After teaching about pressure between solids, and when learners can recall the equation, ask about the effects of: increasing the force, keeping the area the same and then increasing the area, keeping the force the same.	This will differ according to the learner. Most will relate to the concept of a common object such as a drawing pin. Ask: *What would happen if you pushed on the pointed end? Why do you push on the end with the larger area? Why do you cut with a knife blade and not with the handle?* Use numerical examples for some learners if needed: substitute different values for area into the equation, keeping force the same. Show that, since area is the denominator, increasing area gives a lower answer for pressure and this is also true the other way around.

Starter ideas

1 Getting started (5 minutes)

Description: Learners relate everyday objects with sharp edges or sharp points to their function of cutting or pushing into other objects Learners may suggest objects such as pins, scissors, knives. Ask about whether the sharpness of the object affects its ability to function well.

2 Which end of the nail? (5 minutes)

Resources: A nail with a large round end and a sharp point at the other end; hammer; large block of soft wood.

Description: Show learners the nail in contact with the wood the correct way and then upside down, with the round part in contact with the wood. Ask: *Which way is correct? Why? What would happen if the nail was hammered when upside down?* Use the hammer to demonstrate, by tapping **gently**.

If this action blunts the sharp end of the nail, then use another identical nail – this should be explained to learners. Then set the nail the correct way on the wood and ask how to make the comparison fair. Learners should realise that the force from the hammer should be the same, so draw attention to force being one of the key variables. Prompt for how to measure the surface of each end of the nail (area) and draw attention to area being one of the key variables. Carry out the demonstration, trying to reproduce the force that was used in the first part.

Main teaching ideas

1 Think like a scientist: Calculating pressure (20+ minutes)

Learning intention: To measure the force exerted by a person on the floor, to measure the areas in contact with the floor in various positions and to calculate the pressures.

Resources: See the Learner's Book.

Description: See the Learner's Book. Allow learners to volunteer to give their body mass or to be weighed – do not ask them to do this. Care must be taken by all in the class to use the terms 'weight' and 'mass' correctly as both will be determined.

> **Differentiation ideas:** Learners needing more support could be asked to predict how the pressure exerted by the feet on the ground would vary between standing and other activities, such as walking or jumping. Further prompts could be given to identify the fact that these activities require a pushing force on the floor and that pressure increases with force when the area remains constant.

Learners needing more challenge could be encouraged to think whether one or both feet are in contact with the ground during these activities, and extend this to think of the shape of the foot and so the area in contact with the ground. Ask: *How do these changes affect the pressure?*

> **Assessment ideas:** During the activity, ask learners questions about the most appropriate unit to use for area and what the unit of pressure will be if this unit is used. The questions in the Learner's Book also provide assessment opportunities.

2 Pressure from the hand (15–20 minutes)

Learning intention: To measure the force exerted by the hand on a surface, to measure the areas in contact with the surface in various positions, and to calculate the pressures.

Resources: Squared paper or graph paper; bathroom scales; top pan balance; forcemeter.

Description: Tell learners that they will be calculating the pressure exerted by their hand when they are pushing down on a surface. Show the available equipment and ask: *What measurements will be needed? Can pressure be measured directly?*

Each learner uses one hand to push down on the bathroom scales. They will record a measurement in kilograms (kg), which must be converted to a force in newtons (N). Learners can be prompted for how to do this (multiply the mass in kg by 10 N / kg).

They can then measure the area of their hand by drawing around the hand on squared paper.

The force and the area can then be used to calculate the pressure. This can be done using various hand positions, such as palm or fist.

> **Differentiation ideas:** The level of support and guidance given to learners can be varied from guidance at all stages (choosing equipment, converting mass to weight, measuring area, etc.) to virtually no guidance. Learners could be asked to use the force from the hand to calculate, or estimate, the maximum pressure that they could exert on a surface by pushing on an object with a sharp point. Support should be given if learners are converting area units, for example, from cm^2 to m^2 or from mm^2 to cm^2. These conversions can be illustrated using squared paper or graph paper.

> **Assessment ideas:** Ask learners questions during the activity, such as for the equation for pressure, the unit of area they will use, the unit of pressure that will result. Ask learners to write up the activity with methods and results.

3 Balloon pop (10 minutes)

Learning intention: To compare the forces required to burst a balloon, based on using different areas.

Resources: Polystyrene (Styrofoam) sheet or sheet of thick cardboard; large quantity of identical nails; identical balloons; balloon pump; selection of books.

Description: This is a teacher demonstration. Push one nail through the card or polystyrene and set the sheet on a table so that the nail is pointing upward. Inflate a balloon, using a known number of pump strokes, and tie the neck of the balloon. Set the balloon gently on the point of the nail and ask how many books could be placed on the balloon before it bursts. Carry this out with the help of a learner volunteer.

Now push many nails through the sheet so that the points are all at an equal height and as close together as possible.

Tell learners you are going to compare the force required to burst a balloon on many nails. Ask how this can be made a fair test (the balloon must be the same type, the balloon must be inflated by the same volume – do not introduce gas pressure – the nails must be the same). Again, set the balloon gently on the nails then ask learners to set books on the balloon to compare the force.

Safety: Do not use your hands to push down on the balloon; do not allow learners to push down on the balloon with their hands.

> **Differentiation ideas:** Ask learners to give examples from everyday life of large areas being used to reduce pressure; for example, shoulder bags have wide straps. Questions such as these will differentiate by outcome, so learners needing more support can be given examples such as those in the Learner's Book to start. They may then only think of one or two further examples. Learners who need more challenge will be able to think of more varied examples.

> **Assessment ideas:** Ask learners to explain their observations with the balloon in terms of pressure, force and area. They can do this through discussion in small groups or as individuals writing up the demonstration.

Plenary ideas

1 Hands up to ask questions (3–5 minutes)

Description: Learners think of questions they would like to ask the class about pressure. They raise their hands to ask a question, which others try to answer. Those answering the questions must then ask another question to the class. Learners reflect on their own understanding by thinking how easy or difficult it is to think of good questions.

2 Hot seat (5 minutes)

Resources: Stopwatch; small prize.

Description: Ask a learner to volunteer to sit at the front of the class and talk about pressure for 60 seconds. The learner must not use incorrect science, repeat any word, pause or go off the subject. The learner starts talking as soon as you say 'start' and start the stopwatch. Any learner can challenge by clapping their hands once. At this point, stop the timer and the learner who made the challenge must explain why they did so. If their challenge is correct, they take the hot seat and start talking again, as if from the start (so they can use words used by the first learner but then not repeat these further). If the challenge is incorrect, the learner in the hot seat is allowed to continue. The learner still speaking in the hot seat when 60 seconds elapses is the winner.

Homework ideas

1 Learner's Book questions

2 Workbook exercises 3.5A–C

3 Ask learners to list some everyday examples of objects that are designed to increase pressure and other objects that are designed to decrease pressure; they should write a short explanation of each, making reference to the equation for pressure.

Topic 3.6: Pressure in liquids and gases

LEARNING PLAN		
Learning objectives	**Learning intentions**	**Success criteria**
8Pf.06 Use particle theory to explain pressures in gases and liquids (qualitative only).	• Recall how particles move in liquids and gases. • Understand how particle movement causes pressure in liquids and gases. • Predict how changes in liquids and gases affects the pressure.	• Describe the movement of particles in liquids and gases. • Describe how the movement of these particles causes pressure. • Describe how changes in temperature and depth affects pressure in liquids and gases.

LANGUAGE SUPPORT

Learners will use the following words:

depth: distance from the top to the bottom of something, or distance from the surface down to a particular position in a liquid or gas

collide: particles are said to collide when they hit into each other or hit into another object

container: an object that holds something else, for example, a balloon is a container for gas

altitude: a type of height measurement, usually measured vertically upwards from sea level

sea level: a position defined as having zero altitude; the position of the ocean surface measured mid-way between high tide and low tide

atmospheric pressure: the force exerted by the atmosphere on an area of 1 m^2; it is approximately 100 000 N/m^2 at sea level

Common misconceptions

Misconception	How to identify	How to overcome
The air around us exerts no pressure unless wind is blowing.	Ask learners about pressure from the air in the room. Ask: *Is the air exerting any force on surfaces, such as your skin?*	Ask what air is, and then prompt for ideas about particles in a gas. Carry out the collapsing can demonstration and explain this in terms of particles in the air colliding with the sides of the container.

Starter ideas

1 Getting started (5 minutes)

Resources: Paper and pencil.

Description: Learners should recall diagrams showing the arrangement of particles in liquids and gases. Learners should draw these in rectangular boxes. The gas particles should not be touching and should be spaced randomly. The liquid particles should be touching each other and the sides and bottom of the container and also arranged randomly. Learners will sometimes draw the particles in a liquid arranged as particles in a high pressure gas: not touching each other.

2 Mass of air (5–10 minutes)

Resources: Balloon; sensitive top pan balance.

Description: Ask learners *either* whether air has mass *or* which will have more mass: an uninflated balloon or an inflated balloon.

Place the uninflated balloon on the balance and record its mass. Inflate the balloon, tie to seal and place on the balance again. The difference in mass is the mass of air inside.

Main teaching ideas

1 Think like a scientist: Observing the effects of pressure in a liquid (10 minutes)

Learning intention: To show that pressure increases with depth in a liquid.

Resources: Empty 1.5 or 2 litre plastic bottles; adhesive tape; water; waste water collection container.

Description: See the Learner's Book.

> **Differentiation ideas:** Ask: *What determines the pressure: the distance of the hole from the top of the bottle or the depth of the hole from the water surface?*

> **Assessment ideas:** Ask learners to make a conclusion from the observations.

2 Think like a scientist: Observing the effect of temperature on gas pressure (The activity is carried out during the lesson.)

Learning intention: To show that pressure in a gas increases with the temperature of the gas.

Resources: See the Learner's Book.

Description: See the Learner's Book.

> **Practical guidance:** The greater the difference in temperatures between the warm and cold places, the greater the observed difference in pressure will be. If a fridge has an ice-making compartment, then this should be used instead of the main fridge compartment.

> **Differentiation ideas:** Show learners needing more support a loaf of bread that has been sliced, and point out the bubbles. Ask or tell them what happens to bread in the hot oven and prompt them to think what happens to the gas in the bubbles and how this makes the bread rise.

Learners needing more challenge could be asked whether the difference in the pressure of the gas between the high and low temperatures would be greater if a larger bottle were used. It would not, because the pressure on the sides of the bottle is the force from the collisions of the particles *divided by* the surface area of the bottle. If the area is doubled then the number of colliding particles and, therefore, the force, is also doubled.

> **Assessment ideas:** Ask learners to predict the change in the bottle, using ideas about gas particle movement at different temperatures.

3 Collapsing drink can (10–20 minutes, depending on heat source used)

Learning intention: To demonstrate the effect of atmospheric pressure.

Resources: Empty aluminium drink can; large container of cold water; heat source suitable for boiling water; heatproof gloves or tongs.

Pour approximately 100 cm3 cold water into the drink can and boil the water in the can. Quickly lift the can and place it, upside down, into the cold water so that the can is about $\frac{1}{4}$ submerged and vertical. The can will be crushed by atmospheric pressure.

Safety: This activity should be a teacher demonstration; learners should either be behind a safety screen or wear eye protection and stand at least 2 m from the demonstration area.

> **Practical guidance:** Aluminium drink cans work better than steel ones. When turning the hot can upside down, do this over the large container of cold water so that boiling water is not spilled.

> **Differentiation ideas:** Learners needing more support can be asked whether the pressure inside the can or outside the can was greater. Then ask them about what happened to the temperature of the air in the can.

Learners needing more challenge could be given the value of atmospheric pressure (approximately 100 000 N/m²) and the surface area of a can (approximately 0.03 m²) and asked to calculate the force on the can from the atmosphere. Ask: *Is the overall force inward in this investigation greater or less than this calculated value?* (Less, because there is some air pressure still inside pushing outward.)

> **Assessment ideas:** Ask learners to explain their observations in terms of pressure. If necessary, prompt learners by explaining that the pressure inside the hot can is equal to atmospheric pressure because it is open to the air. The pressure inside the can then rapidly decreases when cooled. The pressure becomes lower than atmospheric pressure because the can is sealed by the water and so no longer open to the air.

Plenary ideas

1 What was the question? (5–10 minutes)

Resources: Selection of answers (words and phrases related to the topic of pressure in liquids and gases) displayed at the front of the class.

Description: Learners work in pairs to write questions to match each answer. Learners reflect on their understanding of the topic by considering how easy or difficult it was to think of the questions.

> **Assessment ideas:** Ask learners to volunteer their questions, or the questions can be collected in for assessment.

2 My top tips (5–10 minutes)

Resources: Paper and pens.

Description: Learners work in pairs to write their 'top tips' to others for learning about pressure in liquids and gases.

> **Assessment ideas:** Learners can volunteer to give their top tips to the class and get feedback, or they can be collected in at the end.

Homework ideas

1   Learner's Book questions

2   Workbook exercises 3.6A–C

3   Ask learners to write an explanation of one of the activities they have seen. This should be based on particle theory.

Topic 3.7: Particles on the move

LEARNING PLAN

Learning objectives	Learning intentions	Success criteria
8Pf.07 Describe the diffusion of gases and liquids as the intermingling of substances by the movement of particles.	• Describe how random movement of particles causes diffusion. • Understand how diffusion happens in liquids and gases.	• State how substances in liquids and gases move from regions of higher concentration to regions of lower concentration in terms of particles. • Explain everyday examples of diffusion in terms of particle movements.

LANGUAGE SUPPORT

Learners will use the following words:

concentration: a measure of how many particles are in a particular space or volume; more particles in a space is a higher concentration than fewer particles in the same space

Common misconceptions

Misconception	How to identify	How to overcome
Diffusion is not a random process, and all particles move in the same direction.	After learners have learned about the particle basis of diffusion, ask them whether any particles of the diffusing substance could possibly, at any instant, be moving in the opposite direction to the direction of diffusion.	Use Main teaching idea 3.

Starter ideas

1 Getting started (5 minutes)

Description: The aim is to get learners thinking about diffusion and not necessarily to identify the correct answers, as they have not yet learned the topic. Prompt learners to consider particle movements in gases and liquids. In part **a**, some learners may not consider the smell of food to be caused by particles.

2 Smell of perfume (5 minutes)

Resources: Perfume; filter paper; clamp stand.

Description: Ensure learners are seated in their normal places and not around the front of the room. Turn off any fans and restrict air movement for the duration of the activity. Soak the filter paper with the perfume and hang the paper on the clamp stand. Ask learners to raise their hands when they smell perfume.

Those closer to the filter paper should smell it first. Any learner further away who does not smell the perfume can be allowed to come closer to detect the increase in concentration. Ask for suggestions about how the perfume smell spreads. A common suggestion is that the perfume, or particles, move outward from the paper in straight lines.

Main teaching ideas

1 Activity: Watching diffusion (20 minutes)

Learning intention: To observe diffusion in a liquid and to explain the observation using particle theory.

Resources: See the Learner's Book.

Description: See the Learner's Book.

> **Differentiation ideas:** Learners needing more challenge can be asked to predict whether all coloured, water soluble substances would diffuse through water at the same speed. Ask: *What might affect this?* (Particle size or particle properties, temperature.)

Tell learners needing more support that not all substances diffuse through water at the same rate. Prompt them for how this could be tested, assuming the substance was coloured. Ask which variables should be changed and which should be kept the same.

> **Assessment ideas:** Ask learners to write a description of the activity, possibly as a picture story board.

2 Think like a scientist: Effect of temperature on the speed of diffusion (15–20 minutes)

Learning intention: Observe the effect of changing temperature on the rate of diffusion in a liquid.

Resources: See the Learner's Book.

Description: See the Learner's Book.

Safety: Care should be taken with hot water; the suggested maximum temperature for the water is 60 °C.

> **Practical guidance:** Learners cannot start the diffusion in each container at the same time, so it is important that the beaker at the lowest temperature is started first.

> **Differentiation ideas:** Ask learners who need more challenge to discuss the difficulties with this experiment. These might include starting each temperature at the same time, the fact that each temperature changes over the course of the investigation, and judging when diffusion is complete.

Learners who need more support could be given one of these difficulties, such as starting each one at the same time, and asked how this could be improved.

> **Assessment ideas:** As well as answering the questions in the Learner's Book, learners could present the activity in written or picture form, with an explanation that uses particle theory.

3 Modelling diffusion in gases (5–10 minutes)

Learning intention: To illustrate how particles move during diffusion.

Resources: Beads or small (3 cm diameter or less) balls of two different colours; large tray

Description: Place the beads of one colour in the tray to represent the air. Place beads of another colour, representing the substance that will diffuse, in one corner of the tray. Gently shake the tray to make the 'particles' move. Learners observe the random movement caused by particle collisions and see how the substance diffuses randomly.

> **Differentiation ideas:** Learners needing more support could be asked how this model could be changed to represent a liquid.

Learners who need more challenge could be asked about the strengths and limitations of these models.

> **Assessment ideas:** Ask learners how a higher or lower temperature could be modelled and what this would show.

Plenary ideas

1 Key word list (3–5 minutes)

Resources: Paper and pens.

Description: Learners make a list of key words associated with diffusion. If time allows, they can add short descriptions of each.

> **Assessment ideas:** Learners hand in their lists for assessment as exit slips.

2 Diffusion poem/rap (5–10 minutes)

Resources: Paper and pens.

Description: Learners work in pairs to write a short poem or rap about diffusion.

> **Assessment ideas:** Learners can volunteer to read or perform their composition.

Homework ideas

1   Learner's Book questions

2   Workbook exercises 3.7A–C

3   Learners can make lists of how diffusion occurs when preparing food and drinks at home.

PROJECT GUIDANCE

Making a balance for weighing

This project addresses the following learning objectives:

8PF.04 Identify and calculate turning forces (moment = force × distance).

8SIC.02 Describe how science is applied across societies and industries, and in research.

8SIC.03 Evaluate issues which involve and/or require scientific understanding.

Learners have the opportunity to use their understanding of moments to design a balance for weighing objects.

Take care with the terms 'weight' and 'mass' throughout this activity, as both will be used. For example, the learner may decide to use a 200 g mass for the known load. When using g or kg, the reference must be to mass. When this is converted to weight, it will be 2 N, and then can be referred to as a weight or a load.

The Learner's Book provides some suggestions for the equipment, but ideally learners should be given scope for creativity and allowed to choose their own equipment, within reason. If a metre rule is used as the beam for the balance, sagging can be a problem with larger loads. This can be overcome by using adhesive tape to bind two or three metre rules together, one on top of another.

If masses exceed 500 g, learners should move their balance to the floor. This is part of risk assessment, and learners should be encouraged to develop a risk assessment for their work. If only small masses are to be used, then learners could state that their work involves low risk and so standard laboratory rules apply.

Once complete, learners should be able to demonstrate how their balance works. Some may measure the distance of the unknown weight from the pivot and calculate the weight using the known moment from the other side of the beam. Others may have fixed their known load, and the position of the pivot, and then calibrated the other side of the beam with weights, or even masses. Some may have considered accuracy and devised a way to hang the unknown load on the beam so that the distance of the weight from the pivot can be measured more accurately than setting the load on the beam.

>4 Ecosystems

Unit plan

Topic	Learning hours	Learning content	Resources
4.1 The Sonoran Desert	2-2.5	Introduction to ecosystems, using the Sonoran Desert as an example	**Learner's Book:** Questions 1–4 Activity: Interactions between organisms in the desert Activity: How a species fits into the desert ecosystem **Workbook:** Exercise 4.1, The Sonoran Desert ecosystem **Teacher's Resource:** Template 4.1: How a species fits into the desert ecosystem
4.2 Different Ecosystems	2.5-4	Introduction of a range of different ecosystems; exploration of a local ecosystem; an ecosystem contains many different habitats	**Learner's Book:** Activity: Habitats in an ecosystem Think like a scientist: Investigating a local ecosystem **Workbook:** Exercise 4.2A, A tropical rainforest ecosystem Exercise 4.2B, Hydrothermal vents Exercise 4.2C, Mangroves and fish **Teacher's Resource:** Worksheet 4.2, Planning a school nature reserve Template 4.2: Habitats in an ecosystem
4.3 Intruders in an ecosystem	2-3	How introduced species can affect ecosystems	**Learner's Book:** Questions 1–5 Activity: Why do some introduced species cause problems? **Workbook:** Exercise 4.3A, Beavers in South America Exercise 4.3B, Water hyacinth Exercise 4.3C, Cane toads in Australia **Teacher's Resource:** Worksheets 4.3A–C, The possum problem

Topic	Learning hours	Learning content	Resources
4.4 Bioaccumulation	2.5-4	How non-biodegradable substances may accumulate in organisms, and become magnified along a food chain	**Learner's Book:** Questions 1–2 Think like a scientist: Modelling DDT in a food chain Activity: Biodegradable insecticides **Workbook:** Exercise 4.4, Microplastics **Teacher's Resource:** Worksheet 4.4, Mercury in an Arctic food web
Cross-unit resources			**Learner's Book:** Check your Progress **Project:** Impact of an introduced species **Teacher's Resource:** Language development worksheets 4.1 Writing sentences about ecosystems 4.2 Words and meanings

BACKGROUND KNOWLEDGE

Learners who have followed the Cambridge curriculum at Primary level will have studied adaptations of plants and animals to different environments, at Stage 5. All learners should be familiar with the term 'habitat', which they may have met at Stage 2 and then used again at Stage 4. In this unit, they will begin to appreciate that an ecosystem contains many different habitats, and that organisms have adaptations that allow them to live there.

Learners are likely to be unfamiliar with the correct usage of the term 'ecosystem'. If they know this word at all, it is probable that they will consider an ecosystem to be a place. At this level, they should begin to appreciate that it is a *system* – rather like a transport system or their school's examination entry system. It does indeed include places and objects, but also the interactions between them. This is not an easy concept to understand, and it can help greatly if you take care in how you use the term.

At Stage 6, learners will have studied food chains and food webs, and they met these again at Stage 7 when considering how decomposers fit into food webs. Learners should understand that the arrows in a food chain represent the transfer of energy but, in practice, many are likely still to think of this in terms of 'what eats what'. They will have learned about energy changes, and the dissipation of energy as heat, in Stage 7 Physics. In this unit, they build on understanding of food webs and widen their appreciation of other kinds of interaction between organisms in an ecosystem.

TEACHING SKILLS FOCUS

Organising practical work 2: Working outside the classroom

This unit offers several opportunities to take learners out of the classroom. Such activities have several advantages. In particular, it helps learners to connect the science that they learn in the classroom and laboratory with the real world. For many, it helps to put their learning into a meaningful context, and this in turn can generate interest and deeper understanding.

Ecology is an obvious topic in which investigations outside the classroom can take place. Some schools will be in a fortunate position, with easy access to a range of interesting ecosystems close by. Others will have very little outside space but, even then, there is likely to be at least a small garden, or a tree, or a safe roadside verge.

Biology, however, is not the only science for which going outside the classroom can enhance learning. In chemistry, a rusting fence could provide an introduction to the reactivity of iron with oxygen and water. In physics, learners can measure their speeds as they run on a measured track in the playing field. If learners are stationed with timers at measured intervals along the track, they can collect data and then construct distance/time graphs. Forces, pressure and colour can also be usefully explored outside the classroom.

When planning to work outside, give some thought to the following issues.

- Safety is paramount. Learners must know where they are allowed to go and where they must not go, and you must be certain that they will follow these instructions. Learners should never work on their own; working in pairs is often a good idea, as there is always a chance that a single learner could leave, unnoticed, a group of three or four. Remember that learners are used to being outside when they do sport or physical education – you may want to talk to teachers who regularly supervise these activities for advice, if you are new to the idea of taking learners outside and have concerns about keeping everyone safe.

- Check your school regulations about taking learners outside. If you plan to take them beyond the school grounds, extra procedures may be necessary, such as informing parents or asking their permission.

- If you are going into an area with unmown grass or other vegetation, make sure that everyone has suitable clothing. You should always check the planned working area yourself, before

taking the class to it. Look for any hazards, such as broken glass, or plants or animals that can sting or bite.

- Decide when and where you will give learners instructions about what they are going to do. It is often a good idea to do this inside the classroom. However, consider also taking them outside without explaining what they are going to do, which can generate excitement and interest; then settle them down in a comfortable spot and explain what they are to do. Similarly, equipment can be given out in the classroom, or you can opt to do this outside.

- Make sure that instructions are very clear and comprehensive, so that every learner has no excuse for not being on-task at all times.

- If learners are to record observations and results, it is most convenient to use a clipboard to do this. You may like to ask each pair or group to appoint one person to be the recorder. Pencils are better than pens, as the writing does not run if it gets damp. If learners are working in an area where they may get wet, the clipboards and paper can go inside a plastic bag, big enough for a hand and pencil to go in as well.

- You may like to set a firm time-frame: for example, you could tell learners they have exactly ten minutes to perform a task, and that they must be back at a pre-arranged point at an exact time.

- Ensure that you leave enough time for learners to return to the classroom, discuss their observations and/or results and settle, before the lesson ends.

As a challenge, in this unit, you could try Topic 4.2, *Think like a scientist: Investigating a local ecosystem* and take learners outside to investigate an ecosystem close to your school. You will need to identify an appropriate place first, and study it carefully yourself. See the Topic 4.2 Main teaching ideas section, for suggestions.

Topic 4.1: The Sonoran Desert

LEARNING PLAN

Learning objectives	Learning intentions	Success criteria
8Be.01 Identify different ecosystems on the Earth, recognising the variety of habitats that exist within an ecosystem.	• Appreciate that an ecosystem contains many different habitats, with reference to the Sonoran Desert. • Understand that there are many different types of interaction between living and non-living things in an ecosystem.	• Construct a picture showing some of the interactions in a desert ecosystem. • Explain the difference between a habitat and an ecosystem. • Make a poster or presentation about how a chosen species fits into the desert ecosystem.

LANGUAGE SUPPORT

Learners will use the following words:

adaptations: features of an organism that help it to survive and reproduce in its habitat

nectar: a sugary liquid made by flowers, to attract insects for pollination

pollen: tiny grains produced by flowers

pollinating: transferring pollen grains from an anther (male part of a flower) to a stigma (female part of a flower)

interact: affect one another

environment: surroundings; for an organism, anything external to the organism that affects it

nocturnal: active at night

ecosystem: a network of interactions between living and non-living things; it is generally considered to be self-contained, although in practice all ecosystems interact in at least some ways with other ecosystems

food web: interconnecting food chains, indicating how energy is transferred between organisms in an ecosystem

ecology: the study of organisms in their environment

habitat: the place where an organism lives

Common misconceptions

Misconception	How to identify	How to overcome
An ecosystem is a place.	Throughout this topic, when discussing ecosystems and habitats.	Be vigilant in correcting the use of the term 'ecosystem' to refer to a place; it is very easy to make this mistake, and we all do it! Question 5 addresses this directly.

Starter ideas

1 Getting started (10 minutes, including sharing ideas)

Description: Ask learners to work in pairs to answer the two *Getting started* questions. Allow three or four minutes, then ask for ideas.

2 Introduction to the Sonoran Desert (5–10 minutes)

Resources: Search the internet for a video clip or image(s) of the Sonoran Desert.

Description: Show the video clip or image of the Sonoran Desert. Tell learners that they are going to think about what animals and/or plants live in the Sonoran Desert, and what adaptations they might have, to allow them to survive there. Show the clip or image again, then ask for learners' suggestions.

Main teaching ideas

2 Introducing the concept of an ecosystem (15–20 minutes)

Learning intention: To begin to appreciate that many different species live in a desert, and that they interact with each other and their environment, in ways that include food webs but also other types of interaction.

Resources: Learner's Book illustrations and text.

Note: The website of the Arizona-Sonoran Desert Museum contains a wide range of high-quality information and activities for learners.

Description: With the class, work through the series of photographs and information about different species in the Sonoran Desert, described in the Learner's Book. Use questioning about the photographs to engage learners: for example, ask them to look at the photograph of the Gila (pronounced: heela) woodpeckers and ask how the woodpeckers and the cactus are adapted to live in a desert. Use the terms 'adaptation' and 'interactions' as you talk to the class, and expect learners to use these terms when they are involved in discussion.

> **Differentiation ideas:** This is a whole-class activity. Some learners will need encouragement and direct questioning, to ensure that they are involved in the discussion. Others will ask challenging questions themselves: if you do not know the answers, encourage these learners to find out more information themselves, and perhaps share it with others in the next lesson.

> **Assessment ideas:** Learners' answers to your questions will help determine how well they understand the concept of adaptations and interactions.

3 Activity: Interactions between organisms in the desert (30–45 minutes)

Learning intention: To produce a visual representation, of learners' own design, of some of the interactions between organisms in the Sonoran Desert.

Resources: Per group: a large sheet of paper; coloured pens; (optional) pictures of the animals and plants in the desert, that can be cut out; (optional) scissors and glue.

If internet access is available, learners can also visit the website of the Arizona–Sonoran Desert Museum, where they can find plenty of information about the organisms that live in the Sonoran Desert and how they interact.

Description: If you have already discussed the text about the Sonoran Desert and studied the illustrations, learners can move directly onto this activity. They could work with partners or in groups of three. Ask learners to follow the instructions in the Learner's Book.

When everyone has finished, if time allows, you could ask some groups to explain their pictures to the rest of the class.

> **Differentiation ideas:** This task is suitable for all learners. Some learners will be able to produce intricate diagrams, with many interactions illustrated, and detailed written descriptions. Other learners may produce something much simpler, with more superficial descriptions. Some learners may need help identifying interactions, and with ideas for how to present them visually.

> **Assessment ideas:** Learners' finished pictures will help to show how well they understand that there are many interactions between organisms, including – but not limited to – food webs, within an ecosystem.

4 Activity: How a species fits into the desert ecosystem (45 minutes to construct the poster or presentation; research will need much longer, and some of this could be done outside the classroom)

Learning intention: To research and present information about how a chosen species is adapted to living in a desert.

Resources: Reference material, such as library books, magazines, and the internet. You could suggest some internet sites to learners. The Arizona-Sonaran Desert Museum website is a good place to begin.

If learners want to make a presentation, they may need access to laptops and presentation software.

If learners want to make a poster, they will need paper and coloured pens.

Description: It is best if this activity is done after learners have been taken through all of the information in this topic in the Learner's Book.

It is suggested that learners work in a group of three or four, as this can spread the load of researching information, and reduce the time needed to collect and collate the research.

You could suggest particular species, or allow groups to choose their own. There is no need to restrict this to the Sonoran Desert; you may wish to direct learners to species in their own country in a more familiar ecosystem.

> **Differentiation ideas:** Some learners may need a lot of help selecting a suitable species, and finding information about it. If you know this is likely to be very difficult for some individuals or groups, you could consider preparing information about a species that you can hand to learners, so that their task is to select and present information taken from this, rather than having to research it for themselves. Learners may also require an outline structure to help them to organise their information. *Template 4.1: How a species fits into the desert ecosystem* is available if you feel this would be helpful.

Some learners will be able to organise their own research, and plan their own presentation, without help. They could be asked to record the references for the information that they have found formally, in the same way as for a published paper.

> **Assessment ideas:** Talk to groups as they work, asking questions to determine how well individual learners understand the concepts of adaptations, habitats, ecosystems and interactions – including with non-living components of the environment.

Plenary ideas

1 Presentations by groups (30 minutes)

Resources: Outcomes from *Activity: How a species fits into the desert ecosystem.*

Description: Allow each group 5 minutes to present the outcome of their research on their chosen species. Encourage questioning of each group by the rest of the class.

> **Assessment ideas:** Use learners' presentations, questions and answers to ascertain how well the class has understood the concept of an ecosystem, and the interactions that occur within it.

2 Voiceover (15 minutes)

Description: Show a short video clip of the Sonoran Desert (which you have may have used at the start of the lesson). Ask small groups to write a voiceover for it, using as many of the new words and concepts that learners have covered in this lesson as possible.

Ask each group in turn to read their voiceover as the clip is played again.

> **Assessment ideas:** The voiceovers will give information about how well learners have understood the concepts covered in this lesson.

Homework ideas

1 Learner's Book questions 1–5

2 Workbook exercise 4.1

Topic 4.2: Different ecosystems

LEARNING PLAN

Learning objectives	Learning intentions	Success criteria
8Be.01 Identify different ecosystems on the Earth, recognising the variety of habitats that exist within an ecosystem. 8TWSc.01 Sort, group and classify phenomena, objects, materials and organisms through testing, observation, using secondary information, and making and using keys. 8TWSc.05 Carry out practical work safely, supported by risk assessments where appropriate. 8TWSc.07 Collect and record sufficient observations and/or measurements in an appropriate form.	• Learn about some of the many different kinds of ecosystem on Earth. • Describe some of the different habitats in an ecosystem.	• List some of the habitats in an ecosystem. • Construct a diagram to show interactions between organisms in a local ecosystem, from first-hand observation.

Common misconceptions

Misconception	How to identify	How to overcome
An ecosystem is a place.	In the *Getting started* activity.	Discuss responses to the *Getting started* questions. Do *Activity: Habitats in an ecosystem*, which will help learners to appreciate the difference between the terms.

Starter ideas

1 Getting started (10 minutes, including sharing ideas)

Description: Ask learners to answer the *Getting started* question as a pair-and-share activity. This reinforces understanding of the difference between a habitat and an ecosystem. Learners' responses should show how well they understand the meaning of the term 'ecosystem'.

2 Local ecosystems (10 minutes)

Learning intention: To begin to think about local ecosystems and the habitats within them.

Description: Ask learners to describe an ecosystem they have seen today, and to describe habitats and/ or organisms in that ecosystem. This could be on their journey to school (you could alert them at the end of the previous lesson) or – if they do not travel to school – what they can see out of the classroom window. For example, they could mention a city street, a garden, waste ground, a river, or the games field.

Main teaching ideas

1 Thinking about a range of different ecosystems (15–20 minutes)

Learning intention: To be aware that there are many different types of ecosystem on Earth.

Resources: Learner's Book text and pictures; other pictures of other ecosystems if you would like to introduce a different selection.

Description: Use the text and illustrations of mangrove forest, sea ice and rice paddies to discuss features of different ecosystems. Involve learners in the discussion.

If you asked learners to describe local ecosystems in the *Getting started* activity, you could include these ecosystems in the discussion.

> **Differentiation ideas:** This is a whole-class activity, in which everyone should be able to participate. Ensure that all learners are encouraged to contribute to the discussion.

2 Activity: Habitats in an ecosystem (30–45 minutes)

Learning intention: To describe some of the different habitats in an ecosystem.

Resources: Learner's Book text and pictures; other pictures of other ecosystems if you would like to introduce a different selection; internet access.

Description: Ask learners to follow the instructions in the Learner's Book. They could work individually or in pairs on this activity.

> **Differentiation ideas:** Some learners may need support in finding relevant information, and in presenting it. They could use *Template 4.2: Habitats in an ecosystem* to help them to record their findings.

Learners who need a further challenge could be asked to describe some of the adaptations of the organisms in one or more of the habitats they describe, and explain how these support the organisms' ability to survive and reproduce.

> **Assessment ideas:** Use learners' lists to determine how well they are able to find and summarise relevant information.

3 Think like a scientist: Investigating a local ecosystem (at least one full lesson to visit and study the area; another 40 minutes to draw a diagram showing the interactions in the ecosystem)

Learning intention: To study a local ecosystem, as an example of one of the many different kinds of ecosystem on Earth.

To describe some of the different habitats in a local ecosystem.

Resources: Per group: a clipboard and paper for recording findings; ecology equipment as relevant to the ecosystems to be studied, for example: pitfall trap(s); sweep nets; stick and large sheet of white woven material; hand lenses; camera; identification books; keys (you can develop your own keys, to help learners identify common organisms in the local area).

Description: This is an open-ended investigation. The precise way in which this is carried out will vary according to the ecosystem that you ask learners to study.

Go through the instructions in the Learner's Book with the class. Make sure that learners understand what the purpose of the investigation is: to find different habitats in the ecosystem, and to observe and record living organisms that they find.

Explain and demonstrate any equipment that is available for learners to use. Emphasise that they must treat all living organisms with respect, and that nothing must be harmed.

Discuss safety. You could ask learners to help you to draw up a risk assessment for the activity, and help you to construct a short list of rules that they should follow as they work. Determine the groups that learners will work in; encourage them to work in pairs.

Familiarise learners with the ecosystem to be studied. Ask learners to work through step 1, writing down their ideas and perhaps taking photographs or drawing pictures. Allow 5–7 minutes for this. Then ask learners to move on to step 2, followed by step 3 when they are ready.

As learners work, move between the groups, helping them to look carefully and to identify organisms.

Allow plenty of time for debriefing and discussion. You may want to use learners' findings to produce a display, to which everyone contributes.

> **Practical guidance:** This will depend on the equipment that you decide to use. You may like to check on the internet for guidance on how to use equipment, for example:

- how to set up a pitfall trap
- how to use a sweep net in the air, or in water
- how to use a pooter
- how to use a stick and sheet to capture insects from trees and shrubs.

> **Differentiation ideas:** The open-ended nature of this investigation can be daunting to some learners, who will require guidance to help them work steadily through the different steps, and to record appropriate information.

The investigation is quite demanding and there should be plenty to keep even the most able learners occupied and challenged.

> **Assessment ideas:** Interacting with learners as they work provides an excellent opportunity to determine their understanding of ecosystems and habitats.

Plenary ideas

1 Reflecting on the local ecosystem investigation (10–15 minutes)

Description: Ask the class to think about what they enjoyed and learned while studying the local ecosystem. Chair an open-ended discussion about whether learners feel that this kind of activity helps them to learn and understand a topic. You could read out the learning objective 8Be.01 (*Identify different ecosystems on the Earth, recognising the variety of habitats that exist within an ecosystem*) and ask learners how confident they feel about that. Ask: *Did working in the local ecosystem help? Did you learn anything else from this activity?*

Ask three or four learners to summarise what they think they learnt from this activity.

2 Key words (10 minutes)

Description: Ask learners to write down as many key words as they can think of, that they have met in Topics 4.1 and 4.2. You could set a time of 2–3 minutes for this.

Then ask a learner for the first key word. Write it on the board, and ask for its meaning. Use questioning until you are happy with the description of its meaning, and write it on the board alongside the key word. Repeat with more key words.

> **Assessment ideas:** Use learners' responses to gauge how well the class understands key words, and how confident they are in pronouncing and using them.

Homework ideas

1 Workbook exercises 4.2A–C
2 Worksheet 4.2

Topic worksheets

Worksheet 4.2, Planning a school nature reserve

Topic 4.3: Intruders in an ecosystem

LEARNING PLAN

Learning objectives	Learning intentions	Success criteria
8Be.03 Describe how a new and/or invasive species can affect other organisms in an ecosystem.	• Learn about how new or invasive species can affect an ecosystem. • Apply understanding of invasive species to different contexts.	• Contribute to a discussion about why some introduced species cause problems. • Answer questions about invasive species in at least one context.

> LANGUAGE SUPPORT

Learners will use the following words:

native species: a species that belongs in a country or ecosystem, and has not been introduced by humans

extinct: no longer in existence; the term should really only be used for species that no longer exist on Earth, but is sometimes used for species that no longer exist in one particular country

eradicate: get rid of; totally destroy

invasive species: a species that has been introduced into an ecosystem where it does not belong, and has multiplied and spread widely

Common misconceptions

Misconception	How to identify	How to overcome
There is a tendency to think of effects of one species on another in terms only of food chains and webs.	Throughout oral discussions in this topic (e.g. in *Getting started*, or in *Activity: Why do some introduced native species cause problems?*)	Encourage learners to consider other potential interactions, such as effects on habitat, that can adversely affect a native species.

Starter ideas

1 Getting started (10 minutes, including sharing ideas)

Description: Ask learners to follow the instructions in the Learner's Book. Each group should make a list of what might happen. Allow about 4–5 minutes, then ask groups, in turn, to share their ideas. This will encourage learners to use what they already know to make a prediction, and to think widely about how organisms within an ecosystem interact with one another.

2 Kiwis and stoats (10 minutes)

Resources: Search the internet for two videos – one of a kiwi bird, the other of a stoat.

Description: Show learners a video clip of a kiwi. Explain that kiwis live in New Zealand, and that they nest on the ground and cannot fly. Then show a video clip of stoats. Explain that stoats were introduced from England to New Zealand, and are fierce hunters. Ask learners to suggest how this might cause problems.

Main teaching ideas

1 Discussing the problem of introduced species (10–15 minutes)

Resources: Learner's Book text and pictures.

Description: With the whole class, use the Learner's Book to discuss the problems caused by the introductions of stoats to New Zealand. Explain the meaning of the terms 'native species' and 'introduced species'. Encourage questioning. Ask learners to answer questions 1, 2 and 3.

> **Differentiation ideas:** The discussion is a whole-class activity in which everyone can participate. Some learners may need encouragement to become involved in the discussion, while others may ask challenging questions. Some learners may need support to answer questions 1, 2 and 3; they could perhaps work in a pair or a small group if this helps.

> **Assessment ideas:** Use questions and answers during the discussion to gauge learners' understanding of the way in which networks of interactions in an ecosystem can be damaged by an introduced species. Use learners' answers to questions 1, 2 and 3 to check their understanding of terms.

2 Activity: Why do some introduced species cause problems? (15–20 minutes)

Learning intention: To understand why an introduced species causes problems in an ecosystem, whereas that species is generally not a problem in its native country.

Description: Organise learners into pairs. Ask them to follow the instructions in the Learner's Book.

Allow no more than 5 minutes, then collect ideas from each group. Make a list on the board, writing down all the ideas you are given.

Now ask the class to help you to rationalise these ideas. Encourage learners to suggest how to reword the ideas, to merge two ideas if they are basically the same, or to reduce the number of words in order to make it 'sharper' and more focused.

The two main ideas they are likely to come up with are:

- in its native country, a species has predators and/or diseases that may keep its numbers under control, but in a new country it may have no predators

- in its native country, other native species are likely to have adaptations that help them to survive the predators that also live there, but in a new country native species may not be adapted to survive this predator.

> **Differentiation ideas:** All learners can be expected to have some ideas, but some will need support to clarify and rationalise them.

In the example, an introduced species is a predator. Therefore, learners are likely to think only about this situation. Learners who require a challenge could be asked to think about other possibilities, such as introducing a species that eats the same food as a native species, resulting in competition. (There are other examples of introductions in the three Workbook exercises.)

> **Assessment ideas:** Listen for use of language to check learners' understanding of key terms.

3 The possum problem: Worksheets (20–25 minutes)

Learning intention: To encourage learners to think through a problem caused by introduced species.

What idea is good for: Finding information in a written passage; answering questions in learners' own words.

Resources: Worksheets 4.3A–C The possum problem

Description: Ask learners to follow the instructions on the Worksheet(s). You may wish to read the information with them before they answer the questions.

> **Differentiation ideas:** There is a choice of three worksheets, which differ in the difficulty of the language used, as well as the difficulty of the questions. It is recommended that only learners with strong English language skills attempt Worksheet 4.3C.

> **Assessment ideas:** Use their written answers to the worksheets to assess learners' ability to read and understand written information, and to express their ideas, as well as their understanding of the issues posed by an introduced species.

Plenary ideas

1 Summarising the lesson (5 minutes)

Description: Ask learners, in groups of two to five, to summarise the lesson. Then ask for their ideas: *Can the summary be shorter? Who can give the shortest summary that still includes all the main ideas from the lesson?*

> **Assessment ideas:** Use learners' summaries to determine how well they have understood the ideas covered in the lesson.

2 Write an email (10 minutes)

Description: Ask learners, in groups of two to five, to write an email to explain the lesson to someone who is absent. Allow 3–4 minutes, then ask some learners to volunteer to read out their emails. Ask: *Who has written the best one?*

> **Assessment ideas:** Use learners' emails to determine how well they have understood the ideas covered in the lesson.

Homework ideas

1 Learner's Book question 4
2 Workbook exercises 4.3A–C

Topic worksheets

Worksheets 4.3A–C, The possum problem

Topic 4.4: Bioaccumulation

LEARNING PLAN

Learning objectives	Learning intentions	Success criteria
8Be.02 Describe the impact of the bioaccumulation of toxic substances on an ecosystem.	• Find out about DDT. • Use a model to explain what happens to DDT in a food chain. • Learn what bioaccumulation is, and why it happens.	• Contribute to a discussion about the uses of DDT. • Contribute to modelling the biomagnification of DDT, and answer questions about this activity. • Contribute to a discussion about the use of biodegradable insecticides. • Use the word bioaccumulation correctly.

LANGUAGE SUPPORT

Learners will use the following words:

insecticide: a chemical used to kill insect pests

persistent: describes a substance that remains in the environment for a long time

toxic: poisonous

accumulate: build up

bioaccumulation: the build-up of a substance in an organism's body over time, because it does not break down inside the organism

biomagnification: the increase in the concentration of a substance along a food chain; biomagnification happens because of bioaccumulation in the bodies of organisms at each step of the food chain

biodegradable: can be broken down (decay) naturally by microorganisms, such as bacteria and fungi, into products that are not harmful to the environment

Common misconceptions

Misconception	How to identify	How to overcome
Learners may think that all insecticides show bioaccumulation (and/or biomagnification).	Throughout discussions, where learners may refer to 'insecticides' in general, as though they all show bioaccumulation.	Ensure that you and the learners refer to **specific** insecticides, such as DDT, or to **nonbiodegradable** insecticides, when discussing bioaccumulation and biomagnification. *Activity: Biodegradable insecticides* should also help to correct this misconception.

Starter ideas

1 Getting started (10 minutes, including sharing ideas)

Learning intention: To refresh knowledge of the importance of decomposers, in preparation for thinking about how a lack of breakdown of substances in a food chain can lead to bioaccumulation.

Description: Organise learners into pairs and ask them to answer the three questions. Alternatively, they could do this as a pair-and-share activity. These questions check that learners understand what a decomposer is, and that decomposers cannot break down all substances in the environment.

2 Spraying DDT (5 minutes)

Resources: Search the Internet for a video clip of DDT being sprayed in the 1940s or 1950s, preferably showing people being sprayed.

Description: Show learners a video clip. Explain that this video was filmed a long time ago, when people thought that DDT was perfectly safe. People were often sprayed with DDT to kill parasites. DDT was used like this in countries all over the world at that time.

Main teaching ideas

1 Discussion of the use of DDT and bioaccumulation (15 minutes)

Learning intention: To begin to understand how DDT builds up in an organism's body and passes along a food chain.

Resources: Learner's Book text and illustrations.

Description: Use the information and illustrations in the Learner's Book to discuss the issues relating to the use of DDT – why it is used, why it has been banned in some countries, and why it is still used in others.

Use the terms 'insecticide', 'persistent' and 'toxic', and encourage learners to use and say these words.

> **Differentiation ideas:** This is a teacher-led class discussion, in which all learners can take part. Some learners may need encouragement to take part, and to ask or answer questions. Learners who need a challenge could be asked to read the information before the lesson, and you then hand them the responsibility of leading the discussion.

> **Assessment ideas:** Use questioning during the discussion, and listen to learners' comments, to determine how well they understand the issues covered.

2 Think like a scientist: Modelling DDT in a food chain (30–45 minutes)

Learning intention: To use role-play and modelling to show how DDT accumulates along a food chain.

Resources: For the whole class: at least 200 tokens, some blue, some yellow and some red; a stopwatch; a cup or small bag for each person to put tokens into; one card with 'eagle' written on it; several cards (e.g. eight in a class of 30) with 'small bird' written on them; more cards (e.g. 21 in a class of 30) with 'insect' written on them; one larger bag, big enough to hold all the cards; a method of marking out an area of ground outside (for example, traffic cones – you could perhaps borrow something from the sports department, or you might be able to use a marked-out part of a pitch used for sports); a clipboard and paper so that someone (you, or the 'eagle') can record results.

Description: See the instructions in the Learner's Book.

> **Practical guidance:** This activity works best with a fairly large class. It is possible to do it with smaller numbers, but you need enough learners to be able to have significantly more insects than small birds, as well as one eagle.

If this activity is new to you, make sure that you fully understand exactly how it works, and how you will manage it. You may like to try it out with an older class first – they will probably enjoy helping to fine-tune the way it is done.

It is probably best if you act as the timer.

> **Differentiation ideas:** Everyone can take part fully in this activity. Some learners will need individual help in recording their number of tokens. Being the recorder needs quick thinking and a clear head, so you might choose a learner who needs a challenge to take on this role. (The recorder can also take on the role of the eagle.) The recorder could be given a results chart ready to fill in, or you could ask them to design and draw this themselves.

Some learners will need support answering the questions.

> **Assessment ideas:** Use learners' answers to the questions to assess their understanding of why DDT builds up along a food chain.

3 Activity: Biodegradable insecticides (10–15 minutes)

Learning intention: To appreciate that not all insecticides show bioaccumulation or biomagnification; to appreciate that there are reasons why DDT is still used in some countries and situations.

Description: Ask learners to follow the instructions in the Learner's Book. Allow 5 minutes for them to discuss within their groups, and then ask for their ideas.

> **Differentiation ideas:** Move around the room as groups discuss the questions, and use your own questioning to encourage less confident learners to take part in the group discussion.

Ask challenging questions of learners who will benefit – for example: *Should we be using insecticides at all? Should there be a global ban on DDT, rather than letting individual countries make their own decisions? Who should make these decisions?*

> **Assessment ideas:** Use learners' comments and responses during discussion to determine how well they understand the issues covered in this topic.

Plenary ideas

1 Key words (20 minutes)

Resources: Small cards, each with a different key word from the unit written on it (enough for one word per group and some spare).

Description: Put the small cards into a bag. Organise learners into groups of three. Ask a member of each group to take one card from the bag.

One group then answers questions about their key word, as other groups try to find out what it is. You can set rules about the kind of question that can be asked, and the kind of answer that can be given – for example, the answers can be limited to 'Yes' or 'No'.

The group that first identifies the key word becomes the next group whose key word is to be identified.

> **Assessment ideas:** This is a useful way of checking that the class understands the key words from this unit.

2 Mind maps (20–30 minutes)

Resources: Large sheets of paper; coloured pens.

Description: Ask the class: *What have you learnt about in this unit?* Write a list of their ideas on the board.

Organise learners in pairs, or groups of three or four. Ask them to construct a mind map of everything they have learnt in this unit. They can use the ideas you have written down, or they can use their own ideas.

If time allows, ask each group to explain their mind maps to other groups.

> **Assessment ideas:** Ideas from the class about what they think they have learnt in this Unit will help to tell you how well they have understood the topics covered.

Homework ideas

1 Workbook exercise 4.4

2 Worksheet 4.4

Topic worksheets

Worksheet 4.4, Mercury in an Arctic food web

PROJECT GUIDANCE

Impact of an introduced species

This project addresses the following learning objectives:

8SIC.01 Discuss how scientific knowledge is developed through collective understanding and scrutiny over time.

8SIC.03 Evaluate issues which involve and/or require scientific understanding.

8SIC.05 Discuss how the uses of science can have a global environmental impact.

This project provides an opportunity for learners to apply their knowledge/understanding from this unit to an example close to home.

Learners will make a presentation (as a poster or illustrated talk) of their chosen or allocated topic(s). Decide how to divide the class into groups. You may also like to allocate roles to each member within the group.

Find and select suitable references for groups to use. These could include library books and relevant web pages.

Help groups to select a suitable introduced species to research. Some countries will have much better information available than others, so learners should not be restricted to examples from their own country if this would make it difficult for them to find relevant written information or data.

Ask each group to present their work.

> 5 Materials and cycles on Earth

Unit plan

Topic	Learning hours	Learning content	Resources
5.1 The structure of the atom	2-3	The structure of the atom; models for the structure of the atom; the work of scientists to form the model of the structure of the atom	**Learner's Book:** Questions 1–10 Activity: An atomic timeline **Workbook:** Exercise 5.1A, Labelling the structure of the atom Exercise 5.1B, Models of the structure of the atom Exercise 5.1C, Rutherford's gold foil experiment **Teacher's Resource:** Worksheets 5.1A–C, Wordsearch and meanings Template 5.1A: Researching atomic scientists Template 5.1B: Peer assessment for *Activity: A timeline of discoveries in atomic structure*
5.2 Purity	2-3	The concept of purity in elements; the calculation of percentage purity; concept of purity of product in a reaction	**Learner's Book:** Questions 1–6 Think like a scientist: Finding the mass of salts in seawater Think like a scientist: Reactions with more than one product **Workbook:** Exercise 5.2A–C, Purity

Topic	Learning hours	Learning content	Resources
5.3 Weather and climate	3-4	The difference between weather and climate; the importance of recording the weather data	**Learner's Book:** Questions 1–8 Activity: Recording the weather Activity: Weather data from different sources **Workbook:** Exercise 5.3A, Words and meanings Exercise 5.3B, Weather or climate? Exercise 5.3C, Weather data **Teacher's Resource:** Worksheets 5.3A–C, Comparing weather data Template 5.3A: Results sheet for *Activity: Recording the weather* Template 5.3B: Peer assessment for *Activity: Weather data from different sources*
5.4 Climate and ice ages	2-3	How the Earth's climate has changed in the past ice ages, glacial and interglacial periods; evidence for climate cycles	**Learner's Book:** Questions 1–6 Activity: Where in the world is there ice? **Workbook:** Exercise 5.4A, Wordsearch Exercise 5.4B, Soil cores Exercise 5.4C, Climate cycles **Teacher's Resource:** Template 5.4: Peer assessment for *Comparing the ice covered areas of the Earth 25 000 years ago and today*
5.5 Atmosphere and climate	2-3	How the atmosphere has changed over the lifetime of the Earth; how the changing atmosphere has an impact on the climate; renewable resources	**Learner's Book:** Questions 1–10 Think like a scientist: The greenhouse effect **Workbook:** Exercise 5.5A, Our atmosphere Exercise 5.5B, Changes in the atmosphere Exercise 5.5C, Evidence **Teacher's Resource:** Worksheet 5.5, Looking at temperature data
Cross-unit resources			**Learner's Book:** Check your Progress **Project:** Global warming and climate change debate **Teacher's Resource:** Language development worksheets 5.1 Words and meanings 5.2 Using the correct words

BACKGROUND KNOWLEDGE

Learners are unlikely to have any background knowledge of the structure of an atom so it is worth revising the fact that each type of atom is different. Learners should be familiar with making a timeline listing contributions made by various people. They may have heard of the Large Hadron Collider, which could have aroused their interest.

Although the idea of 'purity' should not be new to learners, the concept of something being pure in science may not mean 'pure' in the same way they understand it. This is a useful reminder with regard to alloys. The fact that impurities in diamonds make them *more* valuable may be a surprise. Learners do not always understand that the products of chemical reactions are often mixed together. The concept of mixtures of salts in seawater may be new to them, as they probably think that only sodium chloride is dissolved in the water.

Learners may think they know about climate and weather but they tend to use the terms interchangeably, so ensure they can distinguish clearly between the two. They are unlikely to have much knowledge of ice ages; they may, as a result of films they have watched, think of them as being very cold without being aware that we are currently experiencing an ice age. You could help their understanding by gathering information about changes in weather for your area over the past 100 million years, to give some perspective on the local climate. Although learners may have heard a great deal about climate change, the idea that it is complicated and involves many factors may be new since the media either take a 'we can fix it with this action' approach or indulge in excessive scaremongering. This topic requires learners to bring in ideas from various science topics and general knowledge.

TEACHING SKILLS FOCUS

Plenaries 2

Plenaries can provide opportunities to assess the learning of the whole class simultaneously.

Remember that they can be planned to summarise learning at any appropriate point in the lesson, not just at the end. Plenaries may often be more appropriately placed at points of transition between activities rather than the end of the lesson. Ensure that learning or consolidation is central to any plenary session. Using mini-plenaries gives the opportunity to identify and address learners' misconceptions at any time during the lesson – and in subsequent lessons.

To be effective, plenaries should be differentiated according to the needs of your class. Your learners must be able to access the plenary task, but some challenge is required so that you can assess what they *don't* know or understand. The suggested plenary ideas allow you to devise your own plenaries to suit your particular classes at the appropriate time.

An effective plenary should give learners time and space to reflect, both on what they have learned and how they have learned it. It should guide them to the next steps in their learning. Reflection points in the Learner's Book could be also used as plenaries. This type of plenary could become the focus for this unit.

One very useful self-assessment task that can be used as a plenary is the RAG123 assessment (which stands for red, amber, green, 1, 2, 3). In this task, learners rate themselves, on a scale of 1–3, by how much they understand the content (1 implies excellent understanding; 3 means misunderstanding of the work). Learners also assess their behaviour during the lesson (red for distracted, green for excellent attitude to learning). It allows learners to reflect at the end of a lesson, topic or unit. You can assess how confident the class feels from their RAG123 scores. You can also use this system to score the class and, as a result, you can set tasks to move them on to the next stage of their learning.

In science, topics can be very discrete and lessons learned in one area do not always seem to learners to be relevant in the next topic of study. However, the RAG123 task focuses on the learner and the learner's attitude, so it is very useful to focus them on the next topic.

CONTINUED

Another useful plenary task is 'Five fingers', as suggested in Topic 5.2. Each learner draws around their hand on a scrap of paper or in their book and writes notes on each finger to answer the questions.

- Thumb – What have you learned? What do you understand?
- Index finger – What skills have you used today?
- Middle finger – Which skills did you find difficult today?
- Ring finger – Who did you help today?
- Little finger – What will you make sure that you remember from today's lesson?

It is useful to collect these and use them to help decide what you need to concentrate on in the next lesson.

This is another type of plenary that structures learners' reflection time. It allows less confident learners to celebrate what they have done well and encourages more confident learners to think about the next steps in their learning.

1 Aim to use the 'Five fingers' plenary task at least once in this unit.

Did it help the learners to focus on the lesson they have just done? Did it help you understand what happened in the lesson from the learners'

perspective? Did it help you to decide if there is anything you need to go over in your next lesson? Have you included enough reflection time for both the learners and yourself? Will the use of this plenary change the way you plan your next lessons?

2 Aim to try a plenary of your own in this unit.

You could start by trying 'Quick-fire questions', as suggested in Topic 5.1: *The structure of the atom*. Ask learners a series of quick-fire questions about the subatomic particles, such as: *Which particle has no charge? Which has the smallest mass? Which particle is not in the nucleus of the atom?*

Learners can answer on a piece of paper, swap with a partner and mark each other's responses. Devise some of your own questions, based on your knowledge of the learners.

Ask learners to write the questions they answered correctly and those they answered incorrectly on sticky notes and stick them in the appropriate places on the board as they leave the room. Then you can use the answers they had wrong as a starter next time.

Were you able to use this information to plan a starter for the next lesson? Were you surprised by the answers the learners gave?

Topic 5.1: The structure of the atom

LEARNING PLAN

Learning objectives	Learning intentions	Success criteria
8Cm.01 Describe the Rutherford model of the structure of an atom.	• To describe the structure of the atom.	• Describe the structure of the atom.
8Cm.02 Know that electrons have negative charge, protons have positive charge and neutrons have no charge.	• To list the particles found in an atom.	• List the particles found in an atom.
	• To describe some of the properties of the particles found in an atom.	• Describe some of the properties of the particles found in an atom.

CONTINUED

Learning objectives	Learning intentions	Success criteria
8Cm.03 Know that the electrostatic attraction between positive and negative charge is what holds together individual atoms. 8SIC.01 Discuss how scientific knowledge is developed through collective understanding and scrutiny over time. 8SIC.04 Describe how people develop and use scientific understanding as individuals and through collaboration, e.g. through peer review. 8TWSc.07 Collect and record sufficient observations and/or measurments in an appropriate form.	• To understand that models of the atom have changed over time. • To look carefully at how results, observations and conclusions can be fairly peer reviewed.	• Describe some of the discoveries that have helped to create the model of the atom used today. • Describe the way that scientific understanding is developed by individuals and by collaboration such as peer review. • Explain how a peer review can be fair.

LANGUAGE SUPPORT

Learners will use the following words:

atom: a tiny particle of matter

sub-atomic particles: atomic particles that are smaller than an atom

protons: positively charged particles found in the nucleus of an atom

neutrons: particles found in the nucleus of an atom that have no electrical charge

electrons: negatively charged particles found surrounding the nucleus of an atom

nucleus: a dense area at the centre of an atom that contains protons and neutrons

electrical charge: a property of an object which causes it to attract or repel other objects with a charge

electrostatic attraction: the force that holds individual atoms together

deflected: the direction of an object was changed

Common misconceptions

Misconception	How to identify	How to overcome
Many learners find it difficult to appreciate that something as small as an atom is made up of even smaller parts.	This will be made very obvious by learners asking … 'but how do you know this?'	While learners cannot understand all the experimental work behind the atomic structure development, the different models shown here will give them a chance to see how ideas change. Work your way through the ideas in the starter. Repetition is the key.
Learners find it difficult to understand that an atom is mainly made up of empty space.	Ask directly: *What is in the space between the subatomic particles?* They will often think it is air.	This is difficult to overcome. You need to continually reinforce this idea of empty space.

Starter ideas

1 Getting started (10 minutes or less)

Resources: Learner's Book and/or three take-away coffee cups with lids (these must be three different sizes). Before the lesson and out of sight of the class, place a large stone or piece of modelling clay into the smallest or the middle-sized cup. Then fill all three with water and put the lids on. Check that the one with the added stone or modelling clay is heavier than the other two cups. Show these to the learners and tell them that the cups have been filled with water.

Description: Ask learners to guess which cup has the most mass. Do this as a show of hands, or ask them each to write it on a sticky note attached to their book or sleeve. Ask them to justify their choice.

Then ask a selected learner, or a volunteer, to come and pick the cups up to gauge their relative masses; tell them to not tell the class what they find out. Ask the selected learner what their initial choice was, and then ask if they want to change their choice. Then ask the class if they want to change *their* choices.

Discuss whether this result was true; did the learner try to trick you all? You should discuss the evidence they have.

Then invite another learner to pick up the cups and ask them again? *Do you want to change your choice?* This should lead into a discussion about how much evidence you need to have. This can be usefully linked to the current evidence about the structure of the atom. *We can't see it, so what evidence do we have and whose evidence do we trust?*

This reminds learners that they need evidence before they can come to a conclusion.

2 Give me five! (10 minutes)

Description: Ask learners to give five facts about atoms. This will be difficult for many learners so allow them a few minutes individually and then a few minutes with a partner, before taking feedback from the class.

Main teaching ideas

1 The story of the structure of the atom (20–30 minutes)

Learning intention: To learn the structure of the atom, the parts and properties and how the Rutherford model was developed.

Resources: Learner's Book.

Description: Work through the model and ensure that the learners are able to name the subatomic particles and their simple properties. Use the ideas of the scientists to build up from the plum pudding model.

> **Differentiation ideas:** In working through this content you will need to keep stopping and checking that learners have understood and to offer extra support to those who need it. It would be useful to stop and do a repetition exercise to ensure that learners can name the subatomic particles and spell these names correctly, and know their simple properties. The time you need to spend on this will depend on the class. As you work through the history, stop and check, asking learners to repeat what you have said.

2 Making a model (20–40 minutes)

Learning intention: To use ideas to build a model.

Resources: Prepared opaque containers or boxes, each containing a heavy object that cannot move about (such as a lump of modelling clay fixed to the container at one end) as well as some small objects that can move and make a noise.

Description: Learners work in small groups of two or three. Ask them to draw what they think is in the box and how the contents are arranged. You could give different groups slightly different containers, for example, some with the heavy object in the middle, and some with the heavy object at the edge. Once learners have decided what they think is the arrangement, they can compare ideas with another group and then with the whole class. Ask: *How reliable is the evidence from the other groups? How can you check it?*

Ask learners to reflect on how difficult this task was. *Did drawing a model of what you thought was there help to visualise it and to understand it? What further information would you like to find out?*

> **Differentiation ideas:** You could make some of the containers very different (easier or more difficult), to suit different groups of learners. If you do this you need to be aware that the different groups will need to question other groups' evidence and to examine their containers.

> **Assessment ideas:** This could be assessed by asking learners to share their reflections, as above.

3 An atomic timeline (30 minutes or more; may be completed for homework)

Learning intention: To investigate some of the scientists involved in developing the early model of the atom.

Resources: Learner's Book; library and or internet access.

Description: Ask learners to make a timeline of discoveries related to early ideas about the structure of the atom. Ask them to add some personal information about the scientists. *Template 5.1A* could be used to support learners while they research the scientists.

This would be a good opportunity to reinforce the ideas of developing scientific understanding both as individuals and through collaboration, including peer review. Ask the learners to explain how they could ensure the review of the work would be fair. Perhaps you could use the example of them reviewing their classmate's work. Is it fair if you say it is great work just because they are your friend or they will be nice about your work? Is it fair that this person might put pressure on you if you said they had made a mistake in their results or there was not enough evidence for the conclusions they made? This is a very good opportunity to discuss the idea of scientific integrity and to discuss the point of peer review. Make sure learners understand they are not just looking to download and print lots of information from the internet.

> **Differentiation ideas:** This will be by outcome, as far as the information is concerned, but be prepared to give additional help and guidance to those who need support understanding or producing the timeline. This could be started as a class exercise on the board.

> **Assessment ideas:** This could be assessed with *Template 5.1B: Peer assessment.*

Plenary ideas

1 Quick-fire questions (10 minutes)

Resources: Prepared questions.

Description: Ask learners a series of quick-fire questions about subatomic particles, such as:

- *Which particle has no charge?*
- *Which has the smallest mass?*
- *Which particle is not in the nucleus of the atom?*

Learners write answers on paper and swap with a partner to mark.

Ask learners to write the questions they got right and those they got wrong onto separate sticky notes and stick these on the board as they leave the room. This way you can use the any incorrect/confused answers as a starter activity in a subsequent lesson.

2 Summarise the lesson (10 minutes)

Description: Ask learners to summarise the lesson in five bullet points, then compare their summaries with a partner. Then ask them to reduce the summary to three bullet points and compare with a partner again. Ask each pair to reduce the summary to one bullet point, write it on a sticky note or paper, and place it on the board or desk as they leave. You could use these to assess what they have taken from the lesson and to inform your next steps.

Learners could consider these questions as they write their summaries: *What was this lesson about? What did I take from it? How can I ensure that I get the most from each lesson?*

Homework ideas

1 Workbook exercise 5.1A–C

2 Research on scientists who worked on early ideas about atomic structure.

Topic worksheets

- Worksheet 5.1A, Wordsearch and meanings
- Worksheet 5.1B, Matching terms and facts
- Worksheet 5.1C, The Large Hadron Collider

Topic 5.2: Purity

LEARNING PLAN

Learning objectives	Learning intentions	Success criteria
8Cm.04 Know that purity is a way to describe how much of a specific chemical is in a mixture. **8Cc.01** Use word equations to describe reactions. **8Cc.04:** Know that reactions do not always lead to a single pure product and that sometimes a reaction will produce an impure mixture of products. **8TWSp.05** Make risk assessments for practical work to identify and control risks. **8TWSc.05** Carry out practical work safely, supported by risk assessments where appropriate. **8TWSa.02** Describe trends and patterns in results, including identifying any anomalous results. **8TWSa.03** Make conclusions by interpreting results and explain the limitations of the conclusions. **8TSWa.05** Present and interpret observations and measurements appropriately.	• Explain what is meant by purity. • Calculate the percentage purity. • Understand why a pure product is needed and that it is difficult to obtain a pure product.	• Define purity. • Calculate percentage purity. • State why a pure product is needed and explain why it is difficult to obtain a pure product.

LANGUAGE SUPPORT

Learners will use the following words:

carat: a measurement of purity of gold

translucent: allows some light to pass through, but not in a way that produces clear images

Common misconceptions

Misconception	How to identify	How to overcome
Some learners think that pure means 'not dirty' and that water that is pure is safe to drink.	Listen to learners' discussions and ask them to explain what they understand by a substance being 'pure'.	Reinforce the idea that a pure substance is one that only contains that substance and nothing else.

Starter ideas

1 Getting started (10 minutes)

Description: Ask learners these three questions to assess the level of understanding about purity:

1 What does it mean if a substance is pure?

2 Which of these items are pure substances?

sodium chloride; oxygen; sea water; gold; orange juice; copper oxide; silver nitrate; soil; black ink; potassium.

3 Of the items in question 2, which are elements, mixtures and compounds?

They could do these on their own then check with a partner. Take feedback from the class.

2 Find words beginning with… (10 minutes)

Resources: Learner's Book.

Description: Write the word 'purity' vertically down the board and challenge learners to find scientific words beginning with those letters. You could allow them to use the glossary at the back of the Learner's Book or allow just those with weaker English to use the book. Take feedback from the class and allow one point for a correct word and two points if no one else has that answer.

Main teaching ideas

1 Purity of elements (20 minutes)

Learning intention: To explain what a pure element is and calculate the percentage purity.

Resources: Learner's Book; construction blocks in a variety of shapes and colours; different gold items (or images) showing the carat marking; images of diamonds (some pure and some with other elements added).

Description: Review the definition of purity. Distribute the construction blocks, saying that each type of brick represents one kind of atom.

Ask learners to work in small groups of two or three to produce a pure substance, a substance that is 50% pure and one that is 90% pure. The groups then swap their 'substances' with another group and check each other's work. Take feedback from the class.

Work through the section about the purity of gold and then ask the groups to sort their bricks so that they can put together a group of 24 identical bricks to represent pure gold, then a group of 18 'gold' bricks with six others for 18 carat gold. Learners repeat the activity to represent the various purities of gold. Doing this with concrete objects helps learners to understand the calculations. Explain that the other metals are likely to be copper or silver.

Work through the information about the diamonds; you could use a range of different images.

> **Practical guidance:** Collect the construction bricks as soon as learners have finished using them, to prevent loss of concentration in the class.

> **Differentiation ideas:** Learners who find the idea of percentages difficult may need help using the bricks to build up the different percentages of purity, and may need to do this exercise several times. Try more challenging calculations with learners who need to be challenged.

> **Assessment ideas:** You could use the questions in the Learner's Book or the Workbook to assess progress.

2 Think like a scientist: Finding the mass of salts in seawater (15 minutes, plus 30–40 minutes for the practical)

Learning intention: To understand the idea of purity in a mixture.

Resources: Learner's Book; an evaporating basin; tongs; Bunsen burner; tripod; pipe clay triangle; safety glasses; top pan balance; seawater sample. (If you are not able to collect samples of real seawater, this can be prepared, using the proportions of salts shown in the diagram. You could make your seawater more or less salty.)

Description: Take time to explain or revisit the idea of getting sodium chloride from seawater. You may need to explain that salts other than sodium chloride are found in sea water and give a simple explanation of what a salt is.

Direct learners to the charts in the Learner's Book so that they realise how little (by mass) there is of sodium chloride in 1000 g of seawater, and that other salts are present. Spend time ensuring learners understand that there are about 35 g of salts and only 68% of that 35 g is actually sodium chloride. You may need to illustrate this visually by showing them 1000 g of seawater, 35 g of 'salts' and then 23.8 g of sodium chloride. Learners may be surprised that there is so little sodium chloride in the water.

Explain the procedure for the practical part of this section. You could demonstrate it, asking learners to assemble the equipment and to explain the next step. It is helpful to ask learners: *What are you going to when you get back to your work area? What is the next step? What equipment do you need? What risks are there? What will you do about the risks?*

> **Practical guidance:** As above. Supervise closely when learners are heating the solution, taking care in case of spitting. Leave the solution for some hours to evaporate fully. Make sure that the evaporating basin is cold before placing it on the top pan balance.

Emphasise that the measurements need to be recorded carefully. Learners can easily lose track of the measurements and, therefore, be unable to work out the percentage of salt.

> **Differentiation ideas:** Some learners may find it difficult to understand the idea of the mass of salt and the calculation of the percentages. Showing them the measured masses, as detailed above, will help. Labelling these masses and leaving them in view, in the laboratory, provides a useful reference point for these learners.

Learners may need different levels of support while carrying out the practical. Those who find organisation challenging may need to be closely supervised when finding the mass, so that you can be sure they have recorded the readings accurately.

You could demonstrate the activity, asking volunteer learners to carry out the various stages. Ask them to explain what they are doing at each step of the process, and what special care they need to take, to demonstrate the experiment to learners who need support.

> **Assessment ideas:** Use questions 1–6 of *Think like a scientist: Finding the mass of salts in seawater* to assess understanding and progress.

3 **Think like a scientist: Reactions with more than one product (40+ minutes, depending on how many reactions you choose to offer)**

Learning intention: To emphasise the idea that there is often more than one product in a reaction and that these are mixed together, so they need to be separated if you require a pure product.

Resources: Test tubes; test tube racks; universal indicator solution; conical flask; measuring cylinder; burette; boiling tube; delivery tube with bung; clamp stands; safety glasses; limewater [LOW HAZARD]; chemical reactants (as in the examples in the Learner's Book or other reactions you choose, depending on what you have available: silver nitrate solution [IRRITANT], use a concentration lower than 0.18 mol/dm^3; sodium chloride solution [LOW HAZARD]; sulfuric acid, use a concentration between 1.5 and 0.5 mol/dm^3 [IRRITANT]; sodium hydroxide solution, use a concentration below 0.5 mol/dm^3 [IRRITANT]; barium chloride solution, use a concentration lower than 0.4 mol/dm^3 [HARMFUL IF SWALLOWED]; sodium sulfate solution [LOW HAZARD]; lead nitrate solution, the safety guidance for the use of lead nitrate is that it is suitable for this age group if used at concentrations below 0.01 mol/dm^3; potassium iodide solution [LOW HAZARD]; copper carbonate powder [HARMFUL IF SWALLOWED, IRRITANT]; hydrochloric acid, a concentration of less than 2 mol/dm^3 should be used, it is an [IRRITANT]).

Description: Demonstrate a simple reaction with only one product, such as magnesium burning in air, and then a reaction that has more than one product. Stress what else is in the test tube apart from the product you want. Go through the word equations for the reactions in the Learner's Book and stress that the products are in a mixture.

Before you allow learners to carry out some or all of the reactions themselves, reinforce the basic safety messages about wearing safety glasses and the dangers of some chemicals they will be using. Insist that they wash their hands after handling chemicals. You may prefer to organise the practical work as a 'circus' set up around the room, so that learners move from one to another, rather than needing a lot of equipment and chemicals at their own work places. You may prefer to place an instruction card at each station, detailing the equipment and the method. You could also include a note about what to do with the used equipment. If you are short of time, you could ask a different group of learners to demonstrate each reaction and then answer questions from the whole class for each reaction in turn. You may choose to carry out reactions that need a burette as a demonstration. If you have burettes available you may like to spend time demonstrating the correct use, paying attention to such details as: setting the burette in the clamp stand, ensuring the tap is closed before filling and using a small funnel to carefully fill it, and running the acid into the tubing below the tap. Then give learners the opportunity to try operating the tap before they carry out the reaction.

> **Practical guidance:** See above. You will need to be vigilant as learners are moving around and question them about each reaction. Remind them to answer questions 7–9 from *Think like a scientist: Reactions with more than one product* for each reaction.

> **Differentiation ideas:** You could decide to limit the range of reactions that your learners do, based on their practical abilities.

Learners may need different levels of support while carrying out the practical activities. Those who find organisation difficult may need to be closely supervised to ensure that they record each reaction before starting on the next one. If a different group of learners demonstrates each reaction, this will provide more support to the less confident learners, but it has the disadvantage of reducing their chances of becoming more proficient at practical work.

> **Assessment ideas:** Use questions 7–9 from *Think like a scientist: Reactions with more than one product* to assess progress and understanding.

Plenary ideas

1 Why does it need to be pure? (10 minutes)

Resources: Sticky notes or paper.

Description: Ask learners to write down examples and an explanation of why a product of a chemical reaction may need to be pure.

2 Five fingers (10 minutes)

Description: Each learner draws around their hand on a scrap of paper or in their book and writes the answers to these questions on the appropriate finger to describe their learning.

- Thumb – What have you learned? What do you understand?
- Index finger – What skills have you used today?
- Middle finger – Which skills did you find difficult today?
- Ring finger – Who did you help today?
- Little finger – What will you make sure that you remember from today's lesson?

You will find it useful to collect these and use them to help decide what you need to concentrate on in the next lesson.

This is another type of plenary that structures learners' reflection time. It allows less confident learners to celebrate what they have done well and encourages more confident learners to think about the next steps in their learning.

Homework ideas

1   Workbook exercise 5.2, Purity

Topic 5.3: Weather and climate

LEARNING PLAN

Learning objectives	Learning intentions	Success criteria
8ESc.03 Describe the difference between climate and weather. **8TWSp.04** Plan a range of investigations of different types, while considering variables appropriately, and recognise that not all investigations can be fair tests. **8TWSc.02** Decide what equipment is required to carry out an investigation or experiment and use it appropriately. **8TWSc.03** Evaluate whether measurements and observations have been repeated sufficiently to be reliable. **8TWSc.06** Evaluate a range of secondary information sources for their relevance and know that some sources may be biased. **8TWSa.01** Describe the accuracy of predictions, based on results, and suggest why they were or were not accurate. **8TWSa.02** Describe trends and patterns in results, including identifying any anomalous results. **8TWSa.03** Make conclusions by interpreting results and explain the limitations of the conclusions. **8TSWa.05** Present and interpret observations and measurements appropriately.	• Learn the difference between weather and climate. • Make observations of the weather. • Look at the differences in living things in different climates. • To evaluate a range of secondary information about weather data.	• Explain the difference between weather and climate. • Make observations of the weather and discuss findings. • Discuss differences in living things in different climates. • Discuss the validity of different data sources and state if any may be biased.

> **LANGUAGE SUPPORT**
>
> Learners will use the following words:
>
> **weather:** the state of the atmosphere in a particular place
>
> **atmosphere:** the layer of gases surrounding the Earth (or another planet)
>
> **humidity:** a measure of the concentration of water vapour in the atmosphere
>
> **visibility:** a measure of how far you can see due to the light and weather conditions
>
> **climate:** the weather conditions prevailing in an area in general and over a long period
>
> **statistics:** the science of collecting and analysing numerical data in large quantities
>
> **meteorology:** the study of weather
>
> **climatology:** the study of climate

Common misconceptions

Misconception	How to identify	How to overcome
Many learners think weather and climate are the same thing.	Ask learners: *What is the difference between weather and climate?*	Explain the difference carefully and reinforce the difference by the correct use of the terms.

Starter ideas

1   Getting started (10 minutes)

Description: Ask learners, in pairs, to suggest as many words as they can that are concerned with weather. Take feedback from the class. You could compile a list, as this will be useful for various tasks in the Learner's Book. It would be a good opportunity to discuss the meanings and spelling of these terms.

2   What's the weather like? (15 minutes)

Resources: Photographs or slide show.

Description: Ask learners, in small groups of three or four, to think about the weather where they live. Ask them to write down how they could describe it to someone who lives in a very different area. Give each group another country or area and ask them to describe what they think the weather is like there. (You could have a series of cards with areas/countries and the groups could pick one, or you could allocate the country.)

Take feedback from the class for the descriptions of both the local weather and that of the other country. This could be set as a homework task, for learners to check and write their own detailed description.

This encourages learners to think about the weather in their part of the world and compare it with that in other parts of the world.

Main teaching ideas

1   Recording the weather (40 minutes, plus time to take readings every day for a week; this could be done at break or before or after school)

Learning intention: To give learners practical experience of recording weather information and basic understanding of the importance of standardisation when comparing data.

Resources: Learners should suggest resources needed. These are likely to include: thermometers; a vessel of standard size and shape, perhaps with a filter funnel for collecting rain; measuring cylinder; compass to establish wind direction; anemometer; camera to record cloud cover.

If you have access to a school weather station, it would be useful for the learners to compare their findings with readings taken in the weather station.

Description: Discuss the need to record weather data around the world. Ask learners, in groups of two to four, to discuss what they think they should measure or observe. Take feedback from the whole class. Ask the class how they think they could record this information and what equipment they will need. They may need to discuss this, in small groups. Take feedback from the whole class. Discuss the standardisation of how measurements and observation are taken, to allow for comparison. Work through the tips in the main text and direct the learners to the questions they will need to answer. Organise the equipment the class decide they need and demonstrate how to use it. The locations in which the measurements and observations are taken is important; for example, rain collection equipment needs to be in an area that is open but where it is not likely to be interfered with by other learners or animals. You could discuss the weather stations and how these provide data that has all been collected in the same way.

Alternatively, you could modify this task and take readings on an hourly basis throughout the day.

It may be easier and more appropriate to use pictograms for recording some of the information, such as cloud cover or wind strength.

> **Practical guidance:** Carry out a risk assessment for activities outside the classroom. Demonstrate how to take observations, depending on what you are able to provide for the learners. For example, place the thermometer in the shade, with the bulb not touching anything other than the air; site rain-collecting equipment appropriately.

> **Differentiation ideas:** You could use *Template 5.3A: Weather recording sheet* for learners who need support with this task. You could restrict the observations so that every group measures temperature and rainfall, but only some groups to do the observations of wind, humidity and cloud cover, as these are likely to be more subjective and some learners may find that this is too difficult or it takes too long.

> **Assessment ideas:** You could assess the reports learners produce on the weather that week or day.

2 Weather data from different sources (30 minutes)

Learning intention: To look at weather data from a variety of sources for a particular place and to consider the reliability and compare the data if appropriate.

Resources: Access to weather data for the areas the learners have chosen. (You could restrict their choices to allow you to prepare data to be printed off if this is easier for you.)

The weather data could come from newspapers, travel agents' websites or brochures, the internet, a weather app, or international or local meteorological agencies. Any data printed off for the learners needs to include the source of the data.

Poster materials; access to computers.

Description: Ask learners to choose a particular place they would like to spend time in and ask them to detail what they would hope the conditions would be to make this ideal. For example: gentle winds and no storms if they were trying to learn to sail, or cold temperatures and a thick layer of snow for skiing. Ask learners to look at the weather data from these sources over a particular time period. Ask: *Does the data differ? How does it differ? Why does it differ? What do you need to know to compare the data? Are all these weather information providers using the same source? How can you find out? Are any of the information providers likely to produce biased information? Why might they do that?*

Organise learners into groups of two or three. Provide them with the data as indicated above. Ask them the questions, then perhaps leave them written on the board.

> **Differentiation ideas:** You could restrict the number of sources for some groups. You could include data from slightly different areas, suitably labelled to ensure that learners are thinking about how to compare appropriately.

> **Assessment ideas:** You could ask groups each to do a presentation about the data. This could be in a variety of formats, such as a poster, a talk, or a computer-based slideshow. Groups could use *Template 5.3B: Peer assessment* to assess one another.

3 Climate zones (15–20 minutes)

Learning intention: To think about climate, as opposed to weather, identify the different climate regions in the world and be able to say where they are.

Resources: Learner's Book; an atlas with climate data; access to pictures or to the internet with printing capability; poster materials.

Description: Ask the learners to look at the photographs in the Learner's Book showing the weather in different countries and answer the questions.

Move on to the section on climate zones and discuss the different types of climate and where they are. Then challenge learners to find pictures to show these different climates; they may need more than one picture to illustrate temperate and Mediterranean zones. Ask learners to make a display, using posters, collages and computer slide shows or animations, to illustrate these climate zones.

⟩ **Practical guidance:** This depends on how you decide to do this task. You could provide all the pictures from magazines, printed from the internet or elsewhere. Then, having worked through the questions, leave learners to work on the display. You will need to supervise them carefully, to ensure they are focussed.

⟩ **Differentiation ideas:** You could give pictures with more obvious clues to groups who need support. You could provide internet access for learners who need a challenge, rather than pictures, so that they carry out their own searches and print information, or produce a computer-based display.

⟩ **Assessment ideas:** Use the questions for assessment and use a modified version of *Template 5.3B: Peer assessment.* Alternatively, you could asses the displays/presentations yourself.

Plenary ideas

1 Emoji exit ticket (10 minutes)

Resources: Paper or sticky notes, or pre-prepared exit tickets.

Description: Ask learners to draw an emoji to describe how they thought they did in the lesson and then to answer these questions: *How well did you understand today's material? What did you learn today? What did you find difficult today?*

⟩ **Assessment ideas:** Use the questions from the Learner's Book for assessment.

2 What's the question? (10 minutes)

Resources: Prepared answers to questions, for example: hot and wet all year, very cold and dry all year, trees bending, there is a rainbow.

Description: Put a small number of answers on the board and challenge learners, individually or in pairs, to write the questions. Learners could consider these points as they decide on the questions: *How well do I think about the answers to questions? Do I give enough detail or too much?*

Homework ideas

1 Workbook exercises 5.3A–C

Topic worksheets

Worksheets 5.3A–C, Comparing weather data

Topic 5.4: Climate and ice ages

LEARNING PLAN

Learning objectives	Learning intentions	Success criteria
8ESc.01 Understand that there is evidence that the Earth's climate exists in a cycle between warm periods and ice ages, and the cycle takes place over long time periods.	• Learn about how the Earth's climate has changed in past. • Find out about ice ages, glacial and interglacial periods. • Look at some of the evidence that the Earth's climate cycles between colder and warmer periods.	• Describe how the Earth's climate has changed in the past. • Explain the difference between ice ages, glacial and interglacial periods. • List some evidence that the Earth's climate cycles between colder and warmer periods.

LANGUAGE SUPPORT

Learners will use the following words:

glacial period: the coldest part of an ice age

interglacial period: a warmer part of an ice age

cycle: a regular changing pattern from one thing to another

ice ages: times when part of the Earth has permanent ice

boulder: large rock

glacier: river of ice formed from snow that has become compressed over a long time

peat bog: an area of wetland where the decay of dead plant material has been delayed

Common misconceptions

Misconception	How to identify	How to overcome
Some learners find the concept of an ice age difficult. They understand frozen parts of the world but think that either the whole Earth was frozen during an ice age, or that the parts that were frozen were always frozen during an ice age. The ideas of glacial and interglacial periods during an ice age are difficult to understand. Most learners cannot grasp the idea that Earth is currently in an ice age.	Ask learners what they understand by an 'ice age' at the start of the lesson and again at the end of the lesson.	When discussing this, give learners the definition of an ice age and wait for them to make the connection between the definition and climate on Earth.

Starter ideas

1 Getting started (10 minutes)

Resources: Learner's Book.

Description: Ask learners to look at the photograph and to discuss, in groups of two or three, why Yuka's body has been preserved for so long. You could also ask why they think the body was found in 1977. They should discuss their ideas in their groups and use the opportunity to discuss why there are no mammoths living now. Take feedback from the class.

2 What do you understand by the term 'ice age'? (10 minutes)

Description Ask learners to say what they understand by the term 'ice age'. Give them one minute thinking time, two minutes to write down their thoughts, two minutes to discuss with a partner, and two minutes to add to their ideas. Take feedback from the class.

Use this as a way to introduce the definition of an ice age and wait for the learners to realise that we are currently in an ice age.

Main teaching ideas

1 Looking at the changes in the temperature in the past (30 minutes)

Learning intention: To introduce ideas about the changing environment on Earth and to see how living things have changed with these changes in climate.

Resources: Learner's Book; atlas showing climate areas; poster materials and access to computers.

Description: Draw learners' attention to the ice sheet map in the Learner's Book and ask them, in their groups, to find out which parts of the Earth are currently covered with ice. Ask them to compare the two maps. How is the area of land covered with ice different? Larger or smaller area? Different regions? They could do this by discussion or they could make a poster, slide presentation or an 'expert' interview, where they act as the scientific expert on a television or radio show and explain how the ice sheets have changed over the past years.

> **Differentiation ideas:** You could use this as an opportunity to try different groupings of learners, to address differentiation. You could look at

suggestions given in the teaching focus at Stage 7, such as grouping by ability or mixing the different abilities up. You could extend this activity to ask if there is any evidence to show that the land was once covered with an ice sheet. Learners may need to do some research to find this out.

> **Assessment ideas:** Assess comparisons that learners have made by using *Template 5.4: Peer assessment*. Use questions 1 and 2 in *Activity: Ice sheets* to assess progress and understanding.

2 Looking at the data (20–30 minutes)

Learning intention: To examine and interpret data.

Resources: Learner's Book.

Description: Explain the facts about ice ages, with the warmer and colder periods, and introduce the vocabulary. Discuss the graph and data with learners, explaining as you work through the section. Ask learners, in pairs, to discuss the data, to be sure they understand the graph. Ask them to answer the questions.

> **Differentiation ideas:** Those with less good graph skills may need to have the graph explained several times, or need help when asked to explain it do their partner.

> **Assessment ideas:** Use the questions to assess their understanding.

3 Evidence for changes in the climate (30–40 minutes)

Learning intention: To provide evidence for changes in the climate.

Resources: Learner's Book; a soil auger (or use a piece of plastic guttering or pipe); slides of different pollen.

Description: Discuss the evidence from glaciers, as in the Learner's Book, and ask learners to answer the questions. You could extend this to include a discussion of the landscape evidence for glaciation, U-shaped valleys and boulders- and other rock debris carried by glaciers to places they would not otherwise have reached.

If possible, demonstrate the use of a soil auger and show learners a core sample. It will probably be necessary to show them one you dug earlier. This may be a good time to remind them about the formation of soils.

Explain that this scientist was able to find pollen in the cores because of the lack of decay. Ask learners to suggest how he could identify the pollen; it might be useful to have available a few slides of different types of pollen, on the board or screen.

Discuss the core sample diagram, so you are sure that learners understand it.

If it helps your learners, you could take them out to take a soil core sample within the school grounds. From this, learners can get a better idea about what the scientist was doing. Learners could look at the soil in the sample and record any differences that they can see.

> **Assessment ideas:** You could ask learners to produce a poster or slide show to illustrate some of the evidence there is for changes in the climate over thousands of years.

Plenary ideas

1 What do you understand by the term ice age? (10 minutes)

Description: Ask learners to think about what they understand by the term 'ice age' and write it down (allow 2 minutes or less). When they have done this, ask learners how their ideas about ice ages have changed over the lesson.

2 Key words (10 minutes)

Resources: Paper and pen or pencil.

Description: Ask learners to write all the key words they can from this lesson. Give a time limit. Then they swap with a partner to complete the meanings of these words. Take feedback from the class.

Homework ideas

1   Workbook exercises 5.4A–C

Topic 5.5: Atmosphere and climate

LEARNING PLAN

Learning objectives	Learning intentions	Success criteria
8ESc.02 Understand that the Earth's climate can change due to atmospheric change. 8TWSm.01 Describe what an analogy is and how it can be used as a model. 8TWSm.02 Use an existing analogy for a purpose.	• Learn about the changes in the atmosphere, starting from the formation of the Earth. • Know that atmospheric changes can affect the climate. • Look at the factors that contribute to global warming. • Interpret data on global temperatures. • Explain why the use of an analogy can be helpful.	• Describe the composition of the atmosphere today and in the past. • Describe how a change in the atmosphere can change the climate. • Give some of the causes and effects of global warming. • Interpret data. • Give an example of an analogy.

LANGUAGE SUPPORT

Learners will use the following words:

photosynthesis: the process by which green plants make food

recycle: use again

fossil fuels: natural fuels such as gas, coal or oil formed from the remains of living organisms

locked up: held so that it is stored; carbon may be locked up in coal or oil until it is burnt

emissions: production and release of a gas

deforestation: cutting down or destroying large areas of trees

greenhouse effect: the trapping of the Sun's heat energy in a planet's atmosphere

global warming: a gradual increase in the overall temperature of the Earth's atmosphere

renewable resources: natural resources that do not run out and can be replaced by normal process within a human's lifetime

bioplastics: materials that are made from natural renewable sources, such as vegetable oils, saw dust or food waste; they are used to replace plastics which are made from petroleum

Common misconceptions

Misconception	How to identify	How to overcome
Some learners find it difficult to understand that we can know about the atmosphere on Earth millions of years ago.	Ask learners: *How can we know this?*	Provide the evidence as clearly as possible. At this stage, some of the evidence is too complicated for learners to understand but the basic ideas can be explained.
Some learners find the whole idea of the greenhouse effect difficult to understand.	After having discussed the greenhouse effect, ask learners to explain how it works.	Explain with the aid of diagrams and animations.

Starter ideas

1 Getting started (10 minutes)

Resources: Learner's Book.

Description: Ask the class the two questions: *What is an ice age? What evidence do we have to show that the Earth's climate was different in the past?*

Ask learners to think about the two questions and write down their ideas. Give them a fixed time without discussion or talking.

Then ask learners to discuss their ideas with a partner. Together, learners clarify their ideas, ready to share them with the class.

2 Finding words that begin with these letters (10 minutes)

Resources: Learner's Book.

Description: Write the word 'atmosphere' vertically down the board. Ask learners to find scientific words starting with each of the letters. You could allow the use of the glossary if you wish. You could restrict the words to those relevant to this topic. Take feedback from the class. You could award one point for each correct word and two points for any word that no one else has. You could extend this to include definitions of the words.

Main teaching ideas

1 Composition of the atmosphere (20 minutes)

Learning intention: To compare the composition of the atmosphere in the past and today.

Resources: Learner's Book.

Description: Lead learners through the factual content in the Learner's Book. Use the data given in the table and the pie charts to compare the two different atmospheres. You could then move on to discuss what happened to change the atmosphere and what this means for the living things on Earth.

Ask learners to answer the questions.

> **Differentiation ideas:** You could extend this, for learners who need a challenge, by researching the atmospheres on other planets and asking what implications there are for life on other planets. Learners could discuss the implications for life on other planets elsewhere in the solar system.

> **Assessment ideas:** You could use the questions in the Learner's Book to assess progress.

2 Evidence for global warming (30+ minutes)

Learning intention: To look at the evidence for global warming.

Resources: Internet access; library.

Description: Lead learners through the factual information about the greenhouse effect in the Learner's Book, and stress the validity of the evidence; Ask: *How do we know this is valid evidence? Where does this evidence come from? Can we trust the source of this evidence? Do they have bias, which might mean they ignore some evidence and emphasise other evidence?*

Ask learners to search the internet to find more evidence. Emphasise that the evidence is complex and that they may need help and guidance to interpret it. This task would probably be best done in small groups of up to four learners.

> **Differentiation ideas:** Provide simplified evidence to the groups who may find this task overwhelming and would need support.

> **Assessment ideas:** Ask groups to present their evidence with a critical discussion about the quality of the evidence.

3 Think like a scientist: The greenhouse effect (30 minutes to set up, time to take readings, and 30 minutes to answer questions)

Learning intention: To demonstrate the greenhouse effect.

Resources: three large plastic bottles, such as 2-litre drinks bottles with lids; three thermometers (standard 0–100 °C classroom thermometers will be suitable, or you could use digital thermometers or data loggers); a means of fixing the thermometers in place (modelling clay, a sticky substance for attaching posters, or thread, wadding, and so on); carbon dioxide supply.

Description: Set the practical up as instructed in the Learner's Book.

Each group will need to discuss when and how often they will take readings. It would be helpful if they then discuss this with the whole class. You will need to give guidance about when they will be able to take measurements, and ensure that they have suitable access, at break time, lunchtime, before or after school, and so on.

> **Practical guidance:** There are a number of ways you can fix the thermometer; it depends what you have available. In addition to the modelling clay option, you could tie thread around the thermometer and allow it to hang with the threads hanging out of the bottle cap, or you could place sticky plastic in the cap and fix the thermometer in it.

Carbon dioxide can be produced by adding acid to a carbonate, such as calcium carbonate. The gas is heavier than air so can be introduced to the bottles through a delivery tube. Then put the cap of the bottle on quickly.

The bottles should be stood upright in a place where they will not be interfered with. They can be in full sunlight. If this is not possible, put them in the classroom, near the window. Making holes in the bottle lids can be difficult, so you could instead replace them with modelling clay to make a seal across the mouth of the bottle.

> **Differentiation ideas:** You could extend this for learners who need a challenge to add more carbon dioxide to some bottles. Learners would need to think how they could assess how much carbon dioxide they have/will add.

> **Assessment ideas:** Use questions 1–6 in *Think like a scientist: The greenhouse effect* to assess what learners have found out. Assess both the planning and the practical aspect of this task.

Plenary ideas

1 Summarising the facts about renewable resources (10 minutes)

Description: Ask learners to list five facts about renewable resources and how using more of them will reduced global warming. They should do this on paper, individually, with no discussion. Then they swap their papers with a partner to compare facts. Between them, they list as many facts as they can.

As they are writing the facts, ask learners to consider: *How can I check that relevant information about global warming/climate change is not biased?*

2 What's the question? (10 minutes)

Resources: Prepared answers to questions, such as: 'about 20%', 'There will be a rise in the sea level' and 'Calcium carbonate'. (The questions to which would be: 'What is the percentage of oxygen in the atmosphere today?', 'What will happen if more of the polar ice caps melt?' and 'What are the shells of many sea creatures made of?'.)

Description: Put a list of 5–10 answers on the board and ask learners to write the questions. They do this individually or in pairs.

This may be developed further if learners write or give answers and ask the other person in the pair to write the question.

You could extend this and use this activity to assess progress.

Homework ideas

1   Workbook exercises 5.5A–C

Topic worksheets

Worksheet 5.5, Looking at temperature data

PROJECT GUIDANCE

Global warming and climate change debate

This project addresses the following learning objectives:

8TWSc.06 Evaluate a range of secondary information sources for their relevance and know that some sources may be biased.

8SIC.01 Discuss how scientific knowledge is developed through collective understanding and scrutiny over time.

8SIC.02 Describe how science is applied across societies and industries, and in research.

8SIC.03 Evaluate issues which involve and/or require scientific understanding.

The Learner's Book gives some information about the increased global temperatures during 2019. You could supply local information about the increasing temperatures and subsequent climate changes and discuss the local impact. You could look at specific studies of islands in the Indian or Pacific oceans showing their vulnerability to the rising sea levels. You could provide news broadcasts or articles about this for the class to study.

You could also find examples in the news media of those who believe that human activity, including the continued use of fossil fuels, deforestation and so on, does **not** contribute to climate change and that there is no proven link.

The class will need access to this information, via the internet or library, but they need guidance on how to select and use the relevant information. You could print copies of sources you would like them to use. Ensure they understand they need to have trust in the sources.

Give each group (of up to four) two large pieces of paper, poster size if possible. Ask them to list their ideas and points they need to make, so that other groups can see them when they are pinned up. Make the point that each group **must** make lists for both points of view. Explain the groups will be chosen at random to represent each viewpoint. Do not allocate groups until they have completed the task on paper or they will only do half the task.

You could choose which group presents which viewpoint or, to be fair, you could use a system of slips of paper marked with letters or numbers. Each group draws out a slip; for example, all the Xs are those who don't believe human activity is having an impact and all the Ys do believe human activity is having an impact. The learners may argue they believe that humans are having an impact so they cannot possibly represent the opposite view. Explain to them that by looking at the other viewpoint they can see what these people believe and provide better evidence and ideas to them.

To run the debate, keep it as formal as possible and choose one group to lead off; pick a group that is not the one with the strongest speakers so that you do not put off the others from contributing. Ask for a contribution or two from those of the same viewpoint. Then ask a group of the opposite view to answer the points made and again ask for contributions from a couple of groups with the same viewpoint. Move around the groups until everyone has contributed.

Then pin up the papers and ask the learners to look for any points that were not made in the debate.

〉6 Light

Unit plan

Topic	Learning hours	Learning content	Resources
6.1 Reflection	2-3	The reflection of light from a plane surface; the law of reflection; drawing ray diagrams to show reflection of light	**Learner's Book:** Questions 1–4 Activity: Mirrors and reflections Think like a scientist: Measuring angles of incidence and reflection **Workbook:** Exercise 6.1A, Making reflections Exercise 6.1B, Ray diagrams Exercise 6.1C, Accurate ray diagrams **Teacher's Resource:** Worksheet 6.1, Reflection in a plane mirror Template 6.1: Results table and graph grid for *Think like a scientist: Measuring angles of incidence and reflection*
6.2 Refraction	2-3	The refraction of light at the boundary between air and glass or air and water; how light changes speed when it passes between different substances; drawing ray diagrams to show how light is refracted	**Learner's Book:** Questions 1–4 Activity: Refraction effects Think like a scientist: Drawing accurate ray diagrams **Workbook:** Exercise 6.2A, Causes of refraction Exercise 6.2B, Predicting refraction Exercise 6.2C, Refraction ray diagrams **Teacher's Resource:** Worksheet 6.2, Refraction in water and glass Template 6.2A: Results table for *Think like a scientist: Drawing accurate ray diagrams* Template 6.2B: Graph grid for *Think like a scientist: Drawing accurate ray diagrams*

Topic	Learning hours	Learning content	Resources
6.3 Making rainbows	2-3	White light is made from many colours; how dispersion of white light can be done with a prism; listing the colours of white light in the correct order	**Learner's Book:** Questions 1–5 Think like a scientist: Making a rainbow **Workbook:** Exercise 6.3A, Colours of the rainbow Exercise 6.3B–C, Making a spectrum
6.4 Colours of light	3-4	What happens when colours of light are added; what happens when colours of light are subtracted; why we see different colours in terms of reflection	**Learner's Book:** Questions 1–5 Activity: Making colours on the screen Think like a scientist: Identify the colour **Workbook:** Exercise 6.4A, Adding primary colours Exercise 6.4B, Subtracting colours of light Exercise 6.4C, Seeing colours **Teacher's resource:** Worksheets 6.4A–C, Coloured filters
6.5 Galaxies	1-2	Galaxies contain dust, gas, stars and other solar systems	**Learner's Book:** Questions 1–5 Think like a scientist: Estimating large numbers **Workbook:** Exercise 6.5A, Our own galaxy Exercise 6.5B–C, Galaxies in space
6.6 Rocks in space	1-2	Asteroids are rocks that are smaller than planets and scientists think that asteroids are rocks left over from the formation of the Solar System	**Learner's Book:** Questions 1–4 Activity: Making a model asteroid Think like a scientist: What happened at Tunguska? **Workbook:** Exercise 6.6A, Describing asteroids Exercise 6.6B–C, Asteroids and planets
Cross-unit resources			**Learner's Book:** Check your Progress **Project:** Investigating refraction **Teacher's Resource:** Language development worksheets 6.1 Reflection and refraction vocabulary 6.2 Light wordsearch 6.3 Correcting the answers

BACKGROUND KNOWLEDGE

Learners will recall sources of light, such as the Sun and lamps. Light from these sources has been described as travelling in straight lines that can be represented in ray diagrams. The concept of reflection of light has been described in terms of how we see objects that are not sources of light. Learners should be familiar with plane mirrors and their uses in everyday life. Learners will also have seen some of the effects of refraction, such as not being able to see clearly through a glass of water or a rain-covered window. Learners may also have seen rainbows, caused either by rain or by a fine spray of water on a sunny day. Learners will also recall that light can pass through transparent objects.

TEACHING SKILLS FOCUS

Lesson starters 2

The lesson starter is the opportunity for you to immediately engage and interest learners. The starter also informs learners what the lesson is about and gives them time to start thinking about this – possibly new – topic. More than this, it gives you a tool with which to assess prior understanding and possibly detect misconceptions in a much less formal way than just asking questions.

For example, in a lesson about reflection of coloured light, you could have various colours of toy plastic bricks set out on a sheet of white paper. This could be positioned in one conspicuous place to be seen by learners as they arrive for the lesson, or several brightly coloured blocks could be placed on tables around the room. As learners arrive they may wonder what this is for, and this is a positive start. The use of a familiar object allows them to identify with that object and helps to break down the barrier that some learners imagine between the science laboratory and real life.

You could start by asking: *How can we see the blocks?* Some may recall that light is reflected from the blocks. Continue by asking why the blocks appear to be different colours. *How does this work?* The light shining on the blocks is the same. It is unlikely that many learners will reach the correct answer, but this does not matter at the start of the lesson. The questions serve to start learners thinking about how this works and helps you to pick up on misconceptions or gaps in prior learning. Any answers that seem strange should be sensitively followed up, as these may indicate errors in understanding.

Your management of a starter activity can completely change a learner's perception of that activity. As a challenge, consider making this change to the start of a lesson: as learners arrive, instead of getting them seated and explaining what the lesson involves, tell them to place their belongings at their desks and come straight to the front for a demonstration.

After trying some different starters, ask yourself:

- What has been the most successful starter activity you have done so far?
- What aspect of the lesson did this starter improve?
- What was it about this starter that made it successful?
- Can you transfer these successful parts of this starter to make other activities equally, or more, successful?

Topic 6.1: Reflection

LEARNING PLAN

Learning objectives	Learning intentions	Success criteria
8Ps.01 Describe reflection at a plane surface and use the law of reflection. **8TWSm.01** Describe what an analogy is and how it can be used as a model **8TWSp.04** Plan a range of investigations of different types, while considering variables appropriately, and recognise that not all investigations can be fair tests. **8TWSc.02** Decide what equipment is required to carry out an investigation or experiment and use it appropriately. **8TWSc.04** Take appropriately accurate and precise measurements, explaining why accuracy and precision are important. **8TWSc.07** Collect and record sufficient observations and/or measurements in an appropriate form. **8TWSa.02** Describe trends and patterns in results, including identifying any anomalous results. **8TWSa.03** Make conclusions by interpreting results and explain the limitations of the conclusions.	• Describe how light is reflected from a plane surface. • Understand the law of reflection. • Draw ray diagrams to show reflection of light.	• Use the law of reflection to state angles of incidence or reflection when provided with one of these angles. • Draw labelled ray diagrams, correctly applying the law of reflection at a plane mirror.

LANGUAGE SUPPORT

Learners will use the following words:

reflection: term given (in this topic) to light (or another type of wave) bouncing back from a surface, without being absorbed

plane mirror: a flat silvered surface usually covered with glass that is designed to reflect as much light as possible

rays: straight lines that represent the path of light

incident ray: a ray of light arriving at a surface

perpendicular: at right angles

normal: in ray diagrams, an imaginary line that is perpendicular to a surface

protractor: equipment used to measure angles on diagrams

set square: piece of equipment in the shape of a right-angled triangle used in drawing diagrams

angle of incidence: the angle between the incident ray and the normal

angle of reflection: the angle between the reflected ray and the normal

ray diagram: the use of labelled lines to show what happens to light when incident on a surface

law of reflection: statement that the angle of incidence and angle of reflection are equal

---

Common misconceptions

Misconception	How to identify	How to overcome
Reflected light is only associated with glare.	Ask learners to give examples of where light is reflected.	The *Think like a scientist* activity in the Learner's Book should help overcome this.

Starter ideas

1 Getting started (5 minutes)

Description: Learners should recall that light travels in straight lines. Giving evidence of this is a little more challenging. The formation of shadows that are the same shape as the object is an example.

2 Sentence completion (5 minutes)

Resources: Prepared slide or sentences written on a board.

Description: Learners complete sentences about the way light travels, for example:

- Light travels in … lines
- We see things because light … from them.
- We can use a … diagram to show how light travels.

Main teaching ideas

1 Activity: Mirrors and reflections (10 minutes)

Learning intention: To recall how and why mirrors are used, and to recall that other objects can cause reflections.

Description: Learners recall some of the uses of mirrors. In the second part of the activity, when asked for other objects that cause reflections, learners may start by recalling shiny objects such as glass or polished metal. However, the activity is designed to differentiate by outcome, and learners should have previously learned that all objects that do not give out their own light can only be seen because of reflection.

> **Differentiation ideas:** For a question that differentiates by outcome, ask learners what other objects, as well as mirrors, reflect light. Learners that need more support will probably suggest shiny

objects in which they can see their own image, or those that cause glare. Learners that need more challenge should realise that all objects cause reflection and that is the reason why we can see these objects. Only those that are shiny will enable a clear reflected image to be produced.

> **Assessment ideas:** Learners could swap answers with other pairs and discuss any similarities or differences in their work.

2 Think like a scientist: Measuring angles of incidence and reflection (30 minutes, to include graph plotting)

Learning intention: To construct accurate ray diagrams using a ray box and a plane mirror, and to investigate how the angles of reflection and incidence are related.

Resources: See the Learner's Book.

Description: See the Learner's Book.

Safety: Some ray boxes become hot after prolonged use; the ray box should only be switched on to take measurements; learners should not touch the ray box until after it has been switched off and allowed to cool.

> **Practical guidance:** The investigation works best if the room can be darkened, or at least direct sunlight be excluded.

> **Differentiation ideas:** Learners that need more support could be given guidance on how to measure the angles from the normal, as many learners may attempt to measure the angles from the mirror surface.

Some combinations of ray boxes and plane mirrors produce two reflected rays: one, faintly, from the outer surface of the glass and the other, more strongly, from the silver surface behind the glass. If effects such as this are observed, then learners that need more challenge could be asked to explain this.

> **Assessment ideas:** Ask learners about patterns in their results or ask them to make predictions while they are doing the investigation. They can also be asked about difficulty in making accurate measurements (a pencil blocks the light ray; the light ray may be quite wide).

3 Laser reflections – direct sunlight can also be used (10+ minutes)

Learning intention: To show reflection from plane mirrors.

What idea is good for: Whole-class activity; teacher demonstration; making observations.

Resources: Laser pointer; small unmounted plane mirrors; adhesive tape or sticky gum; clamp stand; darkened room.

Description: Fix a small plane mirror to the wall above the eye level of seated learners. Direct the light from the laser pointer to the mirror to produce a reflection on another wall. Clamp the laser in this position and mark the position of the reflected beam on the wall. Fix another mirror to the wall in this position, so the beam will be reflected again.

Direct sunlight can also be used for a similar activity.

Safety: Learners should not look directly into the laser beam or into the reflected beam from sunlight; the beams should be directed at a high level so they do not pass, even by accident, into learners' eyes. When using a laser, a suitable hazard warning notice should be displayed on the outside of the classroom door.

> **Differentiation ideas:** At each stage, ask learners to predict, roughly, where the reflected beam will appear. Remind learners that need more support about using the law of reflection.

Reflected light beams are used in some security systems. Learners that need more challenge could be asked to suggest how these systems work. (The reflected beam or beams are directed onto a light sensor. When the beam is broken, the light sensor is no longer activated, and an alarm is switched on.)

> **Assessment ideas:** The questions asked during the activity form part of the assessment, as learners make predictions and explanations based on the law of reflection.

Plenary ideas

1 Taboo words (3–5 minutes)

Description: Learners work in pairs. They take turns at explaining reflection without using one or more taboo words. These taboo words can be keywords such as 'mirror', 'reflection', 'angle of incidence'.

⟩ **Assessment ideas:** Listen to some of the groups' explanations. Ask learners that were not heard to volunteer to share their explanations with the class.

2 What my partner learned today (5 minutes)

Resources: Paper; pens; timer (for you).

Description: Learners work in pairs. Each has 20 seconds to tell their partner what they learned in the lesson. After this time, each learner makes a list of the things that their partner said.

⟩ **Assessment ideas:** Learners can do this activity in their notebooks for assessment with the next homework, or as exit slips.

Homework ideas

1 Learner's Book questions

2 Workbook exercises 6.1A–C

3 Worksheet 6.1

Topic worksheets

Worksheet 6.1, Reflection in a plane mirror

Topic 6.2: Refraction

LEARNING PLAN		
Learning objectives	**Learning intentions**	**Success criteria**
8Ps.02 Describe refraction of light at the boundary between air and glass or air and water in terms of change of speed. 8TWSp.04 Plan a range of investigations of different types, while considering variables appropriately, and recognise that not all investigations can be fair tests. 8TWSc.03 Evaluate whether measurements and observations have been repeated sufficiently to be reliable.	• Describe how light is refracted at the boundary between air and glass or air and water. • Describe how light changes speed when it passes between different substances. • Draw ray diagrams to show how light is refracted.	• Predict which direction (toward or away from the normal) light will bend when passing between air and either glass or water, or going the opposite way. • State whether light will speed up or slow down when crossing a boundary. • Construct ray diagrams for refraction at air-glass and air-water boundaries and the opposite way.

CONTINUED

Learning objectives	Learning intentions	Success criteria
8TWSc.04 Take appropriately accurate and precise measurements, explaining why accuracy and precision are important. 8TWSc.07 Collect and record sufficient observations and/or measurements in an appropriate form. 8TWSa.02 Describe trends and patterns in results, including identifying any anomalous results. 8TSWa.05 Present and interpret observations and measurements appropriately.		

LANGUAGE SUPPORT

Learners will use the following words:

distorted: changed in some way from the original to become less clear

refraction: light changing direction on crossing a boundary from one medium to another due to a change in speed of the light

medium: in this topic, the transparent material through which light is passing

bent: changed direction; in refraction, at boundaries, this is a sudden change

towards the normal: the angle between the light ray and the normal becomes smaller after refraction

away from the normal: the angle between the light ray and the normal becomes larger after refraction

angle of refraction: the angle between the light ray that has been refracted and the normal

lenses: specially shaped pieces of transparent material designed to refract light in particular directions

Common misconceptions

Misconception	How to identify	How to overcome
Light passes through a transparent material without changing direction.	After learning about refraction, ask whether light changes direction when coming through the window.	Present objects such as windows as thin glass blocks and relate this to the *Think like a scientist* activity.

Starter ideas

1 Getting started (5 minutes)

Description: This activity allows learners to think about how light passes through transparent materials. Learners should include materials such as air (gas), water (liquid) and glass (solid) for transparent materials. When they are thinking about why images are distorted through a glass of water, prompt learners to think about how light travels from the object through the glass and the water.

2 Looking through transparent objects (5 minutes)

Resources: Access to a clear glass window; water.

Description: Ask learners whether glass or water, or both, is transparent. Ask what 'transparent' means. If there is rain or condensation on the window, ask: *Why can't we see clearly through the window, if both water and glass are transparent?* If there is no water on the window, dip your fingers in water, then flick the water at the window to make drops of water on the window.

Learners are not necessarily expected to reach the correct explanation, as they have not yet learned about refraction, but they should begin thinking about what happens to light as it passes through these materials.

Take care not to introduce the misconception that refraction is random and unpredictable. Refraction is predictable, but the presence of many curved surfaces on the water drops causes the appearance of disorder.

Main teaching ideas

1 Activity: Refraction effects (10+ minutes)

Learning intention: To show the effect of light changing direction when passing through boundaries.

Resources: See the Learner's Book.

Description: See the Learner's Book.

> **Differentiation ideas:** Ask learners that need more support where other effects such as this may be seen.

After learners have learned about refraction, ask those that need more challenge to draw a ray diagram for a light ray passing through an object of circular cross-section (ignoring the possibility of total internal reflection), using the same principles as for a flat surface.

> **Assessment ideas:** Ask learners: *Is light travelling straight through the materials or bending? What evidence can you give for your answer?*

2 Think like a scientist: Drawing accurate ray diagrams (20–30 minutes, including graph plotting)

Learning intention: To use ray boxes and glass blocks to construct accurate ray diagrams for light being refracted.

Resources: See the Learner's Book.

Description: See the Learner's Book.

> **Differentiation ideas:** Learners may notice partial reflection of the incident light ray at one or both surfaces. Ask learners that need more support for the term that describes this (reflection). Ask learners who need more challenge whether this partial reflection obeys the law of reflection. This could also be an opportunity to overcome the misconception that light can only be absorbed, reflected or refracted and not any two or more of these.

> **Assessment ideas:** Ask learners to compare angles of incidence and refraction at both surfaces. Ask: *Is the light ray bending towards or away from the normal in each case?*

3 Reversing with water (10–15 minutes)

Learning intention: To show refraction effects.

Resources: Paper; marker pens; drinking glass with circular cross-section or glass beaker; water.

Description: Learners draw an image, such as an arrow, on the paper and prop this up on the table. They place the glass or beaker in front of the drawing so they are viewing the drawing through the glass. The drawing should appear distorted. Learners pour water into the glass until they are viewing the drawing through the water. If viewed in the correct way, the drawing will appear reversed.

> **Differentiation ideas:** Ask learners who need more support to name the effect where light changes direction when passing from air into glass or water.

Ask learners who need more challenge to try to explain the observation using a ray diagram. Ask whether a second glass of water could be used to reverse the drawing again, back to its original orientation.

***

Answers: Light travels from the drawing, through the water, to the eyes. On refraction, the light rays from the left and right of the drawing cross over, making the drawing appear reversed.

***

> **Assessment ideas:** Ask what phenomenon is causing the effect (refraction) and ask why light is refracted when passing from air into water or glass (the light slows down). Ask how many boundaries the light crosses (four: air into glass, glass into water, water into glass, glass into air).

Plenary ideas

1 More examples of refraction (3–5 minutes)

Description: Ask learners to give any other examples of where refraction may occur. These should be different from the examples already used in a class activity, but could be variations on them.

> **Assessment ideas:** Ask learners questions about their named example. If a learner says 'glasses' then

ask, for example: *What is light passing from, and what is it passing to, when it is refracted? Where or how does light change speed?*

2 Useful or not? (3–5 minutes)

Resources: Paper and pens.

Description: Learners work in pairs. They divide their paper into two columns, headed 'useful' and 'not useful'. They write examples of refraction in each column; for example, refraction in contact lenses is useful, rain on a window is not useful.

> **Assessment ideas:** The work can be handed in as exit slips.

Homework ideas

1   Learner's Book questions

2   Workbook exercises 6.2A–C

3   Worksheet 6.2

Topic worksheets

Worksheet 6.2, Refraction in water and glass

Topic 6.3: Making rainbows

LEARNING PLAN		
Learning objectives	**Learning intentions**	**Success criteria**
8Ps.03 Know that white light is made of many colours and this can be shown through the dispersion of white light, using a prism. 8TWSm.01 Describe what an analogy is and how it can be used as a model. 8TWSm.02 Use an existing analogy for a purpose.	• Learn how white light is made from many colours. • Discover how dispersion of white light can be done with a prism. • Recall the colours of white light in the correct order.	• Recall that white light is actually a combination of seven colours of light. • Draw a diagram to show how a ray box and a prism can be used to show dispersion of light. • List the seven colours in the order that they occur in the spectrum of white light, starting from red.

CONTINUED

Learning objectives	Learning intentions	Success criteria
8TWSc.01 Sort, group and classify phenomena, objects, materials and organisms through testing, observation, using secondary information, and making and using keys.		
8TWSc.05 Carry out practical work safely, supported by risk assessments where appropriate.		
8TWSc.07 Collect and record sufficient observations and/or measurements in an appropriate form.		
8TWSa.02 Describe trends and patterns in results, including identifying any anomalous results.		
8TWSa.04 Evaluate experiments and investigations, and suggest improvements, explaining any proposed changes.		

LANGUAGE SUPPORT

Learners will use the following words:

spectrum: in this topic, a continuous range of colours, each colour merging with the next

dispersion: the splitting of white light into its component colours

triangular: description of an object that has three straight edges on one face

prism: in this topic, a block of transparent material with a regular shape

Common misconceptions

Misconception	How to identify	How to overcome
Sunlight and light from an electric lamp is colourless/sunlight is yellow.	After learning about dispersion, ask (separately) what colour, or colours of light come from an electric lamp and from the Sun.	This will be more easily overcome in the next topic on colours of light, but in this topic the dispersion experiment can be done to show the component colours of light from a lamp. This is slightly more difficult to do with sunlight, but use of a slit to create a beam of sunlight to shine through the prism will work.

Starter ideas

1 Getting started (5 minutes)

Description: This activity starts learners thinking about the component colours in white light. If learners have never seen a rainbow, show them pictures. Learners should identify that both sunlight and water droplets are required. Some may realise that rainbows are seen when the Sun is behind the observer. Learners may recall some of the seven colours, although possibly not in order.

Note: Some learners may have mythological beliefs about rainbows. These should be respected, but point out that the scientific aspect of colours will be covered in this topic.

2 Draw part of a rainbow (5–10 minutes)

Resources: Paper; colouring pens pencils or crayons representing each of the seven colours of the rainbow, if possible.

Description: Give learners a picture of a rainbow. Without being told how many colours there are, learners draw a cross-section of the rainbow. The idea is that learners see there are different colours, but that the colours merge together. Set a time limit on the activity, as some learners will take a very long time, which is not required.

Main teaching ideas

1 Think like a scientist: Making a rainbow (20–30 minutes, to include both parts)

Learning intention: To show how a prism can be used to disperse white light on a screen and to observe the colours of light directly.

What idea is good for: Making observations; drawing diagrams; viewing a spectrum.

Resources: See the Learner's Book.

Description: See the Learner's Book.

> **Differentiation ideas:** Question 6 from *Think like a scientist: Making a rainbow* will differentiate by outcome, and some learners can be given support with questions such as: *How is the image on the screen similar to a rainbow? How is it different from a rainbow?*

Learners who need a challenge could be asked if they can understand why Newton may have originally only observed five or six colours.

> **Assessment ideas:** Ask learners to recall the seven colours in order, starting from red.

2 Reproducing Newton's experiment (15–20 minutes)

Learning intention: To show dispersion of sunlight in a similar manner to Newton's first demonstration.

What idea is good for: Making observations; drawing diagrams; viewing a spectrum.

Resources: Triangular prism; clamp stand; large board with a small hole; direct sunlight (or desktop lamp); white screen.

Description: Similar to *Think like a scientist: Making a rainbow* with two main differences:

1   The Sun (or a desk lamp) is used as the light source in place of a ray box; the large board forms the slit.

2 The purpose of the large board, besides forming the slit, is to cast a shadow on the screen so that the spectrum can be seen more clearly. The darker the room can be, the better. The clamp stand is used to support the prism, so that it does not need to be held by hand.

Safety: Learners must not look directly into the dispersion pattern produced using the Sun's light.

> **Differentiation ideas:** Ask learners who need more support to give similarities and differences between the dispersion pattern and a rainbow.

Ask learners who need more challenge about how this present day demonstration may differ from Newton's original demonstration. Ask: *What is the significance of us being able to repeat the demonstration 400 years later?*

> **Assessment ideas:** Use class discussion to assess answers.

3 Dispersion in water (15–20 minutes)

Learning intention: To demonstrate that dispersion of white light will also occur with water.

What idea is good for: Making observations; drawing diagrams; viewing a spectrum.

Resources: Ray box; rectangular glass tank such as a fish tank; water; white screen; books or blocks.

Description: Set the ray box on books or blocks and position the tank so the ray of light passes through the corner of the tank, effectively making the corner of the tank act as a triangular prism. Demonstrate on the white screen that dispersion does not occur in the same way as it did with the prism.

Fill the tank with water to a depth where the ray will pass through the water (and the glass sides). Demonstrate that dispersion is observed through water.

> **Differentiation ideas:** Ask learners who need more support to name the parts of the apparatus that represent **a** the raindrops, **b** the Sun in this model of rainbow formation.

Ask learners who need more challenge: What is the purpose of showing that dispersion does not occur with the empty tank? (To show it is not the glass sides that is causing the dispersion.)

> **Assessment ideas:** Ask learners what other materials, besides glass and water might cause dispersion. (Any transparent object – diamonds could be used as an example, although total internal reflection should **not** be introduced.)

Plenary ideas

1 Three skills (3–5 minutes)

Resources: Small pieces of paper printed with three instructions, for example: *Write down one previously learned skill you used in this lesson; Write down one new skill that you learned in this lesson; Write down one skill that you would like to learn.*

Description: Each learner writes their name and responds to the three instructions, handing them in before they leave. Learners are given this opportunity to reflect on their own ability in experimental work, and the skills that they used.

> **Assessment ideas:** From reading the responses, it should be clear what skills have been learned or are required.

2 Summarise the lesson (2–3 minutes)

Resources: Paper and pens.

Description: Ask learners to summarise the lesson in a given number of bullet points. For example, they could be asked to summarise the lesson in four bullet points.

> **Assessment ideas:** Learners could compare each other's bullet points, or volunteer to share their own for class discussion.

Homework ideas

1 Learner's Book questions

2 Workbook exercises 6.3A–C

Topic 6.4: Colours of light

LEARNING PLAN

Learning objectives	Learning intentions	Success criteria
8Ps.04 Describe how colours of light can be added, subtracted, absorbed and reflected. **8TWSp.03** Make predictions of likely outcomes for a scientific enquiry based on scientific knowledge and understanding. **8TWSp.04** Plan a range of investigations of different types, while considering variables appropriately, and recognise that not all investigations can be fair tests. **8TWSp.05** Make risk assessments for practical work to identify and control risks. **8TWSc.02** Decide what equipment is required to carry out an investigation or experiment and use it appropriately. **8TWSc.03** Evaluate whether measurements and observations have been repeated sufficiently to be reliable. **8TWSc.04** Take appropriately accurate and precise measurements, explaining why accuracy and precision are important. **8TWSc.05** Carry out practical work safely, supported by risk assessments where appropriate. **8TWSc.07** Collect and record sufficient observations and/or measurements in an appropriate form.	• Discover what happens when colours of light are added. • Discover what happens when colours of light are subtracted. • Discover why we see different colours.	• Recall the results of the addition of two or more primary colours of light. • Describe the effects of coloured filters on white light and on the primary colours of light. • Predict how white, black and primary coloured objects will appear in white light and light of each of the primary colours.

CONTINUED

Learning objectives	Learning intentions	Success criteria
8TWSa.02 Describe trends and patterns in results, including identifying any anomalous results.		
8TWSa.03 Make conclusions by interpreting results and explain the limitations of the conclusions.		
8TWSa.04 Evaluate experiments and investigations, and suggest improvements, explaining any proposed changes.		
8TSWa.05 Present and interpret observations and measurements appropriately.		

LANGUAGE SUPPORT

Learners will use the following words:

primary colours: the name given to red, green and blue light as they cannot be made from the addition of any other colours of light

magenta: the colour of light that results from the addition of red and blue light; has a bright pink colour

cyan: the colour of light that results from the addition of blue and green light; has a turquoise colour

coloured filters: transparent, coloured pieces of glass or plastic that absorb all other colours of light

transmit: (of a filter) to allow light through

absorbed: the term given to light that is neither reflected nor transmitted

subtraction: taking away

non-luminous: Objects that do not give out their own light.

Common misconceptions

Misconception	How to identify	How to overcome
Colour is a property of objects and not a property of light.	After teaching about why objects appear to be certain colours due to reflection, ask where colour comes from.	Show learners how objects appear in different colours of light, but be careful to restrict this to primary colours only. For example, show a red object in **a** white light, **b** red light, and **c** green or blue light. If colour was a property of the object, then the red object would appear red in any colour of light.

Misconception	How to identify	How to overcome
		You can also show a white object in **a** white light **b** red light **c** green light **d** blue light. Again, if colour was the property of the object, then it would appear white in all colours of light.
A coloured filter adds its colour to light as it passes through.	After teaching about filters, ask what, for example, a green filter would do to white light. Ask whether it does this by adding green to the white light or subtracting the other colours.	Show the effect of two filters together, but take care that these are of primary colours only. For example, show white light passing through a blue filter, then onto a green filter. No light is emitted from the second filter because of subtraction. If filters added colour, then it would not be possible to end up with no light.

Starter ideas

1 Getting started (5 minutes)

Description: Ask learners to list colours. Do not restrict these to the seven colours of the spectrum learned in Topic 6.3. Learners can introduce shades, such as light green, dark green. Other colours can be used, such as pink, purple, orangey-red.

Note: Not everyone sees the exact same colours.

2 Is it red? (2–3 minutes)

Learning intention: To show the effects of different colours of light on objects.

Resources: Light source; coloured filter; two small pieces of paper the same size: one the same colour as the filter, the other white.

Description: Fix the two pieces of paper in front of the filtered light before learners arrive. Call them, as a group, to the front and ask whether one, both or neither of the pieces of paper is the colour of the filter.

Turn off the filtered light and demonstrate that one is red and the other white. Turn the light back on again to show the repeatability of the effect.

Note: When learners see an effect that surprises them, or that they cannot immediately explain, they may attribute this to 'magic'. Do not tell them that this is wrong, but emphasise that, with understanding, they will be able to explain what they have seen.

Main teaching ideas

1 Activity: Making colours on the screen (15+ minutes)

Learning intention: To show how the primary colours of light can be added, in varying quantities, to make all the other visible colours.

Resources: See the Learner's Book.

Description: See the Learner's Book.

> **Differentiation ideas:** Ask learners who need more support what colour would be produced if **a** all the primary colours are set to maximum **b** all the primary colours are set to zero.

Ask learners who need more challenge how other shades of colour could be made, such as lighter or darker magenta (lighter: have red and blue at maximum, and add green; darker: have red and blue lower than maximum and no green).

> **Assessment ideas:** Ask learners: *Why are red, green and blue the colours that can be adjusted? Why are yellow, orange, etc. not included?* (Red, green and blue are the primary colours, and all other colours can be made from addition of these.)

2 Think like a scientist: Identify the colour (10–20 minutes, depending on the number of colours used)

Learning intention: To observe the effects of different colours of light on coloured writing.

Resources: See the Learner's Book.

Description: See the Learner's Book.

> **Differentiation ideas:** Give learners who need more support a summary of whether a primary coloured object will appear the correct colour or black, depending on the colour of light used to illuminate it. This could be provided in a table. Alternatively, they could produce the table themselves, with guidance.

Ask learners who need more challenge: *What would happen if light of another colour, other than a primary colour, was used? Magenta light contains both red and blue light – so what colour would a blue object appear in magenta light?*

> **Assessment ideas:** Ask learners to make predictions and explain them, on the basis of reflection.

3 Explaining addition of colour in light (5–10 minutes)

Learning intention: To understand addition of colour with light.

Resources: Learner's Book image showing adding colours.

Description: Learners will be familiar with mixing paints and that brown is the result of mixing red, green and blue. This can cause confusion when they are learning about adding colours of light. Explain that mixing more pigments results in the mixture becoming darker, whereas mixing more light results in the mixture becoming lighter. Hence, adding all the primary colours of light results in white – the lightest possible.

> **Differentiation ideas:** Encourage learners who need more support to develop their own mnemonic to help recall the colours produced when the different primary colours are added.

Ask learners who need more challenge what the result would be of adding all three primary colours of light, but having one slightly brighter.

For example, if red is slightly brighter than the other two, then a very pale red will result.

> **Assessment ideas:** Ask learners to predict the outcome of mixing each pair of coloured lights, or all three primary colours of light.

Plenary ideas

1 Five top tips (3–5 minutes)

Resources: Paper and pen or pencil.

Description: Learners work in pairs to write five 'top tips' of advice to help others who are learning in this topic.

> **Assessment ideas:** Learners can write the tips with their next homework, or hand them in as exit slips. Alternatively, learners can volunteer to share their tips with the class for discussion.

2 Ask the class (5 minutes)

Resources: Paper and pens.

Description: Learners pretend they are the teacher. Ask: *What questions would you choose to ask the class after teaching this topic?* Learners can then ask some of their questions. Learners reflect on their own understanding of the topic by considering what questions would be important to ask.

> **Assessment ideas:** Assessment can be carried out based on both the questions and the answers.

Homework ideas

1   Learner's Book questions

2   Workbook exercises 6.4A–C

3   Worksheets 6.4A–C

Topic worksheets

Worksheets 6.4A–C, Coloured filters

Topic 6.5: Galaxies

LEARNING PLAN

Learning objectives	Learning intentions	Success criteria
8ESs.01 Describe a galaxy in terms of stellar dust and gas, stars and planetary systems.	• Discover that galaxies contain dust, gas, stars and other solar systems.	• State what a galaxy contains.
8TWSm.01 Describe what an analogy is and how it can be used as a model.		
8TWSm.02 Use an existing analogy for a purpose.		
8TWSm.03 Use symbols and formulae to represent scientific ideas.		
8TWSc.02 Decide what equipment is required to carry out an investigation or experiment and use it appropriately.		
8TWSc.03 Evaluate whether measurements and observations have been repeated sufficiently to be reliable.		
8TWSc.04 Take appropriately accurate and precise measurements, explaining why accuracy and precision are important.		
8TWSc.07 Collect and record sufficient observations and/or measurements in an appropriate form.		
8TWSa.04 Evaluate experiments and investigations, and suggest improvements, explaining any proposed changes.		
8SIC.01 Discuss how scientific knowledge is developed through collective understanding and scrutiny over time.		

LANGUAGE SUPPORT

Learners will use the following words:

galaxy: a collection of dust, gas, stars and solar systems held together by gravity

spiral: a type of galaxy shape with curved arms extending from the centre

Universe: all of space

elliptical: a type of galaxy shape that has an oval shape

irregular: a type of galaxy shape that is not well defined

stellar dust: very small particles that exist in space, mostly smaller than grains of sand; also called interstellar dust or cosmic dust

---

Common misconceptions

Misconception	How to identify	How to overcome
The Sun is not part of a galaxy.	After teaching about galaxies, ask whether the Sun is part of any galaxy.	Explain that the majority of stars exist in galaxies apart from some, known as 'rogue stars' or 'stellar outcasts' that are believed to have once been in galaxies but somehow became separated.

Starter ideas

1 Getting started (2–3 minutes)

Description: Learners consider the relative sizes of objects in space. Learners should know at least some of the relative sizes of these objects, and be able to arrange some of the list correctly.

Note: The activity is to compare the actual sizes of the objects, not their apparent size when viewed from Earth.

2 Where do we live? (5 minutes)

Resources: Internet access.

Description: Use an internet search engine to find images showing where we are in the Milky Way. Images will show the position of the Earth in one of the outer arms of the spiral galaxy. Explain that most of the stars we see in the night sky are part of this galaxy.

Main teaching ideas

1 Think like a scientist: Estimating large numbers (20+ minutes)

Learning intention: To show how the number of a set of objects that are too numerous to count can be estimated.

Resources: See the Learner's Book. Fine sand is not ideal, as the grains are too small.

Description: See the Learner's Book.

> **Differentiation ideas:** Give learners who need more support examples of large numbers that are estimates, such as global human population. Ask them to give reasons why these numbers cannot be known accurately.

Ask learners that need more challenge to suggest other numbers that are estimates and why an estimate is sufficient, in these cases, rather than the exact number. Question 8 from *Think like a scientist: Estimating large numbers* will differentiate by outcome.

> **Assessment ideas:** Learners can answer questions 1–7 from *Think like a scientist: Estimating large numbers* and question 8 of the activity can be used as an extension.

2 What do galaxies look like? (10–30 minutes, depending on structure of activity)

Learning intention: To view images of galaxies.

Resources: Internet access for each group of two to three learners.

Description: There are many websites with high quality images of galaxies outside the Milky Way. Some are actual photographs taken from telescopes such as the Hubble Space Telescope, while others are artists' impressions. Allow learners to perform their own searches or guide them to specific websites, such as the website for the Hubble telescope.

Set learners a task, such as producing a document or slideshow with information about galaxies. They should write the text in their own words and not merely copy from websites.

> **Differentiation ideas:** Ask learners who need more support questions about why we need telescopes to see galaxies that resemble these images. (They are very far away.)

Remind learners who need more challenge about the topic in Stage 7 about the Solar System, and ask them to suggest how galaxies may have formed. (Theory suggests that galaxies also formed from large clouds of dust and gas pulled together by gravity.)

> **Assessment ideas:** Ask learners questions about what galaxies contain.

3 Galaxies in the Universe (10–20 minutes)

Learning intention: To show how our understanding of our galaxy and the rest of the Universe has changed in recent times.

Resources: Access to an internet video resource (optional).

Description: Until 1924, the stars in the Milky Way galaxy were thought to comprise all the stars that existed in the Universe. Edwin Hubble's calculations of the distances of some stars showed them to be much further away than could be possible if they were in our galaxy. It was not until 1995 that hundreds more galaxies were being discovered.

There are videos on the internet telling the same story. Learners could be asked to complete the story themselves, in any form or presentation, but in their own words.

> **Differentiation ideas:** The activity will differentiate by outcome. Learners will, at the very least, discover that our understanding of space and other galaxies has changed dramatically in the last 100 years. Other learners may extend this to find out how galaxies are discovered, together with the implications of these discoveries for estimates of the age and size of the Universe.

> **Assessment ideas:** Ask learners questions, based on Science in Context learning objectives, such as how our understanding in science progresses with time.

Plenary ideas

1 Make a puzzle (3–5 minutes)

Resources: Paper; pen or pencil.

Description: Learners work in pairs. Each learner writes a set of anagrams of the key words associated with this topic. They swap with their partner and attempt to solve each other's anagrams.

> **Assessment ideas:** The activity can be extended by the learners writing a short clue for each of their anagrams.

2 Story board summary (10 minutes)

Resources: Paper and pencils.

Description: Learners summarise the content of the lesson in the form of a story board. A story board is a series of sequential annotated pictures.

> **Assessment ideas:** There should be sufficient time in the activity for you to check content or ask questions of individuals.

Homework ideas

1 Learner's Book questions

2 Workbook exercises 6.5A–C

Topic 6.6: Rocks in space

LEARNING PLAN

Learning objectives	Learning intentions	Success criteria
8ESs.02 Describe asteroids as rocks, smaller than planets, and describe their formation from rocks left over from the formation of the Solar System. 8TWSp.01 Identify whether a given hypothesis is testable. 8TWSp.02 Describe how scientific hypotheses can be supported or contradicted by evidence from an enquiry. 8TWSa.03 Make conclusions by interpreting results and explain the limitations of the conclusions.	• Discover that asteroids are rocks that are smaller than planets. • Know that scientists believe asteroids to be rocks left over from the formation of the Solar System.	• Describe what asteroids are. • Explain the possible origin of asteroids.

LANGUAGE SUPPORT

Learners will use the following words:

asteroids: rocky objects that are smaller than planets, found mostly between the orbits of Mars and Jupiter

asteroid belt: a region in the Solar System with many asteroids, forming an almost circular ring around the Sun between the orbits of Mars and Jupiter and in the same plane as these orbits

craters: bowl-shaped areas whose centres are usually lower than the surrounding land that can be caused by impacts of other objects

impacts: the collisions of smaller objects with larger ones

Starter ideas

1 **Getting started (5 minutes)**

Description: Learners should be able to recall the Sun and planets, and also know that some planets, as well as Earth, have moons. Learners can include artificial objects such as satellites and space probes. Some learners may already have heard of asteroids.

2 **Looking at asteroids (2–3 minutes)**

Resources: Internet access.

Description: Show images of asteroids. Give learners information about the approximate sizes of these objects.

Main teaching ideas

1 **Activity: Making a model asteroid (20–30 minutes)**

Learning intention: To model an asteroid.

Resources: See the Learner's Book.

Description: See the Learner's Book. Follow any safety advice provided with paint and glue products.

> **Differentiation ideas:** The activity will differentiate by outcome, based on the way in which learners construct their models. Some learners may need support with answering the calculation questions, while learners who need challenge can do these without support.

> **Assessment ideas:** Questions in the Learner's Book could be answered individually on paper, or used for class discussion.

2 Think like a scientist: What happened at Tunguska? (10–30 minutes, depending on the structure of the activity)

Learning intention: To show how evidence can be used to support or contradict a hypothesis.

Resources: Internet access (optional).

Description: See the Learner's Book. If internet access is available, other interesting and relevant facts about the Tunguska event can be researched, including statements from people who saw or heard the event.

> **Differentiation ideas:** The questions will differentiate by outcomes.

> **Assessment ideas:** The questions can be answered individually or in small groups, then the answers can be used as the basis for class discussion.

3 The asteroid belt (5–10 minutes)

Learning intention: To describe the asteroid belt.

Description: A common misconception arising from science fiction and computer games is that the asteroid belt is densely packed with asteroids, so that a space probe travelling through the belt would have a higher chance of impacting an asteroid than not.

It should be explained that the total mass of asteroids in the asteroid belt is estimated to be 4% of the mass of the Moon, and that the average distance between any two asteroids in the belt is almost 1 000 000 km.

> **Differentiation ideas:** Remind learners who need more support of the equation $time = \dfrac{distance}{speed}$ and ask them to calculate the time taken to travel 1 000 000 km in a car travelling at a constant speed of 50 km/h with no breaks. If necessary, help them

to convert their answers from hours to days. This will help them comprehend how far apart asteroids are.

Learners who need more challenge could perform this calculation on their own and extend to working out the time taken to fly in an aeroplane doing a constant 900 km/h without breaks. They could convert their answers into days.

> **Assessment ideas:** Learners could be given the radius of the asteroid belt (480 000 000 km) and asked to work out the length of the belt.

Plenary ideas

1 Complete the sentence (5–10 minutes)

Resources: Paper and pens.

Description: Learners work in pairs. Each writes some sentences to be completed by the other in the pair. They swap sentences, complete each other's, and then discuss them.

> **Assessment ideas:** Take the opportunity to check some of the sentences, to ensure the information is correct.

2 Write a mnemonic/Five fingers (5–10 minutes)

Resources: Paper and pens.

Description: Learners write a mnemonic that would help them remember a new word or fact that they learned today. Another useful plenary task is 'Five fingers'. Each learner draws around their hand on a scrap of paper or in their book and writes notes on each finger to answer the questions.

- Thumb – What have you learned? What do you understand?
- Index finger – What skills have you used today?
- Middle finger – Which skills did you find difficult today?
- Ring finger – Who did you help today?
- Little finger – What will you make sure that you remember from today's lesson?

> **Assessment ideas:** Mnemonics can be shared with the class.

Homework ideas

1 Learner's Book questions

2 Workbook exercises 6.6A–C

PROJECT GUIDANCE

Investigating refraction

This project addresses the following learning objectives:

8TWSp.03 Make predictions of likely outcomes for a scientific enquiry based on scientific knowledge and understanding.

8TWSp.04 Plan a range of investigations of different types, while considering variables appropriately, and recognise that not all investigations can be fair tests.

8TWSp.05 Make risk assessments for practical work to identify and control risks.

8TWSc.01 Sort, group and classify phenomena, objects, materials and organisms through testing, observation, using secondary information, and making and using keys.

8TWSc.02 Decide what equipment is required to carry out an investigation or experiment and use it appropriately.

8TWSc.03 Evaluate whether measurements and observations have been repeated sufficiently to be reliable.

8TWSc.04 Take appropriately accurate and precise measurements, explaining why accuracy and precision are important.

8TWSc.05 Carry out practical work safely, supported by risk assessments where appropriate.

8TWSc.07 Collect and record sufficient observations and/or measurements in an appropriate form.

8TWSa.01 Describe the accuracy of predictions, based on results, and suggest why they were or were not accurate.

8TWSa.02 Describe trends and patterns in results, including identifying any anomalous results.

8TWSa.03 Make conclusions by interpreting results and explain the limitations of the conclusions.

8TWSa.04 Evaluate experiments and investigations, and suggest improvements, explaining any proposed changes.

8TSWa.05 Present and interpret observations and measurements appropriately.

When a sugar or salt solution is poured into pure water, the solution can be seen as being different to the water, although both are transparent. This is because the solution refracts light differently to the water, so light passing though the mixture bends where the solution meets the water.

The aim is for learners to investigate how dissolving solutes in water affects the refraction of light. For example, dissolving sugar in water increases the refraction. Learners can relate this to the change in speed of the light. You should not introduce the term refractive index, as this is not required at this stage.

Learners should present results in a logical way and attempt to use their results to answer the original question.

>7 Diet and growth

Unit plan

Topic	Learning hours	Learning content	Resources
7.1 Nutrients	2-3	Carbohydrates, fats, protein, minerals, vitamins and water as nutrients	**Learner's Book:** Questions 1–5 Activity: Protein and carbohydrate in food Think like a scientist: Testing foods for starch Activity: Vitamins poster **Workbook:** Exercise 7.1A, Nutrients and their functions Exercise 7.1B, Analysing information about nutrients Exercise 7.1C, Summarising functions and sources of different nutrients **Teacher's Resource:** Worksheet 7.1, Testing foods for sugar Template 7.1: Table for question 3
7.2 A balanced diet	2.5-3	Concept of a balanced diet, and that different people need different diets	**Learner's Book:** Questions 1–8 Activity: Different diets **Workbook:** Exercise 7.2A, Fibre in food Exercise 7.2B, Energy requirements Exercise 7.2C, Planning a diet **Teacher's Resource:** Worksheets 7.2A–C, My diet today
7.3 Growth, development and health	2-3	Growth and how it happens; development; the effects of exercise and smoking on health	**Learner's Book:** Questions 1–5 Activity: Why do people smoke? **Workbook:** Exercise 7.3A, Interpreting data about smoking Exercise 7.3B, Smoking statistics Exercise 7.3C, Looking at data on giving up smoking **Teacher's Resource:** Worksheets 7.3A–C, Does caffeine affect birthweight?

Topic	Learning hours	Learning content	Resources
7.4 Moving the body	2.5-4	The skeleton; joints; antagonistic muscles	**Learner's Book:** Questions 1–6 Activity: Identifying different kinds of joint Think like a scientist: Using a model arm to investigate how the biceps muscle works **Workbook:** Exercise 7.4A, The skeleton and forces Exercise 7.4B, Antagonistic muscles in the leg Exercise 7.4C, Choosing a hypothesis about bones to investigate **Teacher's Resource:** Template 7.4A: Recording table for *Activity: Identifying different kinds of joint* Template 7.4B: Recording table for *Think like a scientist: Using a model arm to investigate how the biceps muscle works*
Cross-unit resources			**Learner's Book:** Check your Progress **Project:** A diet for Mars explorers **Teacher's Resource:** Language development worksheets 7.1 Words and meanings 7.2 Scrambled letters

BACKGROUND KNOWLEDGE

Learners who have followed the Cambridge curriculum at Primary level will have learned in Stage 4 that animals get their energy from food, and this has been reinforced with the work on food chains and food webs in Stages 4, 6 and 7. They will have learned about the need for a balanced diet at Stage 5, and may know the names and functions of some nutrients.

Learners should also be familiar with the names of some of the bones in the human body, which they studied in Stage 4. They should also know that bones move because pairs of muscles contract and relax. They will have learned about skeletons, and know that vertebrates have a skeleton inside the body and that some other animals have an exoskeleton.

Growth is likely to have been mentioned as one of the characteristics of living organisms. Learners will have learned about physical changes taking place at puberty (which is part of development) in Stage 6. They may know a little about lifestyle and health from the media, and may also remember work done in Stage 6 on disease transmission and good hygiene.

There is a great deal of misinformation about diet and health, and many very poor 'celebrity diets' are available on the internet, so you should be prepared to explain why these do not constitute a good, balanced diet.

TEACHING SKILLS FOCUS

Organising practical work 3: Building learners' skills and confidence

Practical work requires money for laboratories, apparatus and materials. If you do not have a laboratory technician to help you, preparation and clearing away afterwards can take up a lot of your time. So it is worth thinking about what you want to achieve when you do practical work, to make sure that you and your learners get maximum benefit from it.

Experiencing hands-on practical work is the only way that learners can develop practical skills. Achieving even simple skills, such as using a thermometer correctly, reading a scale on a forcemeter or pouring a liquid without spilling it, can help a learner to progress more easily, both in this stage of their learning and later. Knowing that they can do these things gives learners self-confidence. It can be helpful to assess learners on these skills, so that you and they have a record of what they have achieved. Pick out one or two skills that they will use in a practical activity, and give each learner a mark for how well they do it.

Practical work can help learners to understand tricky concepts. For example, they may find it difficult to fully understand how to find the density of an irregular object, if they learn this only in theory. You could give them the instructions and equipment to do this as a practical activity, but then perhaps leave them to work out how to calculate the density. Similarly, using a model arm to investigate the action of the biceps muscle will help some learners to better understand the concepts involved.

Handling apparatus for themselves helps learners to understand what different pieces of apparatus and equipment are for, and how they are used. As learners develop confidence, you should begin to expect them to select suitable equipment themselves. Instead of giving learners exactly what they need, include some items that are not needed, and expect them to make choices. For example, if they are doing an experiment where

they need to measure a volume, you could give them three different pieces of equipment for measuring volume and ask them to choose the best one.

Make sure that learners know what they have to do in a practical activity – you may like to demonstrate first, and then ask questions to check they understand. Ask: *What are you going to do first? What will you do after that?* However, it is useful sometimes to leave instructions open-ended, expecting learners to make some decisions for themselves. This increases their involvement with the work, and also their understanding of the procedure. If the instructions cover every eventuality, learners will begin to use these instructions like a cookery book recipe, without fully understanding what they are doing, or why. Expect learners to develop the ability and confidence to make small adjustments themselves. If they cannot see anything through their microscope, expect them to try to solve the problem themselves. If their electrical circuit does not work, expect them to check connections before asking you to help.

As a challenge, in this unit you could try Topic 7.1, *Think like a scientist: Testing foods for starch*, assessing the learners' practical skills as they work. Start by constructing a list of criteria that you will use. Draw a table, with everyone's names across the top, and the criteria down the side, and attach this to a clipboard. Tell learners what you are going to assess them on – you can share the criteria with them. For example, you could start with:

- collected all apparatus and materials before beginning the experiment
- kept the foods separate
- cleaned the tile between using different foods
- recorded the results clearly and correctly
- worked efficiently and finished within the time allocated
- and so on.

CONTINUED

Decide how you will mark this. It is probably best just to have a 'yes' or 'no' decision – a quick tick on your sheet – as in a large class you will probably not have time to make any more detailed assessments.

After you have carried out a practical activity once, you will have a better idea of what to look for, so your list of criteria may change when you do the same activity with a different class in future.

Topic 7.1: Nutrients

LEARNING PLAN

Learning objectives	Learning intentions	Success criteria
8Bp.01 identify the constituents of a balanced diet for humans as including protein, carbohydrates, fats and oils, water, minerals (limited to calcium and iron) and vitamins (limited to A, C and D) and describe the functions of these nutrients. **8Bp.02** Understand that carbohydrates and fats can be used as a store of energy in animals, and animals consume food to obtain energy and nutrients. **8TWSc.05** Carry out practical work safely, supported by risk assessments where appropriate. **8TWSp.04** Plan a range of investigations of different types, while considering variables appropriately, and recognise that not all investigations can be fair tests.	• Learn about the six types of nutrient that we need to eat. • Find out why we need these nutrients. • Learn about some good sources of these nutrients.	• Complete tables to show sources and uses of nutrients. • Match nutrients to their functions. • Produce a poster that explains sources and uses of vitamins A, C and D. • Analyse information about foods in their own diet, and as provided in secondary data. • Analyse experimental data and plan an experiment to compare sugar content of foods.

LANGUAGE SUPPORT

Learners will use the following words:

protein: a nutrient that is required for making new cells; many important substances in the body are proteins, such as haemoglobin, antibodies and insulin

starch: a carbohydrate whose molecules are made of many glucose molecules linked in a spiralling chain; it is the main energy storage material in plants

carbohydrate: a nutrient that is the main source of energy in our diet; carbohydrates include starch and sugar

fat: a nutrient that is required to make cell membranes, and that is the main energy storage material in animals

oil: a fat that is liquid at room temperature

nutrients: components of food that are used by the body; they include protein, carbohydrate, fat and oil, vitamins, minerals and water

vitamins: substances made by plants and other living organisms, that are required in the diet in small quantities

CONTINUED

vitamin A: required for a strong immune system, and helps vision in dim light

vitamin C: required for making the protein collagen, which is a major component of skin and other body tissues

vitamin D: helps calcium to be absorbed from the digestion system, and helps to keep bones and teeth strong

minerals: inorganic (meaning they do not contain carbon and are not made by other organisms) substances that are required in small quantities in the diet

anaemia: an illness resulting from lack of haemoglobin in the body

Common misconceptions

Misconception	How to identify	How to overcome
Learners often confuse the terms 'food' and 'nutrient'.	As learners take part in discussions.	Make sure that you always use these words appropriately. A food is what is on their plate – rice, fish. A nutrient is one of the components of these foods – carbohydrate, protein. Question 2 addresses this issue directly.
It is not uncommon for learners to think that one nutrient contains another. For example, they may say that 'protein contains a lot of vitamins'.	Throughout this topic and the next, as learners discuss in groups and answer questions.	Continue to emphasise the discrete nature of each nutrient as you work through this topic and the next.

Starter ideas

1 Getting started (10 minutes, including sharing ideas)

Description: Ask learners to pair-and-share, to answer the questions in the Learner's Book. The second question looks briefly at digestion, which will not be covered in this unit, but some learners may remember about digestion from work at Stage 5, and it may be helpful to associate this with the work on nutrients in this topic.

2 What's on this plate? (5–10 minutes)

Resources: A plate or bowl of foods that contain different nutrients.

Description: Show learners the food and ask: *Can you identify these foods? Now, can you tell me some of the nutrients that each of these foods contains?*

If learners cannot name nutrients, use questioning to get them started. For example: *Do you think any of these foods contain protein? Which ones contain fat?*

Learners are unlikely to be able to name all nutrients at this stage, or to identify which nutrients are contained in a particular food. This is fine – the purpose at this stage is just to begin to think about this, and their understanding will increase as they work through this topic.

Main teaching ideas

1 Activity: Protein, carbohydrate and fat in food (15–25 minutes)

Learning intention: To understand which types of food contain protein, carbohydrate and fat.

Resources: Learner's Book; reference books and/ or internet access; a variety of foods available to show learners, to provide a focus for discussion (optional).

Description: Use the text and pictures in the Learner's Book to discuss with learners the sources and functions of proteins, carbohydrates and fats.

Ask learners to do *Activity: Protein and carbohydrate in food.* You could also ask them to think about fat.

> **Differentiation ideas:** Some learners will have difficulty deciding whether the food they have eaten contains protein or carbohydrate. You could provide a table containing this information for foods that they are likely to have eaten.

Learners who need a challenge could be asked to think about starch and sugar separately, rather than just carbohydrates in general.

> **Assessment ideas:** Use oral questioning, and the lists made during the activity, to assess how well learners are able to associate these nutrients with particular foods.

2 Think like a scientist: Testing foods for starch (35–40 minutes extension material)

Learning intention: To gain first-hand experience of testing foods for starch.

Resources: Per group: at least six different kinds of food (you could ask learners, in the previous lesson, to bring some foods with them); some paper plates or small containers to hold the pieces of food (keep them separate); a white tile; a bottle of dilute iodine solution with a dropper.

Description: Demonstrate to learners how to do the starch test. Ask them: *Do you think there are any safety risks in this experiment? What are they?* (The only risk is from the dilute iodine solution; this is not toxic, but if it gets onto hands or clothes it can stain.) *How can you keep safe?*

Once they are sure what to do, ask learners to carry out the activity.

> **Practical guidance:** This is a very simple test. There is no need to cut up or dissolve the food, and no heating is needed.

Learners must be careful not to let one food touch another, or starch could be transferred to a food that does not actually contain any starch.

> **Differentiation ideas:** Give learners who need extra support, or who tend to work very slowly, an outline results chart to complete.

Give learners who need a challenge an apple or other fruit, and ask them to test each of the different parts (seeds, core, flesh, skin) for starch. This requires care and careful observation.

> **Assessment ideas:** This is a good opportunity to assess simple practical skills. You could assess learners on how well organised they are as they work.

3 Activity: Vitamins poster (30 minutes)

Learning intention: To consolidate understanding of sources and uses of vitamins A, C and D.

Resources: Large sheets of paper; coloured pens; magazine with pictures of foods (optional); scissors and glue (optional).

Description: Ask learners to follow the instructions in the Learner's Book.

> **Differentiation ideas:** As always with group work, some learners may need encouragement to ensure that they actively contribute. You could ask groups to allocate specific roles to each person, so that nobody has an excuse to not be on-task at all times.

Learners who require a challenge could add quantitative information to their chart; for example, how much vitamin C is needed per day, and/or how much vitamin C there is in one orange.

> **Assessment ideas:** Listen to learners as they talk among their groups, to estimate how well they understand these three vitamins.

Plenary ideas

1 What's on this plate – now? (5 minutes)

Resources: The plate or bowl of food used in the starter activity.

Description: Show the class the plate of food again. Ask: *What can you tell me now, about the nutrients that these foods contain?*

> **Assessment ideas:** Suggestions will show whether the class has learnt the names of the different nutrients, and whether they can associate them with particular foods.

2 What have we learnt today? (10 minutes)

Description: Organise learners into groups of three. Ask each group to write down three important things they have learnt today.

Allow 4–5 minutes, then ask each group to give you one, two, or all three of their statements.

> **Assessment ideas:** The statements from the groups will help to show how well key information from the lesson has been absorbed.

Homework ideas

1 Workbook exercises 7.1A–C

2 Worksheet 7.1

Topic worksheets

Worksheet 7.1, Testing foods for sugar

Topic 7.2: A balanced diet

LEARNING PLAN

Learning objectives	Learning intentions	Success criteria
8Bp.01 identify the constituents of a balanced diet for humans as including protein, carbohydrates, fats and oils, water, minerals (limited to calcium and iron) and vitamins (limited to A, C and D) and describe the functions of these nutrients 8Bp.03 Discuss how human growth, development and health can be affected by lifestyle, including diet and smoking	• Find out what is meant by a balanced diet. • Think about the nutrients we should try to eat each day. • Learn why we should try not to eat too much of some nutrients.	• Answer questions about the bar chart showing energy requirements. • Match advice about diet with reasons.

LANGUAGE SUPPORT

Learners will use the following words:

balanced diet: daily food intake that contains the correct quantity of energy, and also all of the nutrients that a person requires

fibre: cellulose and other plant fibres that cannot be digested

constipation: slow functioning of the alimentary canal, so that faeces are not passed out regularly

Common misconceptions

Misconception	How to identify	How to overcome
Learners may think that a diet is something you go on to try to lose weight.	As learners take part in discussions.	Use the term 'diet' in the correct way throughout this Topic, and be vigilant for incorrect usage by learners.

Starter ideas

1 Getting started (10 minutes, including sharing ideas)

Learning intention: To remind learners of the six groups of nutrients.

Description: Ask learners to answer the three questions. You could either ask them to write the answers down, or just to think about them, ready to give oral responses. Answers will indicate whether learners know what nutrients are, and have not confused them with foods.

2 Who needs most energy? (5 minutes)

Learning intention: To begin to appreciate that different people need different diets.

Resources: Two images or videos showing people with different energy usage (e.g. a person cycling to work and a person sitting on a bus on the way to work).

Description: Show the class the images or videos. Ask: *Who uses up more energy? Does this mean they should eat different quantities of food?* Use questioning and discussion to introduce the concept that a person's lifestyle can affect the quantity of food they need to eat. Discussion will indicate whether learners appreciate the need to approximately match energy intake with energy output.

Main teaching ideas

1 Finding data in a bar chart (10–20 minutes)

Learning intention: To think about why different people need different quantities of energy in their diet.

Resources: Bar chart and Learner's Book questions 1–5.

Description: Discuss with the class the idea that the energy we use each day comes from our food, and that the energy we take in from our food

should roughly match our energy output. Ask them to answer questions 1–5. This could be done individually, with each learner writing down answers to be marked later, or in groups who then feed back their answers to the class, or as a whole-class oral exercise.

> Differentiation ideas: Some learners may need help to interpret the bar chart and/or to read the scale. Remind them of the importance of including units with their answers.

Learners who require a challenge could use the internet to research some other examples of energy requirements, such as a female marathon runner or a pregnant woman.

> Assessment ideas: Answers to questions can be used to assess ability to read a bar chart accurately, and whether learners understand that life processes such as movement and growth require energy.

2 Activity: Different diets (10–15 minutes)

Learning intention: To understand how a balanced diet is linked to specific aspects of health.

Resources: Learner's Book images and questions.

Description: Ask learners to work in pairs, and follow the instructions in the Learner's Book.

> Differentiation ideas: All learners can attempt this activity; differentiation will be by outcome, with some finding it easier than others to match the advice and reasons. Use questioning to help if learners get stuck.

Learners who need a challenge could be asked to think of one more piece of advice and a reason for it.

> Assessment ideas: Successful matching indicates that learners have a good understanding of what makes a balanced diet, and why this is important for health.

3 My diet today (20–30 minutes; this could be started in class with learners completing it for homework)

Learning intention: To apply knowledge of a balanced diet and nutrients to their own diet.

Resources: Worksheets 7.2A, B or C could be used to help learners to organise their records.

Description: Ask learners to think carefully about what they have eaten and drunk today, and to make a list. For each food or drink, ask them to record which nutrients it contains.

> **Differentiation ideas:** Learners who find this task difficult could be given Worksheet 7.2A, which asks only about protein, fat and carbohydrate. Most learners will be able to complete Worksheet 7.2B, in which they are also asked to estimate relative quantities of the nutrients in each food. Some learners will be able to manage Worksheet 7.2C, in which they also think about three vitamins and two minerals.

Learners could use the internet to check their estimates of which nutrients are present in which foods, but this can be very time-consuming.

> **Assessment ideas:** Entries on the record sheet will indicate how well learners are able to identify which types of food contain which nutrients.

Plenary ideas

1 Diet and health commentary (10–15 minutes)

Description: Organise learners into groups of three. Show the two video clips or images from the starter activity again. Ask learners to write a commentary or a 'day-in-the-life' story for each of them, using what they have learnt about suitable diets for different people.

Play the clips and ask the first group to read their commentary. Repeat for as many groups as there is time for.

> **Assessment ideas:** Learners can assess each other. Ask: *Which group's commentary was the best? What made this one so good?* (The choice may be nothing to do with knowledge of diet, and more to do with how funny the commentary was – but that is fine, so long as the science is correct.)

2 Nutrients mnemonic (10 minutes)

Description: Organise learners into groups of three. Ask them to invent a mnemonic to help them to remember the six groups of nutrients. (They could also include the three different vitamins and the two minerals in their mnemonic.)

Ask each group to read back their mnemonic. Ask: *Whose is the best?*

Tell the class you are going to test their mnemonics, and what they mean, next lesson.

> **Assessment ideas:** You could begin the next lesson by asking some learners to tell you their mnemonic, and the nutrients that it stands for, which will show how well they have remembered the nutrients required in a balanced diet.

Homework ideas

1 Workbook exercises 7.2A–C

2 Learner's Book questions 7 and 8

Topic worksheets

Worksheets 7.2A–C, My diet today

Topic 7.3: Growth, development and health

LEARNING PLAN

Learning objectives	Learning intentions	Success criteria
8Bp.03 Discuss how human growth, development and health can be affected by lifestyle, including diet and smoking.	• Learn how growth takes place. • Find out about the difference between growth and development. • Think about how your diet and how much exercise you take affects your growth, development and health. • Learn how smoking affects health.	• Contribute to discussion about diet, exercise and health. • Answer questions about growth, development and smoking. • Analyse data about smoking. • Analyse data about caffeine and birthweight.

LANGUAGE SUPPORT

Learners will use the following words:

embryo: the earliest stages of development of a new organism; in humans, it develops from the fertilised egg (zygote) and implants into the uterus lining

development in humans: progressive changes in structure, function and behaviour that happen as a person grows from an embryo to an adult

nicotine: a chemical in tobacco leaves that acts as a stimulant and is addictive

tar: a mixture of chemicals found in tobacco smoke that increase the risk of developing many different types of cancer

carbon monoxide: a gas present in tobacco smoke, formed by the incomplete combustion of various compounds in tobacco, which binds with haemoglobin in the blood and reduces oxygen transport

particulates: tiny solid particles in tobacco smoke, which enter the lungs and blood and can cause a wide range of health problems

Common misconceptions

Misconception	How to identify	How to overcome
If the results of an experiment do not support the hypothesis being tested, the experiment 'did not work'.	Worksheets 7.3A–C involve interpreting data that do not support a hypothesis.	Use these worksheets to reinforce the idea that testing a hypothesis means that you do an investigation with an open mind to find out whether the hypothesis might be correct, or whether it is incorrect.

Starter ideas

1 Getting started (10 minutes, including sharing ideas)

Description: Ask learners to work in pairs to answer the two questions and to begin to think about how exercise and smoking may affect health. This could be done as a pair-and-share activity. Learners' responses will indicate what they already know or think about the relationship between exercise, smoking and health.

2 Lifestyle choices (10 minutes)

Learning intention: To begin to think about how smoking, taking exercise and food choices can affect health.

Resources: Images showing people making 'lifestyle choices', such as smoking, exercising, drinking coffee and eating fast food. (You might be able to find a suitable video online, instead of images.)

Description: Show the learners the images and ask them to think about how these 'lifestyle choices' (things that people choose to do) might affect health.

Chair a discussion about how some of the choices might increase the risk of poor health.

Note: Smoking increases the risk of numerous diseases, including lung cancer and heart disease; taking exercise has many beneficial effects on overall health, including mental health; there is no scientific evidence that drinking coffee harms health; eating too much fast food increases the risk of heart disease.

This is an opportunity to identify what learners already think about how these activities might affect health.

Main teaching ideas

1 Growth and development (15–20 minutes)

Learning intention: To understand the difference between growth and development; to begin to understand how diet, exercise and smoking may affect growth, development and health.

Resources: Learner's Book text, illustrations and questions.

Description: Use the text and illustrations in the Learner's Book as a basis for class discussion on these issues. Learners could answer questions 1 and 2 individually, in small groups, or orally as part of a whole-class discussion.

> **Differentiation ideas:** Everyone can take part in the discussion, with directed questioning ensuring that even less confident learners are involved. More challenging questions could be targeted at some learners, looking for a deeper level of understanding. For example, with question 2, you could ask learners: *What else affects your height, apart from your diet?*

You could also ask learners to write short summaries of the effects of the four components of tobacco smoke, outlined in the text.

> **Assessment ideas:** Use answers to questions 1 and 2 to determine understanding of the terms 'growth' and 'development'.

2 Activity: Why do people smoke? (10–15 minutes; longer if learners do research)

Learning intention: To think about issues relating to smoking.

Resources: None unless research is carried out; if learners do research, they will need internet access.

Description: Ask learners to follow the instructions in the Learner's Book.

> **Differentiation ideas:** Learners who would benefit from a challenge could research these questions. They could also talk to people they know, about their attitudes to smoking.

This is an open-ended task. Some learners will provide very simple and relatively superficial answers to the questions, while others will delve more deeply and provide more detailed and thoughtful responses.

3 Does caffeine affect birthweight? – analysing data and drawing conclusions (25–30 minutes)

Learning intention: To develop skills in presenting and analysing data.

Resources: Worksheets 7.3A–C

Description: Ask learners to complete one of the worksheets. You could allocate a particular worksheet to each learner, or you could allow them to choose which one they try.

> **Differentiation ideas:** The three worksheets have different levels of demand. Learners who have difficulty with understanding data provided

to them, or with constructing bar charts, could use Worksheet 7.3A. Worksheet 7.3B is a little more demanding, as learners are required to make decisions about the scales on the bar chart. Worksheet 7.3C is more demanding still, where no help is provided with the bar chart, and where learners are asked to look critically at the design of the investigation and suggest improvements.

> **Assessment ideas:** You can assess ability to draw bar charts, to analyse data and to determine whether results support or disprove a hypothesis.

Plenary ideas

1 Antismoking campaign (10–15 minutes)

Description: Draw a large picture of a cigarette on the board. Tell learners to close their books. Say to learners: *Tell me a sentence we can add to the picture, to explain to people why they should not smoke.*

Take ideas for sentences or snappy slogans, and write them on the board around the picture of the cigarette. Encourage learners to include reference to nicotine, tar, particulates and carbon monoxide.

> **Assessment ideas:** Responses will help to determine how well the class has understood the effects of smoking cigarettes on health.

2 Summarising what you have learnt today (5 minutes)

Description: Ask everyone to sit quietly for one minute, and think of a sentence to summarise what they have learnt today.

Ask each person in turn to say their sentence.

> **Assessment ideas:** Use learners' sentences to gauge how well they have absorbed the main ideas from the lesson.

Homework ideas

1 Learner's Book questions 3 to 5

2 Workbook exercises 7.3A–C

Topic worksheets

Worksheets 7.3A–C, Does caffeine affect birthweight?

Topic 7.4: Moving the body

LEARNING PLAN		
Learning objectives	**Learning intentions**	**Success criteria**
8Bs.01 Identify ball-and-socket and hinge joints, and explain how antagonistic muscles move the bones at a hinge joint.	• Learn about hinge joints and ball-and-socket joints. • Find out how a pair of muscles moves the arm at the elbow.	• Identify hinge joints and ball-and-socket joints in the human body and other skeletons. • Answer questions about how the elbow joint is bent and straightened. • Interpret data from using a model arm, to explain how the biceps works.

LANGUAGE SUPPORT

Learners will use the following words:

skeleton: a structure that supports an animal's body; vertebrates have internal skeletons made of bone and cartilage; arthropods have external skeletons; some invertebrates (e.g. earthworms) have hydrostatic skeletons made up of a fluid-filled cavity

exoskeleton: a skeleton on the outside of the body

joints: places where two bones meet

hinge joint: a joint at which one bone can move in one plane in relation to the other, like a door moving on its hinges

ball-and-socket joint: a joint at which one bone can move in a circular motion in relation to the other

muscles: organs made up of specialised muscle cells, which are able to make themselves shorter (contract)

contraction: (of muscles) getting shorter; this is an active process, in which the muscle uses energy which is obtained through respiration

tendons: strong, non-stretchy cords that attach muscles to bones

biceps: a muscle attached to the scapula and radius, which bends the elbow joint when it contracts

triceps: a muscle attached to the scapula and ulna, which straightens the elbow joint when it contracts

relax: (a muscle) stop contracting

antagonistic muscles: a pair of muscles, such as the biceps and triceps, that work together to cause opposite movements at a joint when they contract; one contracts while the other relaxes

Common misconceptions

Misconception	How to identify	How to overcome
Muscles can make themselves get longer.	When discussing how the elbow joint is moved by the biceps and triceps.	When talking about muscles, always use the words 'contract' and 'relax' to describe what the muscle does. Use the passive tense ('is stretched') to describe how a muscle gets longer. Do not say that a muscle 'stretches'. Encourage learners to use this language.

Starter ideas

1 Getting started (10 minutes, including sharing ideas)

Resources: Learner's Book diagram of skeleton.

Description: Ask learners to answer the two questions. Learners could do this individually, or in small groups, or you could pose the questions as a whole-class activity. Answers will show how much learners already understand about the functions of different bones.

2 The human skeleton (10 minutes)

Resources: A model skeleton.

Description: Show learners a model skeleton. Ask them to name as many bones as they can. Ask: *What are the functions of the skeleton?* (protection, support and movement) Ask: *How do we make*

the bones move? (muscles). Answers will show how much learners already understand about the structure and function of the skeleton.

Main teaching ideas

1 Activity: Identifying different kinds of joint (15 minutes)

Learning intention: To identify hinge and ball-and-socket joints.

Resources: A model skeleton, preferably one with movable joints (optional).

Description: Ask learners to follow the instructions in the Learner's Book. As a follow-up, ask them to answer questions 1 and 2. You can also ask them to look at the X-ray of the arm and shoulder and identify the joints.

> **Differentiation ideas:** Some learners will need support to work methodically through the questions, and to find and name examples of the two types of joint.

Template 7.4A: Recording table for *Activity: Identifying different kinds of joint* is available for learners who need some structure to help them to record their answers.

Some learners will find numerous examples of hinge joints, including all of the joints in the fingers and toes.

> **Assessment ideas:** Use questions 1 and 2 to check that learners can identify hinge and ball-and-socket joints.

2 Antagonistic muscles (20–25 minutes)

Learning intention: To understand how the biceps and triceps muscles bend and straighten the arm at the elbow; to understand what is meant by the term 'antagonistic muscles'.

Resources: Learner's Book text and illustrations.

Description: Use discussion to work through the information in the Learner's Book, to help learners to understand the structure of the bones and muscles in the arm, and how contraction of the biceps and triceps bends and straightens the joint.

Emphasise that muscles can produce a force when they contract (get shorter), but cannot 'make themselves' get longer.

Learners can do the activity to think about how their own biceps muscle behaves as they bend their elbow joint.

Show a video clip of the elbow bending.

> **Differentiation ideas:** Everyone can take part in the discussion. Use directed questioning to involve all learners, and to provide scaffolding to lead learners who are having difficulty towards better understanding.

> **Assessment ideas:** Learners can answer questions 3–6. Use their answers to determine their understanding of the structure of the skeleton and muscles in the arm. Use oral responses during the discussion to check that learners understand how antagonistic muscles work.

3 Think like a scientist: Using a model arm to investigate how the biceps muscle works (30–45 minutes)

Learning intention: To use a model to understand how the biceps muscle moves the arm at the elbow joint.

Resources: A model arm, as shown in the diagram in the Learner's Book; a hanger and masses.

Description: This is best done as a whole-class activity. Make sure that everyone understands how the model represents the bones and muscles in the human arm.

You could record results on the board, or everyone could have their own results chart, ready to complete as the investigation proceeds. Some learners will be able to design and complete their own results chart. *Template 7.4B: Recording table* for *Think like a scientist: Using a model arm to investigate how the biceps muscle works* is available for those who need help with this.

> **Practical guidance:** The model arm can be made from wood or strong cardboard. Wood is more durable, and can be used for many classes over many years.

It is best to make the model approximately life-size, with the 'lower arm' around 25 cm long and the upper arm a similar length or a little shorter. However, exact dimensions are not important.

The top of the 'humerus' must be firmly attached to a support, such as a strong wooden board. The 'elbow joint' should be free to pivot, and should not be attached to the board.

The hooks should be approximately equal distances apart; it will make subsequent recording and calculations easier if they are at a measured distance (for example, at 5 cm intervals) which could be marked on the model.

The masses you need to use, and the range of the scale on the forcemeter, will depend partly on the material of which the model arm is made; the denser and heavier this is, the greater the force that the forcemeter should be able to read, and the greater the number and size of masses you will probably want to place on the hanger.

If you want learners to do calculations of turning forces as part of the analysis of their results, it is important that the angle between the humerus and radius is a right angle, and that the learners pull upwards vertically. You could draw a horizontal line on the board to show where the radius should lie when this angle is correct. Learners can watch the person doing the pulling and tell them whether their pull is vertical or not.

> **Differentiation ideas:** Some learners will find it difficult to associate the model with a human arm, and the forcemeter with a biceps muscle. They can be asked to stand against the model, and bend their own elbow joint, thinking about how their biceps is doing something similar to the forcemeter to pull the radius upwards.

Questions 3, 5 and 7 in *Think like a scientist: Using a model arm to investigate how the biceps muscle works* are quite challenging, requiring learners to make links between what they have learnt in physics and biology lessons. Some learners will be able to deal with these questions on their own, but some may need help to arrive at the right answers. Learners could be asked to calculate turning forces (moments) to explain their answers.

> **Assessment ideas:** Learners could write answers to questions 1–5 in *Think like a scientist: Using a model arm to investigate how the biceps muscle works*.

Plenary ideas

1 Spelling quiz (10 minutes)

Description: Learners work in groups of two or three. Ask them to close their books. Hand out a sheet of paper to each group.

Read out a key word from this topic; you could also use key words from earlier topics in this unit.

Ask learners to write down the word, spelling it correctly.

When all words have been read out, ask learners to exchange their answers with another group.

Write the words on the board, and ask groups to mark the spellings, before returning the sheets of paper to their owners.

You could also, as you go through the spellings, ask learners to tell you the meanings of each word.

> **Assessment ideas:** Use this activity to check that learners are confident in spelling key words correctly, and also to check understanding of their meanings.

2 Mind map (20–30 minutes)

Resources: Large sheets of paper; coloured pens.

Description: Ask the class: *What have you learnt about in this unit?* Construct a list of their ideas on the board.

Learners work in pairs or groups of three or four. Ask them to construct a mind map of everything they have learnt in this unit. They can use the ideas you have written down, or they can use their own ideas.

If time allows, you can ask each group to explain their mind maps to other groups.

> **Assessment ideas:** Ideas from the class about what they think they have learnt in this unit will help to tell you how well they have understood the topics covered.

Homework ideas

1   Workbook exercises 7.4A–C

2   Find out about exoskeleton suits to help people with mobility disorders.

PROJECT GUIDANCE

A diet for Mars explorers

This project addresses the following learning objectives:

8SiC.03 Evaluate issues which involve and/or require scientific understanding.

This project provides an opportunity for learners to apply their knowledge and understanding from this unit to a genuine problem that scientists are trying to solve.

Learners will work in groups to contribute to a display.

Decide how to divide the class into groups. You may also like to allocate roles to each member within the group.

Help to allocate different aspects of the problem to different groups. Some groups might like to work on more than one of the four problems suggested. If you have a large class, you could perhaps find other problems to add to this list.

You may wish to provide a list of useful websites to start everyone off with their research.

You may wish to help groups to think about how their contributions can be pooled with those of other groups, to make a striking display.

Help groups to put their contributions together, and build the display.

⟩8 Chemical reactions

Unit plan

Topic	Learning hours	Learning content	Resources
8.1 Exothermic reactions	2.5-4	Learn about exothermic reactions; plan and carry out an investigation	**Learner's Book:** Questions 1–8 Think like a scientist: Planning and carrying out an investigation into the reaction between acid and magnesium **Workbook:** Exercise 8.1A, Investigating an exothermic reaction Exercise 8.1B, Investigating exothermic reactions between metals and acid Exercise 8.1C, Exothermic reactions with metals **Teacher's Resource:** Worksheets 8.1A–C, Investigation planning Template 8.1: Peer assessment for *Think like a scientist: Planning and carrying out an investigation into the reaction between acid and magnesium*
8.2 Endothermic reactions	2.5-4	Reactions of metals with oxygen	**Learner's Book:** Questions 1–11 Think like a scientist: Carrying out an endothermic reaction Think like a scientist: Endothermic or exothermic? **Workbook:** Exercise 8.2A, Energy changes Exercise 8.2B, Exothermic or endothermic? Exercise 8.2C, Endothermic reactions and processes **Teacher's Resource:** Worksheets 8.2A–C, Falling temperatures Template 8.2A: Results table for *Think like a scientist: Exothermic or endothermic?* Template 8.2B: Self-assessment for *Think like a scientist: Exothermic or endothermic?*

Topic	Learning hours	Learning content	Resources
8.3 Reactions of metals with oxygen	1.5-3.5	Reactions of metals with oxygen; practical skills; interpreting findings from an investigation	**Learner's Book:** Questions 1–8 Think like a scientist: Heating metals in air **Workbook:** Exercises 8.3A–C, Why does iron rust?
8.4 Reactions of metals with water	1.5-3.5	Reactions of metals with water	**Learner's Book:** Questions 1–10 Think like a scientist: Reactions of metals with water **Workbook:** Exercise 8.4, Reactions with water and steam
8.5 Reactions of metals with dilute acids	2-3	Reactions of metals with dilute acids; planning an investigation	**Learner's Book:** Questions 1–4 Think like a scientist: Planning an investigation into the reaction of metals in acid Think like a scientist: Carrying out an investigation into the reaction of metals in acid Activity: Reactivity order **Workbook:** Exercise 8.5A, Investigating reactivity Exercise 8.5B, Reactions of metals with dilute acids Exercise 8.5C, How reactive are these metals **Teacher's Resource:** Worksheets 8.5A–C, Word equation practice
Cross-unit resources			**Learner's Book:** Check your Progress **Project:** Working with chemicals safely **Teacher's Resource:** Language development worksheets 8.1 Selecting the correct word and spellings 8.2 Writing in complete sentences and comprehension

BACKGROUND KNOWLEDGE

Learners will already have some ideas about a range of reactions. They will extend their knowledge in this unit. They know about some exothermic reactions from previous work in the course but will not know the term. It may be difficult for them to grasp the idea of endothermic reactions but their knowledge of endothermic processes should help to make the transition. You will need to make the difference between a reaction and a process very clear: In an exothermic or endothermic *reaction*, new substances are formed; in an exothermic or endothermic *process*, no new substances are formed, there is just a change of state.

They will be using the ideas about symbols for particles and particle and word equations throughout this unit, so it may be helpful to revise the symbols and/or the rules for writing word equations such as 'all on one line', and 'matching acid and salt'.

Most learners understand the idea of reactions being more or less vigorous but now they are beginning to group reactions by type, and to use general equations.

The practical skills learners already have are extended. Learners have more opportunities to plan and carry out investigations. There are templates to help support learners and to help you identify where some learners are having difficulties with their investigation skills.

TEACHING SKILLS FOCUS

Plenaries 3

If you have been developing the use of different plenary activities, and learners are becoming more confident about admitting when they do not understand a topic, now is the time to try 'help style' plenaries. These include *Five fingers* (described in Teaching skills focus, Plenaries 2) and the following ideas.

What did I need help with today?

Ask learners to write down one thing they found difficult, or didn't fully understand, today. Explain that this is completely private, with no names written on the papers. They could even fold the paper over.

Many learners may want to claim that they have no problems, but you need to allow them the opportunity to ask for help, and to reassure them that not everyone understands everything the first time and that it's the teacher's job to help them.

Collect the papers and use them to plan subsequent lessons. You may need to go back over some of the content, especially explaining changes of state and energy changes.

This type of plenary is probably best used when the learners are confident and trust that the teacher and other class members will not ridicule them for not understanding.

Pyramid ideas

Here learners could use the pyramid as shown to answer the questions and reflect on their learning.

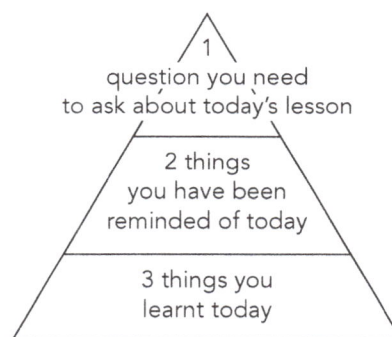

This idea can also be modified to cover vocabulary or any other aspect of the lesson, as shown here.

Quick fire round

Ask learners to write five questions about the subject matter from the lesson. They pass these questions to a partner to answer. They swap back and mark each other's answers. Share some of the questions and answers with the whole class.

Then ask the learners to reflect: *How well did I do and how easy or difficult was it to write the five questions?*

In the hot seat

Ask a confident learner to take the hot seat. It is advisable to set this up with the learner before the lesson. The hot seat can be at the front of the class or in the learner's normal place. Ask the learner a series of five or six questions. The learner may answer correctly or incorrectly Explain to the class that some answers may be incorrect (having agreed this with the volunteer learner beforehand). When the hot-seat learner answers each question, the rest of the class write down whether the answer is correct. If it is incorrect, they give the correct answer. Learners swap answer papers with a partner. Then carry out whole-class marking. Learners share feedback.

Then ask learners to reflect: *How well did I do with these questions? Do I have the confidence in my answers that I should have?*

Plenaries that build in more reflection time are very useful for involving learners in their own progress.

The key to keeping the plenaries interesting and learners engaged, as you would wish, is to use a variety of types, but to include some familiar ones so that learners become used to thinking about their learning.

Just a minute

Some plenaries that learners enjoy, and are useful to enable you to assess progress, are those based on popular television (or radio) quiz shows such as 'Just a Minute'. These often ensure learners have to remember detail from the lesson.

Choose one learner to start by talking about a fact or topic they learned or did during today's lesson. They should talk without repeating any word, hesitating or deviating from the subject. When they make any one of those mistakes, stop the clock and move on to the next person. Continue until the fact has been spoken about for one minute. You could use this for discussing an experiment in a lesson, or the whole lesson.

Use whatever quiz shows are popular locally.

Summary

1   Aim to use the pyramid style plenary at least once in this unit.

When you look at the pyramid answers, focus on the question at the top of the pyramid and provide help.

Where are the learners having difficulties? Are many learners having the same problems? What can you go over in the next lesson to address these issues? Do you need to think about how you present information, more clearly? Are the learners engaging in the learning process and reflecting on where they need to improve?

2   Aim to use at least one 'hot seat' game plenary in this unit.

How did it go? Was the hot-seat learner happy with the task? Could you have made them more comfortable with the process? Were the rest of the class engaged with the task? Were the questions at an appropriate level for them? Did they understand the idea that the hot seat person got some wrong on purpose to catch them out?

Topic 8.1: Exothermic reactions

LEARNING PLAN

Learning objectives	Learning intentions	Success criteria
8Cc.01 Use word equations to describe reactions. **8Cc.02** Know that some processes and reactions are endothermic or exothermic, and this can be identified by temperature change (part). **8TWSp.04** Plan a range of investigations of different types, while considering variables appropriately, and recognise that not all investigations can be fair tests. **8TWSp.05** Make risk assessments for practical work to identify and control risks. **8TWSc.02** Decide what equipment is required to carry out an investigation or experiment and use it appropriately. **8TWSc.03** Evaluate whether measurements and observations have been repeated sufficiently to be reliable. **8TWSc.04** Take appropriately accurate and precise measurements, explaining why accuracy and precision are important. **8TWSc.05** Carry out practical work safely, supported by risk assessments where appropriate. **8TWSc.07** Collect and record sufficient observations and/or measurements in an appropriate form. **8TWSa.01** Describe the accuracy of predictions, based on results, and suggest why they were or were not accurate. **8TWSa.03** Make conclusions by interpreting results and explain the limitations of the conclusions. **8TWSa.04** Evaluate experiments and investigations, and suggest improvements, explaining any proposed changes. **8TSWa.05** Present and interpret observations and measurements appropriately.	• Use word equations. • To learn about exothermic reactions. • Plan and carry out an investigation safely. • Choose appropriate equipment and use it correctly. • Make a risk assessment. • Take enough accurate measurements and present them appropriately. • Describe the accuracy of any predictions based on the results and explain any discrepancies. • Draw conclusions based on the results. • Evaluate the investigation.	• Use word equations. • Describe what happens in an exothermic reaction. • Plan an investigation which considers the variables, selects appropriate equipment and makes a risk assessment. • Carry out an investigation safely using the equipment correctly and controlling any risks. • Take enough accurate measurements and present them appropriately. • Form appropriate conclusions based on results obtained. • Make suggestions to improve the investigation.

LANGUAGE SUPPORT

Learners will use the following words:

fuel: a store of chemical energy

dissipated energy: is transferred to thermal energy and spreads out through the surroundings

combustion: burning

exothermic reaction: a chemical reaction in which energy is transferred into the surroundings

oxidation reaction: any reaction where a substance combines with oxygen

preliminary work: some practical work you do before an investigation to find out how you will carry it out; for example, you might find out the range or interval you will use

Common misconceptions

Misconception	How to identify	How to overcome
Some learners find it difficult to imagine bonds breaking and reforming.	This will be fairly obvious, based on learners' questions. You could ask directly: *What do you understand by the bonds breaking and reforming?*	You could try using construction bricks that fit together. Use different colours to represent the different elements and show how you use energy to break them apart and reform them into new combinations. Exaggerate it somewhat.
Some learners find the idea of preliminary experiments difficult to grasp.	Learners may ask: *Why do we have to do this? What's the point?*	This needs careful explanation. Or you could demonstrate the investigation, using different lengths of magnesium ribbon, as in the Learner's Book, and ask learners how long they need to make the pieces of magnesium ribbon.

Starter ideas

1 Getting started (10 minutes)

Resources: Learner's Book.

Description: Ask learners to look at the equation and to answer the questions on their own. Then compare answers with a partner. Share answers with the class.

This reminds learners about word equations, reactants and products and the language of reactions.

2 Burning (10 minutes)

Resources: Deflagrating spoon; charcoal; gas jar with cover filled with air (or oxygen if you prefer); limewater; heat source (such as Bunsen burner); heatproof mat.

Description: Heat the charcoal on a deflagrating spoon in the heat source until it is alight. Place the spoon in the gas jar and observe the reaction. Once the reaction has ended, test the resultant gas with

limewater for carbon dioxide. As learners watch, ask: *What is happening? What can you see? Can you represent this in a word equation?* Ask them what the reactants and products are.

This is an opportunity to use the specific vocabulary and the rules about word equations. You could allow learners to do this as a practical task. (Although, if you do, it will take much more time.)

Main teaching ideas

1 Burning other substances (30 minutes)

Learning intention: To look at energy changes in some reactions.

Resources: Magnesium ribbon; tongs; safety glasses; heatproof mat; heat source (such as a Bunsen burner); large plastic soda bottle (2 litre) with stopper; eyelet screws on a piece of wood; wires to hold the wood in place; hydrogen gas (generate by adding magnesium to an acid); wires to connect to simple battery circuit to cause a spark; paperclips to hold wires in place; string securely attached across the room.

Look carefully at the diagram in the Learner's Book or refer to one of the many methods given on educational websites.

Description: Learners could carry out the burning magnesium task; it is a repeat but it could serve as a useful risk assessment exercise.

You could carry out the hydrogen rocket experiment. This is a powerful demonstration of the energy released in a reaction. However, it needs to be carried out safely; the basic instructions are in the Learner's Book but you will need to search educational websites for detailed instructions.

> **Practical guidance:** A small piece of magnesium should be placed in the tongs. This should be held at arm's length and ignited in a Bunsen burner. Remind learners to wear safety glasses and not to look directly at the burning magnesium

Safety: You must practise this rocket demonstration before doing it in a class. You must ensure that:

- the string is securely attached
- the stopper flies off in a safe direction
- the rocket moves in a safe direction.

There are many different ways of carrying out the demonstration. A search of the suitable sites on the internet, such as the Royal Society of Chemistry, will provide a number of different methods. It is essential to try the demonstration out before attempting it in the lesson and to select a method suitable for your situation.

> **Assessment ideas:** You could ask learners to write word equations for the reactions they have seen or carried out. You could ask them to describe the changes in energy that they observe. You could use questions from the Learner's Book.

2 Exothermic reactions with water and acid (30 minutes, or more if you allow the learners to carry out the reaction with acid themselves)

Learning intention: To demonstrate other exothermic reactions.

Resources: For potassium in water: safety screen; safety glasses for everyone; glass trough filled with water; small piece of potassium; knife to cut the

potassium; forceps to remove the potassium from the container; ceramic tile to cut the potassium on.

For magnesium in acid: magnesium ribbon; dilute acid; measuring cylinder; thermometer; test tube; test tube rack; ruler; clamp to hold the thermometer away from the bottom or side of the test tube.

Description: Demonstrate the potassium in water experiment and ask learners to record what happens. Ask them to discuss the energy changes during this reaction and to write the word equation.

The magnesium in acid experiment seems easy, but you need to draw attention to the fact that you need to be able to compare findings and, for that comparison to be valid, learners need to use the same technique, using the same quantities of the reactants in the same way. You could ask them directly why it is important that you measure the length of the magnesium and the volume of acid. Then lead a discussion from there. In this task, holding the discussion is just as important as doing the experiment. Learners want to do the practical task, but they need to be sure why they are doing it in the right way. It often means that the task takes much longer but, in order to get learners to understand the issues, it is essential. If you simply tell learners what to do, they will not be prepared for unfamiliar situations.

> **Practical guidance:** Place the potassium on the tile and cut it with the knife or scalpel. **Do not** touch the potassium with your hand at any time. Use forceps to transfer a small piece of potassium to the trough of water.

See above for the magnesium and acid reaction. Discuss why the thermometer is held in a clamp rather than just resting on the bottom of the test tube.

Safety: The potassium in water experiment needs to be done **only** as a demonstration, with a safety screen, so that all learners – and you – are protected. Everyone must wear safety glasses as the potassium may spit and explode. Use forceps to remove a small piece of potassium from the container. The potassium must be stored under oil as it may react with the water vapour in the air.

> **Differentiation ideas:** Since this is a practical/ demonstration that everyone can observe, differentiation can only be by the questions you choose to ask each group or individual. The discussion of the energy changes could lead to

you asking various groups: *Where does the energy come from? What happens to the energy?* Then ask learners to ask each other the same questions and to assess the replies. They should ask themselves: *Have I understood?* and *Has my partner understood?*

> **Assessment ideas:** You could ask learners to discuss the energy changes in these reactions and to write the word equations. Questions from the Learner's Book could be used.

3 Think like a scientist: Planning and carrying out an investigation into the reaction between acid and magnesium (divide into two sessions; 30–40 minutes for the planning and preliminary work and 40–50 minutes for the investigation)

Learning intention: To plan an investigation and to carry out practical work safely.

Resources: The learners should make their own list of equipment and resources but these are likely to be: safety glasses; magnesium ribbon; ruler; dilute acid (you could provide several for them to choose from, or just one); measuring cylinder suitable for $10\,cm^3$; test tubes and test tube rack; thermometer; clamp to hold thermometer; insulation material.

Worksheets 8.1A–C Planning the investigation

Description: Learners work in groups of no more than three. Discuss the task, as in the Learner's Book, and the issues that need to be addressed. You could ask the groups to discuss it and then take feedback from the whole class. You may decide to let all groups plan the same investigation or to let them plan different ones. Give the groups time-limited sessions to reach a certain point and then discuss their progress, especially if sustained concentration is difficult for the class. You could ask them to carry out the preliminary work all together, or as it fits in with their planning. Safety issues need to be considered if some groups are sitting and discussing close to where others are carrying out practical work.

Make a point of checking plans before learners do the investigation in full. It may be that you need to collect the plans and go over them before the practical session.

During the practical session, circulate and ask the groups what they are doing, and refer back to their plans. Try to ensure they are being precise and accurate in their measurements and ask them to explain why that is necessary. You need to leave plenty of time for learners to present the results and discuss the findings.

> **Differentiation ideas:** You could use the worksheets to help the learners with the planning task. These offer three levels of support. You could choose not to give a worksheet to those learners who need a challenge.

> **Assessment ideas:** Use learners' plans to assess progress and the questions 1–3 from *Think like a scientist: Planning and carrying out an investigation into the reaction between acid and magnesium.* Use *Template 8.1: Peer assessment* to assess the practical work.

Plenary ideas

1 Exit ticket emoji (10 minutes)

Resources: Sticky notes or paper.

Description: Ask learners to draw an emoji for how they thought they did in the lesson and then to answer these questions: *How well did you understand today's material? What did you learn today? What did you find difficult today?*

You could provide learners with a prepared worksheet, with a space for the emoji followed by the three questions each with space after them and allow them to fill it in and then leave it at the end of the lesson for you to use it to inform your planning of the next session.

2 Five fingers (10 minutes)

Description: Each learner draws around their hand on a scrap of paper or in their book and writes answers to these questions in the appropriate place on each finger.

- Thumb – What have you learned? What do you understand?

- Index finger – What skills have you used today?

- Middle finger – Which skills did you find difficult today?

- Ring finger – Who did you help today?
- Little finger – What will you make sure that you remember from today's lesson?

You will find it useful to collect these and use them to help decide what you need to concentrate on in the next lesson.

This type of plenary is a way of structuring learners' reflection time. It allows the less confident learners to celebrate what they have done well and encourages the more confident learners to think about the next steps in learning.

Homework ideas

1 Workbook exercises 8.1A–C

Topic worksheets

Worksheets 8.1A–C, Investigation planning

Topic 8.2: Endothermic reactions

LEARNING PLAN

Learning objectives	Learning intentions	Success criteria
8Cc.01 Use word equations to describe reactions. 8Cc.02 Know that some processes and reactions are endothermic or exothermic, and this can be identified by temperature change. 8TWSp.05 Make risk assessments for practical work to identify and control risks. 8TWSc.01 Sort, group and classify phenomena, objects, materials and organisms through testing, observation, using secondary information, and making and using keys. 8TWSc.05 Carry out practical work safely, supported by risk assessments where appropriate. 8TSWa.05 Present and interpret observations and measurements appropriately.	• Use word equations. • Learn about chemical reactions that take in energy. • Learn about the use of exothermic and endothermic reactions and processes. • Carry out an investigation to distinguish between exothermic and endothermic reactions. • Carry out practical work safely using risk assessments. • Present and interpret observations and measurements.	• Use word equations. • List some chemical reactions that are endothermic. • Explain the difference between an endothermic reaction and an endothermic process. • Carry out an investigation to distinguish between exothermic and endothermic reactions. • Describe some uses of exothermic and endothermic reactions and processes.

LANGUAGE SUPPORT

Learners will use the following words:

endothermic reaction: a chemical reaction in which energy is transferred from the surroundings

endothermic process: a process (such as change of state) in which energy is transferred from the surroundings

Common misconceptions

Misconception	How to identify	How to overcome
Some learners find it difficult to explain the temperature changes where there is a drop in temperature, as they find talking about transfers of heat energy difficult and talk about 'cold moving from one place to another'.	Ask learners to explain what is taking place with these energy changes. You could use this as a plenary question to see how well they have grasped the ideas.	To overcome this you need to be clear in the language that you use. The use of heat energy transfer diagrams could help.

Starter ideas

1 Getting started (10 minutes)

Resources: Learner's Book.

Description: When you make any scientific measurements, you are told that you need to be 'accurate' and 'precise'. Ask learners what they think this means. Ask them to discuss their ideas with a partner.

Then ask learners to look at the three archery targets. They need to identify which archer has been:

- precise but not accurate
- neither precise nor accurate
- both and precise.

Once learners have discussed this with their partner, Take feedback from the class.

2 Words beginning with... (10 minutes)

Resources: Learner's Book.

Description: Write the word 'endothermic' vertically down the board and challenge learners to find words that start with those letters. Decide whether to allow them to use the Learner's Book and a glossary, or not. You could restrict them to words about energy and energy transfers or scientific equipment. Take feedback from the class, giving one point for each correct answer, two points if nobody else in the class has that word.

Main teaching ideas

1 Carrying out an endothermic reaction (30 minutes)

Learning intention: To carry out an endothermic reaction.

Resources: A test tube; test tube rack; stirring rod; thermometer; spatula; lemon juice or citric acid; sodium hydrogencarbonate.

Description: Ask learners to follow the instructions in the Learner's Book and complete this reaction. Circulate and help with reading the temperature, as some learners will find it difficult to believe that the temperature decreases. You will need to go over the energy changes carefully, making sure you are using the correct terminology.

> **Practical guidance:** The students should pour some of the lemon juice or citric acid into a beaker and take and record the temperature. They should then add about three spatulas of sodium hydrogencarbonate and stir the mixture. Once the reaction is complete (once the fizzing has stopped), they take and record the temperature again. Encourage learners to feel the outside of the beaker and experience the drop in temperature.

> **Assessment ideas:** Use questions 1 and 2 from *Think like a scientist: Carrying out an endothermic reaction* to assess how well learners were able to carry out the experiment.

2 Another way to cool down (20 minutes if you demonstrate this; 40 minutes if you do it as a practical; 30–60 more minutes if you choose to ask learners to plan and carry out an investigation)

Learning intention: To demonstrate an endothermic process, to carry out practical work and to plan an investigation.

Resources: Learner's Book; Worksheets 8.2A–C; safety glasses; beaker; water; glass rod; thermometer; spatula; potassium chloride.

Description: You could do this as a demonstration, with or without learners' help. The class could do this as a practical activity, and then use their experience to help them tackle the planning and interpretation of results in Worksheets 8.2A–C.

> **Differentiation ideas:** Use the different worksheets 8.2A–C. You may have to provide more practical support for those with poorer practical skills. Using the self-assessment template may help learners to focus on their practical skills and to reflect on how they can improve them.

> **Assessment ideas:** You could use *Template 8.3: Self-assessment* to assess the practical skills and/or Worksheets 8.2A–C to assess progress and understanding.

3 Think like a scientist: Endothermic or exothermic? (40–50 minutes)

Learning intention: To investigate different reactions and processes to decide if they are endothermic or exothermic.

Resources: Beakers or polystyrene cups or other insulated containers; stirring rod; thermometer (not to be used for stirring the solutions); chemicals as listed below; safety glasses; *Template 8.2: Results table*.

For the various reactions and processes you could offer:

1 sodium hydroxide and dilute hydrochloric acid

2 potassium chloride and water

3 melting ice cubes

4 copper sulfate solution

5 ammonium nitrate and water

6 boiling water until steam comes off

7 steam from a kettle directed at a cold surface

8 dilute hydrochloric acid and magnesium ribbon

9 sodium hydrogencarbonate and citric acid

Description: This is best done as a 'circus' of experiments, with equipment for each reaction or process set up at a different point around the room. You may not be able to offer all the reactions and processes listed, but try to make sure you offer at least some that are exothermic, some that are endothermic, some that are reactions, and some that are processes. Provide a card with instructions and the list of resources at each station, to avoid confusion. If you are short of time, different groups could undertake some of the experiments and then give feedback on their results to the whole class. The experiments you choose will depend on what you have available. It is sensible to provide labelled beakers of reagents rather than a stock bottle. You may need to top these up as the lesson proceeds. Most of these experiments require the temperature to be taken before and after a reaction or process has occurred and some, such as melting ice or producing steam, may be too difficult to measure. It would be a useful discussion point about the lack of change in temperature between the ice and the melted ice.

Circulate and keep an eye on the different stations where learners are working, in case any learners need support.

Once everyone has finished, you could hold a review of their findings and a discussion about how difficult it was to take the temperature or carry out the reaction or process. At this point you can check that learners understand the difference between a reaction and a process.

> **Practical guidance:** Learners should be practising the skills to enable them to work in a safe and methodical manner, record findings accurately, and be able to interpret the results to identify an exothermic or endothermic reaction or process. An explanation of what is taking place would be helpful.

Safety: Care needs to be taken when working with acids and alkalis or when using steam. Copper sulfate is a skin irritant and can cause eye damage so should only be used at low concentration. Learners should wear safety glasses and wash hands after using copper sulfate solution and/or magnesium powder.

> **Differentiation ideas:** You could restrict some of the processes or reactions and allow those who need a challenge to do some that are more difficult to measure. You could use *Template 8.2: Results table* with some of the learners.

> **Assessment ideas:** You could use questions 1–4 of *Think like a scientist: Endothermic or exothermic?* to assess understanding. You could also use the class discussion to assess their skills and explanations.

Plenary ideas

1 What did I need help with today? (10 minutes)

Resources: Paper or sticky notes.

Description: Ask learners to write down one thing they found difficult, or didn't fully understand, today. Explain that this is completely private, with no names written on the papers. They could even fold the paper over.

Many learners may want to claim that they have no problems, but you need to allow them the opportunity to ask for help, and to reassure them that not everyone understands everything the first time and that it's your job to help them.

Collect the papers and use them to plan subsequent lessons. You may need to go back over some of the content, especially explaining changes of state and energy changes.

This type of plenary is probably best used when the learners are confident and trust that you and other class members will not ridicule them for not understanding something.

Asking learners to concentrate on what they didn't understand can seem hard on them, but they need to reflect on what they cannot explain or understand, so that they have the confidence to ask for help so that they can improve.

Learners might also reflect on their practical skills and how to improve them using *Template 8.2: Results table*.

2 Pyramid ideas (10 minutes)

Resources: Drawing of a pyramid with questions as shown here.

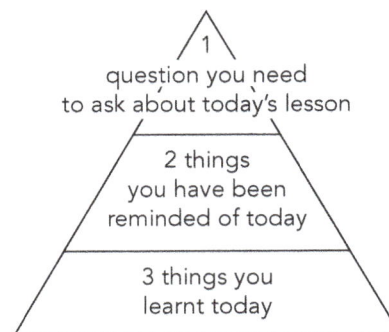

Description: Ask learners to complete the pyramid. Learners could reflect on both what they have learnt and what they need to follow up on.

Homework ideas

1   Workbook exercises 8.2A–C

Topic worksheets

Worksheets 8.2A–C, Falling temperatures

Topic 8.3: Reactions of metals with oxygen

LEARNING PLAN

Learning objectives	Learning intentions	Success criteria
8Cc.01 Use word equations to describe reactions. **8Cc.03** Describe the reactivity of metals (limited to sodium, potassium, calcium, magnesium, zinc, iron, copper, gold and silver) with oxygen, water and dilute acids (part). **8TWSc.05** Carry out practical work safely, supported by risk assessments where appropriate. **8TWSc.07** Collect and record sufficient observations and/or measurements in an appropriate form. **8TWSa.03** Make conclusions by interpreting results and explain the limitations of the conclusions.	• Use word equations. • Investigate the reactions of some metals with oxygen. • Carry out practical work safely. • Compare the reactivity of some metals with oxygen, making conclusions based on the results obtained.	• Use word equations. • Describe the reactions of some metals with oxygen. • Carry out an investigation safely. • Compare the reactivity of some metals with oxygen using information obtained from practical work.

LANGUAGE SUPPORT

Learners will use the following words:

reactive: how readily a substance takes part in a reaction

prevent: to stop something happening

inert: chemically inactive

rust: a chemical reaction in which iron combines with oxygen in the presence of water to form iron oxide

collapse: suddenly fall down or give way

Common misconceptions

Misconception	How to identify	How to overcome
Some learners do not realise that rusting involves oxygen; they think it is just water.	Ask directly, and use some of the Workbook and Learner's Book questions.	Relate the reaction to the other metals studied.

Starter ideas

1 Getting started (10 minutes)

Description: Ask learners to think back to what they learned about the properties of metals in Stage 7. Give learners one minute, individually, to write down all the properties they can remember. Learners compare their list with a partner and add any new ones to their own list. Then the pair compare their new lists with another pair and add any more properties. Learners share their final lists with the class.

2 Finding words that begin with … (10 minutes)

Resources: Learner's Book.

Description: Write the word 'oxygen' (or 'oxidation') vertically down the board and challenge learners to find words that start with those letters. Decide whether to allow them to use the Learner's Book and a glossary, or not. You could restrict them to words about reactions or scientific equipment. Take feedback from the class, giving one point for each correct answer and two points if nobody else in the class has that word.

Main teaching ideas

1 Heating metals in air (30 minutes)

Learning intention: To give practical experience of the reactions of metals with oxygen.

Resources: Safety glasses; Bunsen burner; heatproof mat; tongs; small pieces of metal such as magnesium, zinc, iron and copper.

Note: heat sources other than Bunsen burners (such as spirit burners and solid fuel burners) will be difficult to use in this task as they may not get hot enough. Do **not** place metals on a hot plate as this is not safe.

Description: Allow learners to use small pieces of the metals listed above. They should place a small piece in tongs and heat it in the Bunsen burner flame. Learners record their observations.

> **Practical guidance:** Safety glasses must be worn. Watch that learners are holding the tongs at arm's length and not behaving irresponsibly. You will need to remind the learners not to touch the hot metal or to touch the jaws of the tongs when they try to pick up the next piece of the metal as they too will be hot. Remind them not to place the hot metal or tongs on the work surface but to place them on a heatproof mat.

> **Differentiation ideas:** You could restrict the metals used by any groups who may need support with practical work. For learners who need a challenge, ask why they think they have not been given other metals, such as gold or sodium.

> **Assessment ideas:** Use the questions in the Learner's Book and your own observations of their practical skills.

2 Looking at the reactions of very reactive and very unreactive metals (20 minutes)

Learning intention: To impress on learners that metals react differently.

Resources: Potassium, sodium and/or calcium metal; scalpel; tile; surgical gloves; gold and silver objects; a silver object that has oxidised.

Description: Explain to learners that they have seen different levels of reactivity in the metals they tested. Discuss the common properties of metals and then demonstrate cutting one of the soft metals. Draw learners' attention to the shiny surface that is visible as soon as it is cut, and the dull surface after it has reacted with the air. Discuss the reactivity of gold. Ask: *Does it change when it is in the air? Why not?* If possible, show learners an oxidised silver object and talk about the difference between gold and silver jewellery. You could use images if you do not have objects to show them.

> **Practical guidance:** Wear gloves and safety glasses whilst doing the demonstration, in case the metals come into contact with the moisture on your body.

3 Rusting investigation (30 minutes, plus time to see results)

Learning intention: To demonstrate the conditions needed for rusting.

Resources: Four test tubes (two with stoppers); test tube rack; four identical iron nails; calcium chloride; boiled water; oil.

Description: Set the test tubes up as shown in the Learner's Book. You could demonstrate this to the class and then produce a pre-prepared set that you have had set up for a few weeks.

> **Practical guidance:** Showing a set of the test tubes that you have prepared several weeks in advance makes more impact, as learners can see results at once. However, it is still helpful to demonstrate *how* the experiment was set up first, before you show the older one.

> **Assessment ideas:** Use the question in the Learner's Book to assess learners' understanding.

Plenary ideas

1 Summarise the lesson (10 minutes)

Description: Give learners a short time to summarise the lesson, in five bullet points. Then ask them to summarise it in three points. Again, only allow a short time. Then ask learners to summarise the lesson in one bullet point. Finally, ask learners to share their individual summary points with the class.

As learners are writing their summaries, they could consider the question: *How can I get to the main point of the lesson and not get confused with the details?*

> **Assessment ideas:** You could use the Workbook exercise to assess understanding.

2 Just a minute (10 minutes)

Resources: Stopwatch.

Description: Choose one learner to start by talking about a fact or topic they learned or did during today's lesson. They should talk without repeating any word, hesitating or deviating from the subject. When they make any one of those mistakes, stop the clock and move on to the next person. Continue until the fact has been spoken about for one minute. You could use this for discussing an experiment in a lesson, or the whole lesson.

> **Assessment ideas:** You could use the task above to assess the use of scientific vocabulary.

Homework ideas

1 Workbook exercise 8.3

Topic 8.4: Reactions of metals with water

LEARNING PLAN

Learning objectives	Learning intentions	Success criteria
8Cc.03 Describe the reactivity of metals (limited to sodium, potassium, calcium, magnesium, zinc, iron, copper, gold and silver) with oxygen, water and dilute acids (part). 8Cc.06 Understand that some substances are generally unreactive and can be described as inert. 8TWSp.05 Make risk assessments for practical work to identify and control risks. 8TWSc.05 Carry out practical work safely, supported by risk assessments where appropriate.	• Describe the reactions of some metals with water. • Carry out an investigation safely, after carrying out a risk assessment. • Compare how reactive some metals are with water.	• Describe the reactions of some metals with water, including those that do not react. • Carry out an investigation safely. • Compare how reactive some metals are with water.

LANGUAGE SUPPORT

Learners will use the following words:

sandpaper: rough paper used for smoothing or polishing surfaces

reactivity: how reactive something is

Common misconceptions

Misconception	How to identify	How to overcome
There is sometimes confusion between the reaction of magnesium with water and with steam.	It will become apparent if a learner is confused by the way they muddle the reactions.	Be clear about the products that are formed. Write the equations clearly, next to one another, and explain that a hydroxide is formed in the reaction with water.

Starter ideas

1 Getting started (10 minutes)

Description: Ask learners to think back to the reactions of metals with oxygen, which they studied in the previous topic. Ask them to write down the name of the most reactive metal they learned about and try to make a list of the metals in order of how reactive they are. Learners compare their lists with a partner and make one list between them, to share with the class.

2 Equation practice (10 minutes)

Resources: Prepared equations some written incorrectly.

Description: Show the class five equations, with some aspect written incorrectly (for example, not all on one line; wrong metal on the right of the equation compared with the left; acid and salt name not matching; and so on). Ask learners to copy them but write them correctly.

Main teaching ideas

1 Think like a scientist: Reactions of metals with water (30–40 minutes)

Learning intention: To investigate the reactions of some metals with water.

Resources: Learner's Book; test tubes; test tube rack; sandpaper; small pieces of metals such as magnesium, zinc, iron and copper; forceps; water.

Description: You may choose to demonstrate one of the reactions first. Alternatively, learners can follow the instructions in the Learner's Book and carry out the investigation themselves.

If no reaction happens, learners should try again, using hot water.

Circulate and ask questions about the relative reactivity and about learners' detailed observations. Many of the metals do not react with hot water. Very few of these metals will react and the learners may find this dull. Point out that discovering that a reaction does **not** happen is just as important to a scientist as finding that a reaction does happen. It will be difficult to form a reactivity list, but encourage learners to use the information from this investigation and the one in the previous topic to justify what they are able to conclude.

> **Practical guidance:** Learners take a small piece of one of the metals provided and use sandpaper to clean the surface of the metal. Learners may need help with this. They place a small piece of each of the metal samples into test tubes half full of water. Learners record their observations in a table and explain what happened. Stress that learners need to make detailed observations. It may be easiest for them to add a number of metals to their tubes of water at the same time to enable a direct comparison. Learners may need to leave the metal to react for some time. If nothing happens, they could try testing the metals again, this time using hot water. Remind learners that the pieces of metal must be removed before the water is poured down the sink. This will prevent blocking of sinks.

> **Differentiation ideas:** You could ask questions as you circulate; for example: *What would happen if you placed a gold ring in water? Why will you not be given sodium to test in water?* Try to match the complexity of the questions to the learners' progress.

> **Assessment ideas:** Use questions 1–3 from *Think like a scientist: Reactions of metals with water*, to assess learners' understanding and observations.

2 Reactions of sodium and potassium with water (20 minutes)

Learning intention: To observe the reactions of sodium and potassium with water.

Resources: Glass trough filled with water; potassium and sodium metal; scalpel; tile; surgical gloves; long forceps; safety glasses for all the class; safety screens to protect the class and yourself adequately.

Description: Once the safety measures are in place, cut a small piece of sodium and use the long forceps to place it in the trough of water. Do this by leaning around the side of the screen so that you and your face are protected. Learners should record their observations. Then repeat the activity with a small piece of potassium. Learners can then compare the reactions.

Note: Use the sodium first, as the potassium reaction is then more impressive.

> **Practical guidance:** See previous activity. This should **not** be done unless you have practised it.

> **Assessment ideas:** Use questions from the Learner's Book to assess.

3 Reactions of other metals with water and steam (30 minutes)

Learning intention: To observe reactions of other metals with water and steam.

Resources: Safety glasses.

Water reaction: large beaker three-quarters full of water; filter funnel; small piece of calcium; test-tube(s) filled with water.

Steam reaction: boiling tube with stopper and tube; ceramic wool soaked in water; piece of magnesium ribbon; Bunsen burner.

Description: Water reaction: Set up the demonstration as in the Learner's Book. Demonstrate the reaction and allow the gas to displace the water in the test tube until it is full. While you are waiting, identify the word equation for this reaction. Test for hydrogen.

Steam reaction: Set up the demonstration as in the Learner's Book. Heat the magnesium and the ceramic wool intensely. Point out the steam being given off. When you have a sufficiently strong flow of hydrogen, you could ignite it – but be careful where the learners are standing, in relation to the apparatus. While waiting, spend some time discussing the word equation and what is happening in this reaction. Ask: *Where does*

the oxygen to form magnesium oxide come from? What is another way to form magnesium oxide?

> **Differentiation ideas:** A discussion about the difference between the reaction of magnesium in water (which is a very slow reaction but produces magnesium hydroxide and hydrogen) and the reaction with steam (that produces magnesium oxide and hydrogen) should stretch some of the more confident learners. This may be an appropriate time to remind learners about the difference between steam and water vapour.

> **Assessment ideas:** Use the questions in the Learner's Book to assess and/or use questioning about the word equations and the magnesium reactions with water and steam, as above.

Plenary ideas

1 Higher or lower? (10 minutes)

Resources: Cards with the names of the metals: sodium, potassium, calcium, magnesium, zinc, iron, copper, gold and silver.

Description: Choose one card and ask learners if the metal is more reactive or less reactive than the next card you choose. Learners could put their thumbs up for more reactive and thumbs down for less reactive. You could ask do this based on the reactions in water and/or the reactions with oxygen.

> **Assessment ideas:** Use the plenary to assess understanding. You could extend this activity by asking learners to make a poster or list to show the metals in order, from most reactive to least reactive. If you provide sets of cards that can be moved around as learners get more information, they can modify their lists.

2 In the hot seat (10 minutes)

Resources: Prepared questions.

Description: Ask a confident learner to take the hot seat. It is advisable to set this up with the learner before the lesson. The hot seat can be at the front of the class or in the learner's normal place. Ask the learner a series of five or six questions. The learner may answer correctly or incorrectly Explain to the class that some answers may be incorrect (having agreed this with the volunteer learner beforehand). When the hot-seat learner answers each question, the rest of the class write down whether the answer is correct. If it is incorrect, they give the correct answer. Learners swap answer papers with a partner.

Then carry out whole-class marking and take feedback.

> **Assessment ideas:** Use the questions as outlined in the description.

Homework ideas

1   Workbook exercise 8.4

Topic 8.5: Reactions of metals with dilute acids

LEARNING PLAN

Learning objectives	Learning intentions	Success criteria
8Cc.03 Describe the reactivity of metals (limited to sodium, potassium, calcium, magnesium, zinc, iron, copper, gold and silver) with oxygen, water and dilute acids (part). **8TWSp.04** Plan a range of investigations of different types, while considering variables appropriately, and recognise that not all investigations can be fair tests. **8TWSp.05** Make risk assessments for practical work to identify and control risks. **8TWSc.02** Decide what equipment is required to carry out an investigation or experiment and use it appropriately. **8TWSc.05** Carry out practical work safely, supported by risk assessments where appropriate. **8TWSa.02** Describe trends and patterns in results, including identifying any anomalous results. **8TWSa.03** Make conclusions by interpreting results and explain the limitations of the conclusions. **8TWSa.04** Evaluate experiments and investigations, and suggest improvements, explaining any proposed changes. **8TSWa.05** Present and interpret observations and measurements appropriately.	• Investigate reactions of metals with dilute acids. • Plan and carry out an investigation safely, using a risk assessment, choosing appropriate equipment correctly and considering the variables. • Suggest improvements to be made to the investigation. • Present observations appropriately. • Form conclusions based on the results of the investigation, recognising the limitations of the practical work. • Describe the trends in the results.	• Describe the reactions of some metals with dilute acid. • Plan and carry out an investigation safely, using a risk assessment, choosing appropriate equipment correctly and considering the variables. • Suggest improvements to be made to the investigation. • Present observations appropriately. • Form conclusions based on the results of the investigation, recognising the limitations of the practical work. • Describe the trends in the results. • Compare how reactive some metals are with dilute acid.

Learners will use the following words:

salt: a compound formed when a metal reacts with an acid for example magnesium chloride

reagents: chemicals that are used in a reaction

Common misconceptions

Misconception	How to identify	How to overcome
Some learners may require more practice with word equations.	Learners produce inaccurate or incomplete equations when asked.	Individual help and more examples of word equations for learners to complete.

Starter ideas

1 Getting started (10 minutes)

Description: Give learners 2 minutes to write down as many of these word equations as they can. The word equations for the reactions between: oxygen and sodium; oxygen and magnesium; oxygen and iron; water and potassium; water and calcium; magnesium and steam.

Stop them after 2 minutes. Learners swap papers with a partner and check each other's work. Ask them to be prepared to share answers with the class.

2 Spelling the names of the common acids (10 minutes)

Description: Call out the names of the common acids and common salts and ask learners to write them down. Learners swap papers with a partner and correct each other's spelling.

Main teaching ideas

1 Planning an investigation (30–40 minutes)

Learning intention: To practise planning an investigation.

Resources: Learner's Book.

Description: Talk through the investigation idea and the diagrams in the Learner's Book. Split the class into groups of two or three and point out the questions they need to consider. Allow the groups time to discuss the questions before they write

a plan. You could bring the class back together and discuss the ideas, as a class, before the groups write up their plans. Circulate while they are discussing and writing, asking appropriate questions to cover points they may have missed or to help them to make the point more clearly. Learners often know what they mean to say, but fail to write it clearly.

> **Differentiation ideas:** You could provide apparatus for some groups to make it a little easier to make decisions. Take care with questioning; you could give more support to learners who need this, with questions such as: *Would that work? Is that a fair test? How can you be sure that is accurate?*

> **Assessment ideas:** You could use learners' write-ups as a means to assess the plans.

2 Carrying out the investigation (30 minutes)

Learning intention: To carry out the investigation.

Resources: Safety glasses; test tubes; test tube rack; measuring cylinders; small pieces of metal (such as magnesium, iron, copper, zinc and iron); dilute acid (you could provide a range of different acids in a variety of concentrations, no stronger than $1 \, \text{mol/dm}^3$, depending on what the learners have chosen); forceps; top pan balance.

Description: Do not allow the groups to carry out the investigation until you have seen and approved their plans. You could decide to provide a plan that all groups can use. Circulate while they are setting up the practical to ensure high safety standards.

If learners have decided to use the same mass of metal in their investigation, they will need a top pan balance. You may choose to provide prepared similar-sized samples of metal rather than asking learners to find the mass.

Learners will need to place the *same* volume of the *same* concentration of the *same* type of acid into the test tubes or beakers. They then need to add the samples of metal and observe the reactions. Learners should record their observations. The best method may be to add a number of metals to their tubes of acid at the same time, to enable direct comparison. The learners should then use their results to make a reactivity list.

> **Practical guidance:** Remind learners that the pieces of metal must be removed before the water is poured down the sink. This will prevent blocking of sinks.

> **Differentiation ideas:** As you circulate, you will need to help those who find the organisation of practical work difficult, and you can ask questions to stretch those who need a challenge.

> **Assessment ideas:** Use the practical to assess practical skills. Tell the class you will be looking for good organisation and safe working, as well as assessing the results they obtain. You could do this by using a modified template, for self- or peer review.

3 A reactivity order (15 minutes)

Learning intention: To produce a list showing the order of reactivity of the metals used.

Resources: Sticky notes; poster materials.

Description: Ask learners to write the name of each of the metals they used on a sticky note and to stick these on to a pre-drafted table, in the order of their reactivity (most reactive at the top), based on the information from the investigation.

Ask learners to compare their order with other groups. Are they the same or similar?

Use the class results to make an order on which you all agree.

Ask: *Does this order tie in with the results from the investigations of the reactions of metals with oxygen and water?* This should provide some discussion.

Now ask learners to write sticky notes for the metals they could not use (sodium, gold, silver, calcium and potassium) and fit those into the list.

When they are satisfied with the order, they should make a poster to show their list, and illustrate it with diagrams to show the various reactions with oxygen, water and/or dilute acids.

> **Practical guidance:** Keep groups small (two to three learners per group).

> **Differentiation ideas:** Some groups may require more help, both with the order and the poster.

> **Assessment ideas:** You could assess the posters for creativity as well as accuracy.

Plenary ideas

1 Quick-fire round (10 minutes)

Resources: Prepared questions.

Description: Ask learners to write five questions about the topic of the lesson. They swap questions with a partner and answer each other's questions. Learners then swap back and mark each other's answers. Share some of the questions and answers with the whole class.

> **Assessment ideas:** You could use questions and answers to assess what the learners have taken from the lesson.

2 Five fingers (10 minutes)

Description: Each learner draws around their hand on a scrap of paper or in their book and writes answers to these questions in the appropriate place on each finger.

- Thumb – What have you learned? What do you understand?
- Index finger – What skills have you used today?
- Middle finger – Which skills did you find difficult today?
- Ring finger – Who did you help today?
- Little finger – What will you make sure that you remember from today's lesson?

You will find it useful to collect these and use them to help decide what you need to concentrate on in the next lesson.

This type of plenary is a way of structuring learners' reflection time. It allows the less confident learners to celebrate what they have done well and encourages the more confident learners to think about the next steps in learning.

> **Assessment ideas:** You could use the workbook exercises and the end of topic progress test.

Homework ideas

1   Workbook exercises 8.5A–C

Topic worksheets

Worksheets 8.5A–C, Word equation practice

PROJECT GUIDANCE

Working with chemicals safely

This project addresses the following learning objectives:

8SIC.03 Evaluate issues which involve and/or require scientific understanding.

Organise the learners into groups of two or three. This works best because they all have to contribute something and no one can opt out.

Open the session with a discussion about all the decisions learners had to make today. Ask them to do the same and share their decisions with the class. Make the point that learners accomplish many of the risk assessments they make – about crossing the road, for example – without giving it a lot of thought. If, however, they don't pay attention, the results can be very bad. It's the same in the laboratory. These things become part of what learners do as a matter of course, but if they don't pay attention, the results can be very serious.

The picture in the Learner's Book provides a focus about safety in the laboratory. Most learners enjoy looking for the detail in the pictures and in spotting more items than the next person. Set a time limit for the identification of hazardous items and then ask the groups to share what they have found with the whole class. You could award points for each correct item found and extra points for correct items that no one else found.

The main point of the task is to provide help and guidance for learners who are just starting the course. Give credit for originality and a good strong message. You could do a peer assessment, based on one of the peer assessment templates suitably modified for each group, and devise a scoring system so the group with the best project wins a prize. All the items could be used as displays in laboratories or learners' books. This is an opportunity for creativity and a chance for learners to use all the good laboratory practice they have picked up over the whole course.

>9 Magnetism

Unit plan

Topic	Learning hours	Learning content	Resources
9.1 Magnetic fields	2-3	What is meant by a magnetic field; drawing the magnetic fields that surround magnets and understanding how magnetic fields interact	**Learner's Book:** Questions 1–4 Activity: Showing a magnetic field pattern Think like a scientist: Detecting a magnetic field **Workbook:** Exercise 9.1A, Magnetic field patterns Exercise 9.1B, Magnetic fields Exercise 9.1C, Interaction of magnetic fields **Teacher's Resource:** Worksheet 9.1, Magnetic fields
9.2 The Earth as a giant magnet	2-3	The Earth has a magnetic field; the core of the Earth acts as a magnet	**Learner's Book:** Questions 1–5 Think like a scientist: Detecting the Earth's magnetic field **Workbook:** Exercises 9.2A, The Earth's magnetic field Exercise 9.2B, Direction of the Earth's magnetic field Exercise 9.2C, The strength of the Earth's magnetic field **Teacher's Resource:** Worksheet 9.2, Earth's magnetic field
9.3 Electromagnets	2-3	How to make an electromagnet; some applications of electromagnets	**Learner's Book:** Questions 1–5 Activity: Making an electromagnet **Workbook:** Exercises 9.3A–C, Electromagnets **Teacher's Resource:** Worksheet 9.3, Making electromagnets

Topic	Learning hours	Learning content	Resources
9.4 Investigating electromagnets	3-4	What affects the strength of an electromagnet; how these variables affect the strength of an electromagnet	**Learner's Book:** Questions 1–4 Think like a scientist: Investigating electromagnet strength **Workbook:** Exercises 9.4A–C, Strength of electromagnets **Teacher's Resource:** Worksheet 9.4, Investigating electromagnets Template 9.4A: Results table and graph grid for *Think like a scientist: Investigating electromagnet strength, Part 1* Template 9.4B: Results table and graph grid for *Think like a scientist: Investigating electromagnet strength, Part 2* Template 9.4C: Results table and graph grid for *Think like a scientist: Investigating electromagnet strength, Part 3*
Cross-unit resources			**Learner's Book:** Check your Progress **Project:** Investigating magnetism **Teacher's Resource:** **Language development worksheets** 9.1 Magnetism vocabulary 9.2 Magnetism crossword 9.3 Correcting the passage

BACKGROUND KNOWLEDGE

Learners will recall facts about magnets, and the forces between magnets when opposite poles or like poles are brought together. The terms 'north', 'south', 'attract' and 'repel' should already be familiar. Learners may also be aware of different shapes of magnet, such as bar magnets and horseshoe magnets. Learners may also know that a magnetic compass is a piece of equipment that points towards geographic north and can be used for navigation.

Learners should be able to draw circuit diagrams for series circuits and be familiar with the circuit symbols for a cell, a switch and an ammeter. Learners should recall that adding more cells into a series circuit, while other variables remain the same, would increase the current in that circuit. Learners should also recall examples of magnetic materials, including iron and steel, and some may also recall that nickel and cobalt are magnetic. The principle of planning an investigation, considering variables and carrying out a fair test are required skills.

TEACHING SKILLS FOCUS

Lesson starters 3

An effective lesson starter sets the mood for the lesson and, as well as influencing learning can also influence behaviour and therefore be a powerful tool for classroom management. For example, suppose a teacher wishes to begin a lesson by assessing learners' prior learning about magnets. There are many ways to go about this, but consider two approaches.

1   The desks are clear of books and equipment when learners arrive. You begin by saying: *You are going to have a test before we start this topic.*

2   Learners arrive to find coloured cards and some objects on the desk. You begin by saying: *We are going to play a game.*

Approach 1 is direct and functional, letting learners know exactly what is going to happen. However, it is unlikely to interest learners or motivate them to enjoy the lesson. By using the word 'you', you can imply a dividing line between yourself and the learners. Learners' stress levels are likely to rise, and this can lead to challenging behaviour. The test itself is likely to be done in silence, giving the teacher a sense of control.

Approach 2 is visually stimulating as there are interesting objects already set out. The idea of playing a game is more likely to motivate learners to engage and enjoy the activity. Research shows that we learn best when we are happy and our stress levels are low. You use the word 'we', which is inclusive and friendly. During the game, learners may be moving around the room and talking but, if they are engaged with the task, this should be a productive, peer learning experience. The game is also likely to generate immediate assessment information without the need for marking written tests.

The game in approach 2 can assess the same learning outcomes as the test, but may require a little more advance preparation. You must ask yourself whether this extra preparation is a worthwhile exchange for a positive, engaging, friendly and motivating learning environment.

You should also try the same starter activity with two different classes. Some activities are more effective with certain learner groups. Ask yourself:

*   *Was the activity more successful with group X than group Y and if so, why?*

*   *How could the activity be modified for group Y to make it equally as successful?*

*   *How can this aspect of differentiation be transferred to main lesson activities for these groups?*

If you have regular department – or whole school – teacher meetings, you could suggest that the discussion of starter activities is put on the agenda. All teachers can then volunteer to share ideas. This is especially interesting across different subjects, as some aspects of all activities are transferrable. A successful starter used in a languages lesson will have strategies that are also useful in science.

Topic 9.1: Magnetic fields

LEARNING PLAN

Learning objectives	Learning intentions	Success criteria
8Pe.01 Describe a magnetic field, and understand that it surrounds a magnet and exerts a force on other magnetic fields. **8TWSm.03** Use symbols and formulae to represent scientific ideas. **8TWSc.01** Sort, group and classify phenomena, objects, materials and organisms through testing, observation, using secondary information, and making and using keys. **8TWSc.02** Decide what equipment is required to carry out an investigation or experiment and use it appropriately. **8TWSc.07** Collect and record sufficient observations and/or measurements in an appropriate form. **8TWSa.02** Describe trends and patterns in results, including identifying any anomalous results. **8TWSa.03** Make conclusions by interpreting results and explain the limitations of the conclusions. **8TWSa.04** Evaluate experiments and investigations, and suggest improvements, explaining any proposed changes.	• Describe a magnetic field. • Understand that magnetic fields surround magnets. • Understand how magnetic fields interact.	• Draw a magnetic field pattern around a magnet. • State the direction of magnetic field lines. • Draw the magnetic field patterns between poles of different magnets.

LANGUAGE SUPPORT

Learners will use the following words:

magnet: an object that has been permanently magnetised

magnetic: a material that will be attracted to a magnet

magnetic field: the area around a magnet where the effect of the magnet can be detected

compass: a magnetic compass contains a magnetised needle that is free to turn, so the needle will point in the direction of magnetic field lines

magnetic field lines: the lines that make up the pattern of a magnetic field; the lines point from north to south around the outside of a magnet

like poles: two magnetic poles that are the same: north and north, or south and south

Common misconceptions

Misconception	How to identify	How to overcome
The north pole of a bar magnet is stronger than the south pole.	After teaching about magnetic field patterns, show learners a bar magnet and ask how the strength of the magnet compares at both poles.	Allow learners to compare the number of objects, such as paperclips, that can be lifted by each pole of the same magnet.
Commonly used metals such as copper and aluminium are magnetic, or that all metals are magnetic.	Provide learners with a list of metals that they will have heard of. Ask: *Which are magnetic?*	Allow learners to investigate different metals with a bar magnet and discover that some are non-magnetic.

Starter ideas

1 Getting started (5 minutes)

Description: Learners may recall fridge magnets, magnets holding cupboard doors closed, magnets keeping paperclips or pins together, the magnetic compass and similar uses.

2 Magnet game (5–10 minutes)

Resources: For each learner: a red card and a blue card.

Description: The red card represents a north pole and the blue card represents a south pole. Learners hold one card in each hand and role play as bar magnets, acting out the forces that would occur when one of their poles approaches someone else's pole.

Main teaching ideas

1 Activity: Showing a magnetic field pattern (10–20 minutes, depending on structure of activity)

Learning intention: To show the pattern of a magnetic field.

Resources: See the Learner's Book. More than one type of magnet is ideal, for example a bar magnet and a horseshoe magnet.

Description: See the Learner's Book.

> **Differentiation ideas:** Learners who need more support can be asked: **a** how the pattern resembles the diagram of the magnetic field in the Learner's Book, and **b** where the greatest numbers of iron filings are concentrated.

If the magnet is quite strong, there may be a clear area a few centimetres away from each pole. If this does not appear, it can be created by gently tapping the paper. Learners who need more challenge could be asked what causes this. (If the magnet is strong,

iron filings are pulled toward the poles. When the force of attraction is greater than the friction between the iron filings and the paper, then the iron filings will move. Tapping the paper makes the iron filings bounce a little, which lowers the friction between them and the paper.)

> **Assessment ideas:** Ask learners questions about the field pattern and how it resembles what they have drawn or seen in the Learner's Book. Ask them to reach a conclusion about the relative strength of the two poles of the same magnet.

2 Think like a scientist: Detecting a magnetic field (20–30 minutes, to include recording results)

Learning intention: To detect and investigate magnetic fields.

Resources: See the Learner's Book.

Description: See the Learner's Book.

> **Practical guidance:** Advise learners to take care not to move the ruler during the investigation. If they find this difficult, then the magnet and the ruler can be held in position using adhesive tape. Another, marked, magnet or a magnetic compass can be used, remembering that a compass points from north to south. The magnet could also be suspended and allowed to align with the Earth's magnetic field, remembering that there is a magnetic south close to the Earth's geographic north pole.

> **Differentiation ideas:** Questions 4 and 5 in *Think like a scientist: Detecting a magnetic field* will differentiate by outcome. Some learners may need support with these questions, especially question 5, but learners needing more challenge should be able to do these without support.

> **Assessment ideas:** Ask learners about their methods, such as fair testing, during the investigation. Ask learners to write up or make a presentation of their work.

3 Drawing magnetic fields (10 minutes)

Learning intention: To help learners draw magnetic field patterns correctly.

Resources: Paper; ruler; pencil.

Description: Some learners have difficulty drawing curved lines and may draw sketchy, fuzzy lines that lack accuracy. Allow learners to use a ruler to draw a bar magnet, or provide a template for them to draw around. Ensure learners have a smooth surface to work on, so the pencil can move smoothly. Advise learners to draw curved lines by placing the pencil onto the paper at the start of the line and not lifting the pencil until the line is complete. Turn the paper so the hand can pivot around the wrist as natural 'compasses'. That means only drawing curves that are inverted U-shapes or C-shapes (mirror image C-shapes if learners are left-handed).

> **Differentiation ideas:** Allow learners who need more support drawing the curved lines to trace magnetic field patterns from a good-quality template. They could then develop this by placing guidance dots around the magnet. The dots can then be joined with a curved line.

Encourage learners who need more challenge to check their magnetic field lines are symmetrical.

> **Assessment ideas:** Lines in magnetic field patterns should be unbroken and should touch the edge of the magnet. There should be an arrowhead on every line, pointing from north to south. Learners can use these criteria to assess each other's drawings.

Plenary ideas

1 Describing a magnetic field (3–5 minutes)

Description: Learners are asked to volunteer to describe to the class, in words, the appearance of a magnetic field pattern. Add challenge by making a certain word, or words taboo (they cannot be used in the description).

> **Assessment ideas:** After listening to the description, ask learners to volunteer to give feedback on the basis of what was good about the description and what could be even better.

2 Five bullet points (2–3 minutes)

Resources: Paper; pens

Description: Ask learners to summarise the key facts about magnetic fields in five bullet points.

> **Assessment ideas:** Learners could complete this activity in their notebooks, for assessment at the same time as the next homework, or as exit slips.

Homework ideas

1   Learner's Book questions

2   Workbook exercises 9.1A–C

3   Worksheet 9.1

Topic worksheets

Worksheet 9.1, Magnetic fields

Topic 9.2: The Earth as a giant magnet

LEARNING PLAN

Learning objectives	Learning intentions	Success criteria
8ESp.01 Know that the reason the Earth has a magnetic field is that the core acts as a magnet.	• Learn that the Earth has a magnetic field and that the core of the Earth acts as a magnet.	• Draw the magnetic field pattern around the Earth. • Recall the differences between the Earth's magnetic poles and the geographic poles.

CONTINUED

Learning objectives	Learning intentions	Success criteria
8TWSm.01 Describe what an analogy is and how it can be used as a model.		• Recall that the core of the Earth is the source of the magnetic field.
8TWSm.02 Use an existing analogy for a purpose.		
8TWSc.01 Sort, group and classify phenomena, objects, materials and organisms through testing, observation, using secondary information, and making and using keys.		
8TWSc.05 Carry out practical work safely, supported by risk assessments where appropriate.		
8TWSc.07 Collect and record sufficient observations and/or measurements in an appropriate form.		
8TWSa.02 Describe trends and patterns in results, including identifying any anomalous results.		
8TWSa.04 Evaluate experiments and investigations, and suggest improvements, explaining any proposed changes.		

LANGUAGE SUPPORT

Learners will use the following words:

naturally occurring: present without human activity

geographic north pole: one of the points where the Earth's axis of rotation meets the Earth's surface; conventionally shown toward the top of maps

magnetic north: a point near the geographic north of the Earth toward which the needle of a magnetic compass points; this pole is actually a south magnetic pole

navigate: plan the route of a journey

magnetised: a magnetic material that has been temporarily or permanently turned into a magnet is said to be magnetised

Common misconceptions

Misconception	How to identify	How to overcome
The Earth's magnetic field at the Earth's surface is very strong.	Question 1 of Workbook exercise 9.2C. Alternatively, ask: *Which is stronger: the magnetic field from the Earth or the magnetic field 1 cm from the end of a bar magnet?*	Hang a paperclip or iron nail that is **not** magnetised from a piece of string. Bring a bar magnet close so the suspended object moves. Remove the bar magnet and ask why the object is not visibly pulled by the Earth's magnetic field.

Starter ideas

1 Getting started (5 minutes)

Resources: Desktop globe or map of the world (optional, but helpful).

Description: Learners may not immediately associate magnetism with the Earth. It is sufficient at this stage that they can describe, or point out on a globe, the north and south poles.

2 Looking at a compass (5 minutes)

Resources: Magnetic compass

Description: Show learners the compass and ask whether they know what it is. Demonstrate that wherever the compass is placed around the room, it still points in the same direction. Ensure that there are no sources of magnetism, or large magnetic objects close by. Ask: *What does it do? What is it used for?* Then bring a magnet brought close to the compass to show that it responds to a magnetic field. Ask: *Where is the magnetic field in the room coming from?*

Main teaching ideas

1 Think like a scientist: Detecting the Earth's magnetic field, part 1 (10–20 minutes)

Learning intention: To show the behaviour of a bar magnet in the Earth's magnetic field.

Resources: See the Learner's Book.

Description: See the Learner's Book.

> Practical guidance: Knowing which direction is north would be useful and helpful.

> Differentiation ideas: Learners who need more support may need prompting about what happens between like poles and what happens between

opposite poles, before being able to reach the conclusion that the north of a bar magnet cannot be attracted to another north pole.

Ask learners who need more challenge: *What variables affect the speed at which the bar magnet lines up in its final direction?* (Mass of the magnet – the lower the mass, the faster it will turn; stiffness of the string – the stiffer the string, the more slowly it will turn; the strength of the Earth's magnetic field – the stronger the field, the faster it will turn.)

Depending on your geographic location, it may be possible to notice the bar magnet dipping slightly from horizontal. Learners could be shown a diagram of how the Earth's magnetic field lines are angled to the surface to explain this.

> Assessment ideas: Ask learners: *What piece of navigation equipment works on this principle?* Questions in the activity in the Learner's Book also provide assessment.

2 Think like a scientist: Detecting the Earth's magnetic field, part 2 (20 minutes)

Learning intention: To make a magnetic compass.

Resources: See the Learner's Book.

Description: See the Learner's Book.

> Practical guidance: Confirm that the object to be magnetised has not been previously magnetised. Do this by bringing the object to a magnetic compass. Only if the object is magnetised will it repel one end of the compass needle. The unmagnetised object can be shown floating, with no directional preference, before the activity.

> **Differentiation ideas:** Ask learners: *What changes would need to be made to this design to make it more practical for navigation?* This question will differentiate by outcome.

> **Assessment ideas:** Ask learners questions about the words 'magnetic' and 'magnetised'. Questions in the activity in the Learner's Book also provide assessment.

3 Why does the Earth have a magnetic field? (5–10 minutes)

Learning intention: To think about theories of what causes the Earth's magnetic field.

Description: Learners need to know that the core of the Earth causes the magnetic field. What property of the core, however, makes it generate this field? Explain that scientists are still not completely sure and are still investigating and collecting evidence. It is a good idea, on occasions such as this, to remind learners that scientists do not have all the answers to how things work, but this is the goal of science.

Present theories suggest that the rotation of the Earth causes forces inside the core. These forces make the molten iron flow around in curved paths. The movement of electrons in the iron is thought to generate the magnetic field.

Scientists know that the direction of the Earth's magnetic field has reversed 183 times in the last 85 million years. They know this from looking at the direction of magnetic particles in rocks that have formed over this time period. Scientists think it takes about 7000 years for it to reverse completely.

> **Differentiation ideas:** Learners who need more challenge could be told the distance from the north to south poles and, using the time of 7000 years, calculate the speed at which each pole would need to move in a complete reversal. (Using $speed = \dfrac{distance}{time}$, learners can give their answer in any unit – conversion of units is not required in this activity.)

Learners who need more support can do the same activity but with support at each step in the working.

> **Assessment ideas:** Ask learners what the movement of electrons in a metal is called (flow of current).

Plenary ideas

1 One minute challenge (1 minutes)

Resources: Small pieces of paper, approximately 10 cm by 5 cm.

Description: Learners write their names and then have 1 minute to write as many key words associated with this lesson's topic as possible.

> **Assessment ideas:** Learners can compare their word lists or hand them in for you to assess.

2 How to remember (5–10 minutes)

Description: Learners choose one thing that they will find easy to remember from the topic. They then choose one thing that they may find difficult to remember. Ask: *What is the difference? How can the more difficult one be made easier to remember?*

> **Assessment ideas:** Learners can work in pairs and discuss their ideas.

Homework ideas

1   Learner's Book questions
2   Workbook exercises 9.2A–C
3   Worksheet 9.2

Topic worksheets

Worksheet 9.2, Earth's magnetic field

Topic 9.3: Electromagnets

LEARNING PLAN

Learning objectives	Learning intentions	Success criteria
8Pe.02 Describe how to make an electromagnet and know that electromagnets have many applications. **8TWSm.03** Use symbols and formulae to represent scientific ideas.	• Make an electromagnet and recall some applications of electromagnets.	• Describe how to make an electromagnet. • Draw a circuit diagram for an electromagnet. • Recall some applications of electromagnets.

LANGUAGE SUPPORT

Learners will use the following words:

permanent magnets: magnets that cannot be switched on and off and that do not require electricity to operate; the magnetic field around them is constant

electromagnet: type of temporary magnet that operates when current flows so the magnetism can be switched on and off

coil: wire wrapped around repeatedly in the shape of a cylinder

core: material around which the coil of an electromagnet is wound

Starter ideas

1 Getting started (5 minutes)

Learning intention: To allow learners to think about applications of electromagnets.

Description: Learners work in pairs or small groups to discuss uses for a magnet that can be switched on and off. These may include lifting magnetic objects and dropping them again.

2 Lifting scrap metal (5–10 minutes, depending on the structure of the activity)

Learning intention: To show learners the effect of a magnet that can be switched on and off.

Resources: Search the internet for a video of an electromagnet lifting scrap metal.

Description: Learners watch the video, then discuss what is happening. Ask: *What types of metals are lifted? How are they being dropped again? What process is being carried out?*

Main teaching ideas

1 Activity: Making an electromagnet (20 minutes)

Learning intention: To allow learners to make their own electromagnet.

Resources: See the Learner's Book.

Description: See the Learner's Book.

> **Practical guidance:** The wire provided to make the coil should be long enough so that the cell is not short-circuited. A cell, **not** a power supply, should be used, as learners will be tempted to change the voltage. This is part of the next topic.

Safety: Only dry cells (non-rechargeable) should be used. Rechargeable cells should **not** be used as these can deliver large currents when the resistance in the circuit is small. There is a risk of overheating and even explosion.

> **Differentiation ideas:** Questions 1–3 in *Activity: Making an electromagnet* will differentiate by outcome.

> **Assessment ideas:** Learners can be given a selection of circuit diagrams for an electromagnet, some of which are incorrect, and asked to select the correct one(s).

2 Controlling fire doors (10–20 minutes, depending on the structure of the activity)

Learning intention: To explore one application of electromagnets.

Resources: Search the internet for a video showing a fire door controlled by an electromagnet.

Description: Learners watch the video, more than once if needed, then answer and discuss questions.

> **Differentiation ideas:** Ask questions in different ways. For example, for learners who need more support: *What material must the plate on the door be made from, so it sticks to the electromagnet?* For learners who need more challenge: *What else is needed, apart from the electromagnet and current, to make this work?*

> **Assessment ideas:** Questions such as those suggested above in *Differentiation ideas*.

3 Drawing a coil (10 minutes)

Learning intention: To show learners how to draw a coil around a core.

Resources: Ruler and pencil.

Description: Learners often find it difficult to draw a coil around a core. They frequently draw a complete helical shape around a narrow rectangle that then looks as if the core is transparent.

Start by drawing the core, either as the outline of a nail or just a rectangle. It is easier to begin if the long axis of the shape is horizontal. Draw two vertical lines for the wires at either end of the core. These should just touch the core.

Next, start at one side and draw a line meeting one of the wires, crossing the core at a slight angle to vertical.

Now repeat these angled lines along the rectangle, so the last one lines up with – but doesn't touch – the other vertical line.

Finally, add labels to the coil and the core.

> **Differentiation ideas:** Learners who are better at drawing can make their angled lines slightly curved, to make the pattern look more like a coil. However, remind them that a science diagram is not the same as a realistic picture.

Give learners who need more support a good-quality exemplar, followed by a template of a core. They can then copy the coil and draw this on the template to get practice.

> **Assessment ideas:** Learners can practise drawing this, with the core in both the horizontal and vertical positions.

Plenary ideas

1 What equipment is needed? (3–5 minutes)

Resources: Prepared list of equipment, some of which is needed to make an electromagnet

Description: Learners choose, from the list, the essential components for making an electromagnet. If the list includes a switch, then learners could discuss whether this is essential or optional.

> **Assessment ideas:** From looking at the lists, it should be clear whether learners have understood the topic.

2 Mistake in the diagram (5–10 minutes)

Resources: Paper and pencil.

Description: Learners work in pairs. Each learner draws a diagram of an electromagnet but with one deliberate mistake. Learners swap diagrams and identify each other's mistake.

> **Assessment ideas:** The activity is based on peer assessment.

Homework ideas

1 Learner's Book questions

2 Workbook exercises 9.3A–C

3 Worksheet 9.3

Topic worksheets

Worksheet 9.3, Making electromagnets

Topic 9.4: Investigating electromagnets

LEARNING PLAN

Learning objectives	Learning intentions	Success criteria
8Pe.03 Investigate factors that change the strength of an electromagnet.	• Investigate which factors (or variables) affect the strength of an electromagnet and investigate how these variables affect the strength of an electromagnet.	• State the factors that affect the strength of an electromagnet.
8TWSm.03 Use symbols and formulae to represent scientific ideas.		• Describe what changes would be made to each of these factors to make the electromagnet stronger or weaker.
8TWSp.03 Make predictions of likely outcomes for a scientific enquiry based on scientific knowledge and understanding.		
8TWSp.04 Plan a range of investigations of different types, while considering variables appropriately, and recognise that not all investigations can be fair tests.		
8TWSp.05 Make risk assessments for practical work to identify and control risks.		
8TWSc.01 Sort, group and classify phenomena, objects, materials and organisms through testing, observation, using secondary information, and making and using keys.		
8TWSc.02 Decide what equipment is required to carry out an investigation or experiment and use it appropriately.		
8TWSc.03 Evaluate whether measurements and observations have been repeated sufficiently to be reliable.		

Learning objectives	Learning intentions	Success criteria
8TWSc.04 Take appropriately accurate and precise measurements, explaining why accuracy and precision are important.		
8TWSc.05 Carry out practical work safely, supported by risk assessments where appropriate.		
8TWSc.07 Collect and record sufficient observations and/or measurements in an appropriate form.		
8TWSa.01 Describe the accuracy of predictions, based on results, and suggest why they were or were not accurate.		
8TWSa.02 Describe trends and patterns in results, including identifying any anomalous results.		
8TWSa.03 Make conclusions by interpreting results and explain the limitations of the conclusions.		
8TWSa.04 Evaluate experiments and investigations, and suggest improvements, explaining any proposed changes.		
8TSWa.05 Present and interpret observations and measurements appropriately.		

LANGUAGE SUPPORT

Learners will use the following words:

factors: in science, another word for variables

soft iron: iron that is easily magnetised and easily demagnetised

demagnetised: a material that has lost its magnetism is said to be demagnetised; will no longer attract magnetic objects

Common misconceptions

Misconception	How to identify	How to overcome
Increasing the length of the core, while keeping all other factors constant, will increase the strength of the electromagnet.	Ask learners to describe the factors that affect the strength of an electromagnet.	Allow learners to make a core from a longer nail or another object such as the vertical support unscrewed from a clamp stand, and to test the strength of this in comparison with the shorter one. Ensure all other variables remain the same.

Starter ideas

1 Getting started (5 minutes)

Description: If necessary, prompt learners to think about strength in this activity. They should realise that a stronger electromagnet is required for sorting scrap metal than the electromagnet used in the circuit that makes a toaster 'pop up'. There is less of a difference in strength between the electromagnets in the fire door application and the bell, although the fire door one is stronger.

2 Differences in electromagnets (5–10 minutes)

Resources: Search online for a video of an electromagnet lifting scrap metal, or other powerful electromagnet.

Description: Ask learners to recall the electromagnet they made in Topic 9.3. Ask them to describe similarities and differences between their electromagnets and the one in the video. This allows learners to think about different strengths of electromagnets.

Main teaching ideas

1 Think like a scientist: *Investigating electromagnet strength, Part 1* (20+ minutes)

Learning intention: To investigate the effect of changing the number of turns in the coil on the electromagnet strength.

Resources: See the Learner's Book.

The ammeter and extra cells are not required for this part of the investigation.

Description: See the Learner's Book. *Template 9.4A: Results table and graph grid* for *Think like a scientist:*

Investigating electromagnet strength, Part 1 is available for learners who could benefit from using it.

> **Differentiation ideas:** Prompt learners who need more support to construct their own sentences describing the trends in the results.

Ask learners who need more challenge to predict whether the same number of coils packed close together or further apart will affect the strength. Learners could also look for a numerical trend: *When the number of turns doubles, does the number of paperclips attracted also double?*

> **Assessment ideas:** Observe learners while they are carrying out the investigation to assess their approach to the task. Ask questions on any aspect of their procedure, such as: *Show me how you got this result. Do you think you need to repeat this?*

2 Think like a scientist: *Investigating electromagnet strength, Part 2* (15+ minutes)

Learning intention: To investigate the effect of changing the material in the core, on the electromagnet strength.

Resources: See the Learner's Book.

The ammeter and extra cells are not required for this part of the investigation.

Various metals and non-metals should be included, in addition to the iron nail or core used in part 1. For example, copper nails, stainless steel nails, galvanised nails, and similar sized pieces of wood and plastic.

Description: See the Learner's Book. Template 9.4B: Results table and graph grid for *Think like a scientist: Investigating electromagnet strength, Part 2* is available for learners who could benefit from using it.

> **Differentiation ideas:** Remind learners who need more support of the difference between magnetic and magnetised.

Ask learners who need more challenge to predict the results in advance, using their knowledge of magnetic and non-magnetic materials. *Are all metals magnetic? Can all magnetic materials be magnetised equally?*

> **Assessment ideas:** Observe learners while they are carrying out the investigation, to assess their approach to the task. Ask questions on any aspect of their procedure: *Show me how you got this result. Do you think you need to repeat this?*

3 Think like a scientist: *Investigating electromagnet strength, Part 3* (20+ minutes)

Learning intention: To investigate the effect of changing the current in the coil on the electromagnet strength.

Resources: See the Learner's Book.

Description: See the Learner's Book.

Safety: If using a power supply, the voltage should be limited to 8 V or less and the wire to make the coil should be as long as possible.

Alternatively, the output of the power supply can be constant and a variable resistor or potential divider can be used to control the current in the wire.

Learners should be reminded that an ammeter is connected in series with the coil.

> **Differentiation ideas:** Learners who need more support can be given help to set up the equipment, or the equipment can be set up for them.

Ask learners who need more challenge to make the circuit themselves, working only from a circuit diagram. Ask them also to predict the results in more detail than just the trend. For example: *How will increasing the current from to affect the number of paperclips lifted by the electromagnet?*

> **Assessment ideas:** Observe learners while they are carrying out the investigation, to assess their

approach to the task. Ask questions on any aspect of their procedure: *Show me how you got this result. Do you think you need to repeat this?*

Plenary ideas

1 What did your partner learn? (5 minutes)

Resources: Paper and pens.

Description: Learners work in pairs. One learner describes three things that they learned in the lesson. Then their partner does the same. Each learner should try to think of something different to say, to avoid a 'leader-follower' scenario.

> **Assessment ideas:** Learners can ask each other questions about what the other has learned, or individuals can volunteer to ask the whole class questions about what they have learned.

Reflection ideas: Learners can compare what others have learned with what they have learned.

2 Questions to the answers (5–10 minutes)

Resources: Paper; pens.

Description: Either, you provide the answers and learners write the questions, or learners work in pairs and write the answers for their partner to compose the questions. Answers can include statements such as: 'This will make the electromagnet stronger.'

> **Assessment ideas:** Completed questions with answers can be passed to other learners for checking and discussion.

Homework ideas

1   Learner's Book questions

2   Workbook exercises 9.4A–C

3   Worksheet 9.4

Topic worksheets

Worksheet 9.4, Investigating electromagnets

PROJECT GUIDANCE

Investigating magnetism

This project addresses the following learning objectives:

8TWSc.06 Evaluate a range of secondary information sources for their relevance and know that some sources may be biased.

8SIC.01 Discuss how scientific knowledge is developed through collective understanding and scrutiny over time.

8SIC.03 Evaluate issues which involve and/or require scientific understanding.

8SIC.04 Describe how people develop and use scientific understanding as individuals and through collaboration, e.g. through peer-review.

Learners can use the internet or books to find information, but they must present this information in their own words. Encourage learners to only use information at a level they can understand and they should certainly not include any information at too high a level. Also encourage learners to consider which of their secondary sources are likely to be the most reliable.

Information about early discoveries may include Greek (discovery of lodestone), Chinese (first literary reference to magnetism), Arab (properties of magnetic material), Indian (use of magnetite by physicians to remove arrows from wounds), or UK (the first magnet to be made, in 1600).

Animals are known to use magnetism for navigation, and it is now known that many other organisms, including bacteria, use magnetic fields for orientation. Examples include newly hatched sea turtles finding their way to the sea, migrating birds that travel long distances and mammals that live underground.

The Earth's magnetic field protects the Earth from harmful radiation from the Sun that would otherwise remove ozone from the atmosphere. Ozone, in turn, protects the Earth from excess ultraviolet radiation.

Not all planets in the Solar System have magnetic fields: Mars and Venus have almost no magnetic field, since their cores are completely solid. The gas giant planets Jupiter, Saturn, Uranus and Neptune have the strongest magnetic fields.

The strongest known natural magnets are called magnetars, which are collapsed stars of around 20 km diameter and mass 2–3 times that of the Sun. They have extremely strong magnetic fields that last about 10 000 years.

Encourage learners to make their presentations as interesting and appealing as possible.

> Glossary

absorbed – the term given to light that is neither reflected nor transmitted

accumulate – build up

adaptations – features of an organism that help it to survive and reproduce in its habitat

aerobic respiration – the controlled release of energy from glucose (and other nutrient molecules) through a series of reactions using oxygen, inside mitochondria

air sac – a tiny blind-ending sac in the lungs, in which gas exchange takes place between the air and the blood; also known as an alveolus

altitude – a type of height measurement, usually measured vertically upwards from sea level

alveoli – air sacs in the lungs, where gas exchange takes place with the blood

analogy – the use of one structure, idea or process to explain another

angle of incidence – the angle between the incident ray and the normal

angle of reflection – the angle between the reflected ray and the normal

antagonistic muscles – a pair of muscles, such as the biceps and triceps, that work together to cause opposite movements at a joint when they contract; one contracts while the other relaxes

antibodies – chemicals produced by white blood cells, that bind with pathogens and help to destroy them

asteroid belt – a region in the Solar System with many asteroids, forming an almost circular ring around the Sun between the orbits of Mars and Jupiter and in the same plane as these orbits

asteroids – rocky objects that are smaller than planets, found mostly between the orbits of Mars and Jupiter

at rest – not moving

atmosphere – the layer of gases surrounding the Earth (or another planet)

atmospheric pressure – the force exerted by the atmosphere on an area of $1\ m^2$; it is approximately $100\,000\ N/m^2$ at sea level

atom – a tiny particle of matter

average speed – calculated by dividing distance travelled by time taken; as actual speed may vary during the journey, the result of the calculation is an average value for the speed

away from the normal – the angle between the light ray and the normal becomes larger after refraction

balanced – forces acting on an object are balanced if the sizes of the forces are equal and they are in opposite directions

balanced diet – daily food intake that contains the correct quantity of energy, and also all of the nutrients that a person requires

ball-and-socket joint – a joint at which one bone can move in a circular motion in relation to the other

bent – changed direction; in refraction, at boundaries, this is a sudden change

biceps – a muscle attached to the scapula and radius, which bends the elbow joint when it contracts

bioaccumulation – the build-up of a substance in an organism's body over time, because it does not break down inside the organism

biodegradable – can be broken down (decay) naturally by microorganisms, such as bacteria and fungi, into products that are not harmful to the environment

biomagnification – the increase in the concentration of a substance along a food chain; biomagnification happens because of bioaccumulation in the bodies of organisms at each step of the food chain

bioplastics – materials that are made from natural renewable sources, such as vegetable oils, saw dust or food waste; they are used to replace plastics which are made from petroleum

blood plasma – the liquid part of blood

boulder – large rock

breathing – movements caused by muscles, which cause air to move into and out of the lungs

bronchiole – one of many small tubes that carry air through the lungs, from the bronchi

bronchus – one of two tubes that convey air from the trachea into the lungs

calculate – use a mathematical process to derive an answer

capillaries – the smallest type of blood vessel

carat – a measurement of purity of gold

carbohydrate – a nutrient that is the main source of energy in our diet; carbohydrates include starch and sugar

carbon monoxide – a gas present in tobacco smoke, formed by the incomplete combustion of various compounds in tobacco, which binds with haemoglobin in the blood and reduces oxygen transport

cartilage – a tough but bendy material that provides support to the trachea

change direction – an object moves in a curved path or at an angle to its original movement

chromatogram – the resulting separation of substances after carrying out chromatography

climate – the weather conditions prevailing in an area in general and over a long period

climatology – the study of climate

coil – wire wrapped around repeatedly in the shape of a cylinder

collapse – suddenly fall down or give way

collide – particles or objects are said to collide when they hit into each other or hit into another object

coloured filters – transparent, coloured pieces of glass or plastic that absorb all other colours of light

combustion – burning

compass – a magnetic compass contains a magnetised needle that is free to turn, so the needle will point in the direction of magnetic field lines

concentrated (solution) – a solution in which a large mass of solute is dissolved

concentration – a measure of how many particles are in a particular space or volume; more particles in a space is a higher concentration than fewer particles in the same space

conserved – no change happens; used in this course with regard to mass and energy

constant – not changing; the word uniform is also used for constant

constipation – slow functioning of the alimentary canal, so that faeces are not passed out regularly

container – an object that holds something else, for example, a balloon is a container for gas

contract – of muscles: get shorter

contraction – (of muscles) getting shorter; this is an active process, in which the muscle uses energy which is obtained through respiration

control variables – factors that are kept the same in an investigation so that the test is fair

core – material around which the coil of an electromagnet is wound

craters – bowl-shaped areas whose centres are usually lower than surrounding land that can be caused by the impacts of other objects

cyan – the colour of light that results from the addition of blue and green light; has a turquoise colour

cycle – a regular changing pattern from one thing to another

deflected – the direction of an object was changed

deforestation – cutting down or destroying large areas of trees

demagnetised – a material that has lost its magnetism is said to be demagnetised; will no longer attract magnetic objects

dependent variable – the variable that changes in an investigation as a result of changing the independent variable; this variable is measured

depth – distance from the top to the bottom of something, or distance from the surface down to a particular position in a liquid or gas

development in humans – progressive changes in structure, function and behaviour that happen as a person grows from an embryo to an adult

diffusion – the net movement of a substance from a place of higher concentration to a place of lower concentraction, as a result of the random movement of particles

dilute (solution) – a solution in which a small mass of solute is dissolved in a large volume

direction – the path of movement of an object or the line along which a force acts

dispersion – the splitting of white light into its component colours

dissipated energy – is transferred to thermal energy and spreads out through the surroundings

dissolving/dissolve – the complete mixing of a solid with a liquid so that a transparent solution is formed

distance/time graph – a type of graph in which the distance moved by an object is displayed on the vertical axis and the time elapsed is on the horizontal axis

distorted – changed in some way from the original to become less clear

ecology – the study of organisms in their environment

ecosystem – a network of interactions between living and non-living things; it is generally considered to be self-contained, although in practice all ecosystems interact in at least some ways with other ecosystems

electrical charge – a property of an object which causes it to attract or repel other objects with a charge

electromagnet – type of temporary magnet that operates when current flows so the magnetism can be switched on and off

electrons – negatively charged particles found surrounding the nucleus of an atom

electrostatic attraction – the force that holds individual atoms together

elliptical – a type of galaxy shape that has an oval shape

embryo – the earliest stages of development of a new organism; in humans, it develops from the fertilised egg (zygote) and implants into the uterus lining

emissions – production and release of a gas

endothermic process – a process (such as change of state) in which energy is transferred from the surroundings

endothermic reaction – a chemical reaction in which energy is transferred from the surroundings

environment – surroundings; for an organism, anything external to the organism that affects it

eradicate – get rid of; totally destroy

exoskeleton – a skeleton on the outside of the body

exothermic reaction – a chemical reaction in which energy is transferred into the surroundings

expired air – air that is breathed out

extinct – no longer in existence; the term should really only be used for species that no longer exist on Earth, but is sometimes used for a species that no longer exists in one particular country

factors – in science, another word for variables

fat – a nutrient that is required to make cell membranes, and that is the main energy storage material in animals

fibre – cellulose and other plant fibres that cannot be digested

food web – interconnecting food chains, indicating how energy is transferred between organisms in an ecosystem

force – an action that, if unbalanced, will change the direction of movement of an object or will change the shape of an object

fossil fuels – natural fuels such as gas, coal or oil formed from the remains of living organisms

fuel – a store of chemical energy

galaxy – a collection of dust, gas, stars and solar systems held together by gravity

gas exchange – the movement (by diffusion) of gases into and out of organisms; in the lungs, oxygen diffuses into the blood and carbon dioxide diffuses out

geographic north pole – one of the points where the Earth's axis of rotation meets the Earth's surface; conventionally shown toward the top of maps

glacial period – the coldest part of an ice age

glacier – river of ice formed from snow that has become compressed over a long time

global warming – a gradual increase in the overall temperature of the Earth's atmosphere

glucose – a sugar that is used in respiration

greenhouse effect – the trapping of the Sun's heat energy in a planet's atmosphere

habitat – the place where an organism lives

haemoglobin – a red pigment in red blood cells that combines reversibly with oxygen and transports oxygen from the lungs to all respiring cells

hinge joint – a joint at which one bone can move in one plane in relation to the other, like a door moving on its hinges

humidity – a measure of the concentration of water vapour in the atmosphere

ice ages – times when part of the Earth has permanent ice

impacts – the collisions of smaller objects with larger ones

incident ray – a ray of light arriving at a surface

independent variable – the variable that is directly changed by the investigator in an experiment

inert – chemically inactive

insecticide – a chemical used to kill insect pests

insoluble – a substance that will not dissolve in a given solvent

inspired air – air that is breathed in

interact – affect one another

interglacial period – a warmer part of an ice age

interval – the size of the gap between measurements

invasive species – a species that has been introduced into an ecosystem where it does not belong, and has multiplied and spread widely

irregular – a type of galaxy shape that is not well defined

joints – places where two bones meet

larynx – the organ at the top of the trachea that contains the vocal cords

law of reflection – statement that the angle of incidence and angle of reflection are equal

lenses – specially shaped pieces of transparent material designed to refract light in particular directions

lever – a rigid bar that pivots on a fixed support

like poles – two magnetic poles that are the same: north and north, or south and south

limewater – a dilute solution of calcium hydroxide; it goes cloudy when mixed with carbon dioxide

locked up – held so that it is stored; carbon may be locked up in coal or oil until it is burnt

m/s – metres per second; metres divided by seconds; the standard scientific unit of speed

magenta – the colour of light that results from the addition of red and blue light; has a bright pink colour

magnet – an object that has been permanently magnetised

magnetic – a material that will be attracted to a magnet

magnetic field – the area around a magnet where the effect of the magnet can be detected

magnetic field lines – the lines that make up the pattern of a magnetic field; the lines point from north to south around the outside of a magnet

magnetic north – a point near the geographic north of the Earth toward which the needle of a magnetic compass points; this pole is actually a south magnetic pole

magnetised – a magnetic material that has been temporarily or permanently turned into a magnet is said to be magnetised

medium – in this topic, the transparent material through which light is passing

meteorology – the study of weather

metres – the standard scientific unit of length, used to measure distance in this topic

mitochondria – small structures (organelles) found in the cells of animals, plants and fungi, in which aerobic respiration takes place

moment – the turning effect of a force, calculated as the force multiplied by the distance of the force from the pivot

muscles – organs made up of specialised muscle cells, which are able to make themselves shorter (contract)

native species – a species that belongs in a country or ecosystem, and has not been introduced by humans

naturally occurring – present without human activity

navigate – plan the route of a journey

nectar – a sugary liquid made by flowers, to attract insects for pollination

neutrons – particles found in the nucleus of an atom that have no electrical charge

newton metre (N m) – the standard unit of moment; other units of moment include and N cm and N mm

newtons per metre squared – the international standard unit of pressure; meaning the number of newtons of force on every square metre of area; written as N/m^2

nicotine – a chemical in tobacco leaves that acts as a stimulant and is addictive

nocturnal – active at night

normal – in ray diagrams, imaginary line that is perpendicular to a surface

nucleus – a dense area at the centre of an atom that contains protons and neutrons

nutrients – components of food that are used by the body; they include protein, carbohydrate, fat and oil, vitamins, minerals and water

oil – a fat that is liquid at room temperature

opaque – a material through which light cannot pass

opposite – the direction of two forces is opposite if the angle between the forces is 180°

oxidation reaction – any reaction where a substance combines with oxygen

oxyhaemoglobin – the compound formed when oxygen combines with haemoglobin

paper chromatography – a method for separating mixtures of dissolved chemicals using special paper

particulates – tiny solid particles in tobacco smoke, which enter the lungs and blood and can cause a wide range of health problems

pathogens – organisms that cause disease, e.g. bacteria, viruses

peat bog – an area of wetland where the decay of dead plant material has been delayed

per – in each; the word per can appear between two different units, for example metres per second

permanent – fixed; does not dissolve in water or will not lose its magnetism

permanent magnets – magnets that cannot be switched on and off and that do not require electricity to operate; the magnetic field around them is constant

perpendicular – at right angles

persistent – describes a substance that remains in the environment for a long time

phagocytosis – the actions of phagocytes, certain white blood cells, when they take in and destroy pathogens (the terms phagocyte and phagocytosis are not required in the specification)

photosynthesis – the process by which green plants make food

pivot – the point about which a lever turns

plane mirror – a flat silvered surface usually covered with glass that is designed to reflect as much light as possible

point – in the context of objects, the tip of a sharp object

pollen – tiny grains produced by flowers, which contain their male gametes

pollinating – transferring pollen grains from an anther to a stigma

preliminary work – some practical work you do before an investigation to find out how you will carry it out; for example you might find out the range or interval you will use

pressure – the result of a force exerted on an area; the pushing effect of a force

prevent – to stop something happening

primary colours – the name given to red, green and blue light as they cannot be made from the addition of any other colours of light

prism – in this topic, a block of transparent material with a regular shape

protein – a nutrient that is required for making new cells; many important substances in the body are proteins, such as haemoglobin, antibodies and insulin

protons – positively charged particles found in the nucleus of an atom

protractor – equipment used to measure angles on diagrams

range – the difference between the highest and lowest values

ray diagram – the use of labelled lines to show what happens to light when incident on a surface

rays – straight lines that represent the path of light

reactive – how readily a substance takes part in a reaction

reactivity – how reactive something is

reagents – chemicals that are used in a reaction

recycle – use again

red blood cells – the most common type of cells in blood; they have no nucleus; they transport oxygen

reflection – term given to light (or another type of wave) bouncing back from a surface, without being absorbed

refraction – light changing direction on crossing a boundary from one medium to another due to a change in speed of the light

relax – (of a muscle) stop contracting

renewable resources – natural resources that do not run out and can be replaced by normal process within a human's lifetime

respiration – a series of chemical reactions that take place in all living cells, in which energy is released from glucose

respiratory system – the system involved with providing oxygen to the blood and removing carbon dioxide, so that respiration can take place in cells

rust – a chemical reaction in which iron combines with oxygen in the presence of water to form iron oxide

safety precautions – in an experiment, these are adjustments made to reduce the risk of accident or reduce the risk of injury from an accident; they are specific to the experiment and more than just basic school laboratory rules

salt – a compound formed when a metal reacts with an acid for example magnesium chloride

sandpaper – rough paper used for smoothing or polishing surfaces.

saturated solution – a solution in which no more of the solute will dissolve; note, this term is extension material

sea level – a position defined as having zero altitude; the position of the ocean surface measured mid-way between high tide and low tide

second – the standard scientific unit of time

set square – piece of equipment in the shape of a right-angled triangle used for drawing diagrams

sharp – having a pointed end with a small area at the end of the point; having the ability to cut or push into something else

skeleton – a structure that supports an animal's body; vertebrates have internal skeletons made of bone and cartilage; arthropods have external skeletons; some invertebrates (e.g. earthworms) have hydrostatic skeletons made up of a fluid-filled cavity

sketch – make a drawing; in the context of a graph, sketch means to show the shape of the graph without plotting values, so there will only be named variables on the axes and not a numbered scale; axes on sketch graphs usually have arrowheads

slow down – get slower, decelerate or reduce in speed

soft iron – iron that is easily magnetised and easily demagnetised

solubility – a measure of how soluble a solute is in the particular solvent

soluble – a substance that will dissolve in a given solvent

solute – a substance that is dissolved

solution – a mixture in which particles of a substance (solute) are mixed with particles of a liquid so that the substance can no longer be seen.

solvent – a liquid in which other substances will dissolve

solvent front – the level the solvent has reached as it travels up the paper, while carrying out chromatography

spectrum – in this topic, a continuous range of colours, each colour merging with the next

speed – distance travelled per unit time

speed up – get faster, accelerate or increase in speed

spiral – a type of galaxy shape with curved arms extending from the centre

starch – a carbohydrate whose molecules are made of many glucose molecules linked in a spiralling chain; it is the main energy storage material in plants

stationary – not moving

statistics – the science of collecting and analysing numerical data in large quantities

stellar dust – very small particles that exist in space, mostly smaller than grains of sand; also called interstellar dust or cosmic dust

sub-atomic particles – atomic particles that are smaller than an atom

subtraction – taking away

suggest – put forward an idea

surface area – in the context of pressure between solids, this is the area of contact between the two solids

tar – a mixture of chemicals found in tobacco smoke that increase the risk of developing many different types of cancer

tendons – strong, non-stretchy cords that attach muscles to bones

towards the normal – the angle between the light ray and the normal becomes smaller after refraction

toxic – poisonous

trachea – a tube leading from the back of the throat, through which air travels into the lungs; it has C-shaped rings of cartilage in it to support it

translucent – allows some light to pass through, but not in a way that produces clear images

transmit – of a filter, to allow light through

transparent – a material through which light can pass in a way that produces clear images

triangular – description of an abject that has three straight edges on one face

triceps – a muscle attached to the scapula and ulna, which straightens the elbow joint when it contracts

turn – rotate around an axis or change direction

unbalanced – forces acting on an object are unbalanced if the effects of the forces do not cancel

unit – part of any physical quantity that defines what is being measured, for example metres, seconds

Universe – all of space and everything in it

variables – factors that can be changed in an investigation

visibility – a measure of how far you can see due to the light and weather conditions

vitamins – substances made by plants and other living organisms, that are required in the diet in small quantities

vocal cords – bands of muscle that stretch across inside the larynx, which we vibrate to make sounds

voicebox – another name for the larynx

weather – the state of the atmosphere in a particular place

white blood cells – blood cells with a nucleus; they help to protect against pathogens

windpipe – another name for the trachea

> Acknowledgements

The authors and publishers acknowledge the following sources of copyright material and are grateful for the permissions granted. While every effort has been made, it has not always been possible to identify the sources of all the material used, or to trace all copyright holders. If any omissions are brought to our notice, we will be happy to include the appropriate acknowledgements on reprinting.

Thanks to the following for permission to reproduce images:

Cover Mehmet Hilmi Barcin/Getty Images